Not First in Nobody's Heart

Ron Paquin
05

this book graciously donated
from the personal collection of
George Hill Jr.

Not First in Nobody's Heart
The Life Story of a Contemporary Chippewa

Ron Paquin *and* Robert Doherty

RJP PRESS
301 LAKE STREET
ST. IGNACE, MICHIGAN 49781

© Ronald Paquin, St. Ignace, Michigan 49781
All rights reserved
Authorization to photocopy items for internal or personal use, or the internal or personal use of specific clients, is granted by RJP Press, provided that the base fee of $.10 per copy is paid directly to the Copyright Clearance Center, 27 Congress Street, Salem, MA 01970. For those organizations that have been granted a photocopy license by CCC, a separate system of payments has been arranged. The fee code for users of the Transactional Reporting Service is 0-8138-1837-0/92 (clothbound edition) and 0-8138-1836-2/92 (paperbound edition) $.10

⊚ Printed on acid-free paper in the United States of America

First edition, 1992
Second edition, 1996

Library of Congress Cataloging-in-Publication Data

Paquin, Ron.
    Not first in nobody's heart: the life story of a contemporary Chippewa / Ron Paquin and Robert Doherty. – 2nd ed.
        p. cm.
    ISBN 0-8138-1837-0 (cloth). – ISBN 0-8138-1836-2 (paper)
    1. Paquin, Ron. 2. Ojibwa Indians – Biography. 3. Ojibwa Indians – Social conditions. 4. Mackinac Island (Mich.:Island) – Social conditions. I. Doherty, Robert, 1935–   .II. Title.
E99.C6P377   1992
977.4′923 – dc20
                                                                       91-47568
[B]

FRONTISPIECE: *Ron Paquin, Lake Michigan, 1981.* Photo courtesy of Robert G. Doherty.

Contents

Preface vii

"Well, Here Goes" 3

Reform School 20

High School Days 32

On the Skids 45

Busted 55

The Loony House 64

Moving Up the Line 76

Cassidy Lake 86

On Parole 112

Locked Up Again 120

Settling Down 132

Work 154

Fishing 166

Broken Dreams 196

Taking Stock 215

Afterword 223

In Memoriam 260

Preface

Sitting on a prison cot in 1965, Ron Paquin began telling his life story to a fellow inmate, who wrote it down. The guards ordered Paquin to quit and took the manuscript away from him, but he never forgot his plan to write a book about himself. Years later, he began anew, this time using a tape recorder. Driven by the need to vent old feelings and by the hope that his story might spare innocent children from the torments he had experienced, Paquin felt compelled to tell others about his life. He had already recorded a partial autobiography when I first interviewed him in 1979 while I was researching a book on Native American fishing rights. He told me about his book and let me listen to his tapes. Shortly afterward, we began the ten-year collaboration that led to *Not First in Nobody's Heart*.

A Chippewa who has always lived in the north woods, Paquin describes his life among working-poor people in Michigan's tourist-dominated Mackinac Straits area—men and women whose existence is mostly hidden by Mackinac Island's elegance. Paquin grew up unwanted by his heartless parents. He suffered life at its worst but somehow found the strength to heal himself to the point that he could give others the love long denied to him.

Because Paquin's stories disclose intimate details about other people, he and I decided to give fictitious names to the persons who appear in this book, except for well-known public figures and members of Paquin's family. We have also changed other details, shifting the dates and locations of events and names of businesses, for example, in order to preserve anonymity and to protect the privacy of individuals and institutions. Paquin's stories are true in essence, then, but any similarity between them and actual people or circumstances is coincidental. I want to thank the Central Research and Development Fund of the University of Pittsburgh for two grants that helped me complete this book. My thanks also to Joe and Helen Rishel, who painstakingly transcribed many of Paquin's tape recordings, and to Grace Tomcho, who skillfully typed and edited several versions of a messy manuscript. I am especially grateful for the kind support and encouragement of Richard Kinney, the director of Iowa State University Press. Without him, *Not First in Nobody's Heart* would never have come into being.

Beulah, Michigan
June 1991
  ROBERT DOHERTY

Not First in Nobody's Heart

LEFT TO RIGHT *Donny, cousin Dorothy, and me. My twin brother, Donny, and I was born September 4, 1942, behind Al Wright's Bar in a little cabin, to Alec and Theresa Paquin of St. Ignace, Michigan.... We stayed with our parents for just lacking two years.*

"Well, Here Goes"

Well, here goes. My name is Ronald Joseph Paquin. I was born September 4, 1942, behind Al Wright's Bar in a little cabin, to Alec and Theresa Paquin of St. Ignace, Michigan. My twin brother, Donny, and I was delivered by the doctor there. We stayed with our parents for just lacking two years, I think, and my mother took sick, so my aunt went and got us. And it was bad, I guess, as far as our physical shape was. We was covered with sores from not being changed. We wasn't being looked after as babies should be, in other words. My aunt took care of us medically and got us straightened around.

We wasn't happy at my aunt and uncle's, the Hartwicks. They showed us some affection for a while, but then we got to be probably like a burden to them maybe. I don't know. There was a lot of beatings that went on too. My aunt had quite a time with that razor strop. She'd beat us on our bare butts. I mean, she did it real bad.

My aunt had a girl that she was taking care of, her sister's daughter. Mary Ann is her name, and to this day we're close, almost like brother and sister. She was the family favorite. She got what I'd call love – a spoiled kid is what she was. Now, you can't blame her, being a kid, for taking this affection. I would've if I had a chance. But we took a lot of beatings for what she'd do. We got blamed for everything that happened, whether we did it or not.

When they fed us, Nanny – Mary Ann – got what she wanted. She ate what she liked, and if she didn't care for something, she didn't have to eat it, but the twins did, fat or not. My uncle ate like a pig. He'd hog the good food, the lean meat. He'd grab the lean, most of it, and give us the fatty parts. To this day I can't eat fat. That doesn't turn a kid bad, I know. I'm just explaining what went on.

Now, that part wasn't so tough. I think that as a kid, even at that age, I could tolerate the razor strop, and we was dressed good. If I remember right, we was.

We had this baby-sitter all the time. Well, she was one sick bitch. We never told anyone what went on, because we was scared. We must have been, when this was going on, probably six and a half or seven years old. She stripped naked, bare naked, and forced sexual intercourse on us kids. And she did this all the time when my mother and dad—I called my aunt and uncle Mom and Dad then— was gone. We feared that bitch. She'd make us kiss her there and on her tits and then she'd lay us on her and force intercourse. What she was getting out of it, I don't know, but I wasn't getting nothing.

That was one of the reasons we wanted to leave. But that wasn't the only thing going on. There was this colored guy that stayed up the hill from us. He liked us boys and everything. He got us our first boxing gloves when we was four years old. He taught me to box even at that young age. But he'd try homosexual stuff on us, try to bribe us with candy. He'd lay on the bed bare-assed and say, "Come on, do it to me," and all that. He wanted us to suck him, to do oral sexual stuff with him. I never did. I wouldn't do it. He never got to where he would force us, but he'd try to pull it. And goddamn, that's a hell of a situation for a kid—homosexual on one part, a sex maniac on the other.

We went to Groscap school, an elementary school just outside St. Ignace. We'd meet this guy there. He was nice to us, and one day he told us who he was. He said, "I'm your brother Floyd." We talked to him, and we kept asking our aunt and uncle. "Naw," they said. My aunt Virginia visited us at the Hartwicks', and she finally told us, "Mary and Francis aren't your parents. Your real parents are Theresa and Alec." We was very curious then. We liked Floyd. We decided we didn't want to stay at my aunt's no more. We wanted to go home to our real mom and dad. Besides we had to get away from them sex fiends. We feared that baby-sitter. She threatened more than the colored guy did. I never told about her till now.

They sent us back to our parents like we asked. What a mistake! The novelty wore off. You'd think they'd be glad to get their sons back, but they wasn't. We got deprived of everything that the other kids got, and they didn't get much. She wouldn't feed or clothe us—not one thing that a parent should do. And greedy! I never seen a woman so greedy. She'd hide stuff like peanut butter and crackers and canned goods, making sure her fat ass got fed. You'd walk in the house, you'd smell something good cooking, but you didn't have it on the table. She was cooking and eating it while everybody was

LEFT TO RIGHT *Cousin Mary Ann, Donny, and me. When my mother took sick, my aunt went and got us, and we lived at my aunt and uncle's for quite a few years. We called our aunt and uncle Mom and Dad.*

gone. We was lucky to get potatoes. I seen lots of times we'd get meals with just potatoes—nothing else. Sometimes there wasn't no meals at all. And, I don't know, she cared less about us. We noticed that right off. I don't know why my mother and father hated me so much. There wasn't never no love for me in their house. We thought it was bad at the Hartwicks'; that wasn't nothing. We got beat plus half-starved at home. No clothes. Nothing worked out. We started roving, staying away from home. And we begun stealing.

The house was a log cabin with four rooms in it. There was Donny and I, six brothers and sisters, and my mother and dad living there. And it was filthy, a real mess—no running water or electricity, no inside facilities. We heated it with a cookstove that run on wood and had the reservoir on the side for heating water.

But the place was filthy. My ma never cleaned it. There was bedbugs everywhere. I don't know if you know about bedbugs, but they're about the size of a ladybug, they smell awful, and they bite. The way you get bedbugs is by creating filth. That's where they come from. There was so many mice that if you left something on the table, there was foot marks and turds and everything else from them eating on it.

She wouldn't wash the sheets, and most of us kids had a wetting-the-bed problem. I know I did. I had that till I was eleven years old. I don't know what caused it, but my aunt made me eat spoons of salt. She held the sharp edge of a knife against my bare cock and said she'd cut it off if I didn't stop peeing in my bed. I worried about the homosexual, and I feared that nympho baby-sitter, but I never did have nightmares, which I always had from a month or so after I went to my mother and dad's. I walked in my sleep—didn't know where I was at half the time. And it was a confusion to me, finding out I had parents but getting no love from them.

Now, this may be hard to believe. My mother had chickens. She took care of them goddamn chickens better than us kids. The other kids could have eggs, but if me or Donny wanted one, we had to buy it from her. We'd sell pop bottles; she charged us a nickel an egg. We had to actually buy them from her to have one. And she wouldn't give us no blankets. I don't know what was the matter with her. To this day I can't figure it out.

We hated my mother, and with these chickens we figured to pay her back, I guess. I'm not sure what kind of chickens they was; they was all white. She had about thirty of these chickens, maybe more. We was crazy mad at her, Donny and I. I figured we should kill them sons of bitches. I told Donny, "If we don't get no eggs, she won't either and not nobody else." We opened the chicken coop one day.

We had like little trials for them and then sentenced them to death: "You old cackler, you won't lay no more goddamn eggs after we get done with your ass." We strung a rope over the rafters. We put a noose over their heads and yanked them up real fast. Snapped their necks, I imagine. They didn't live long, I know that. Just flopped around and died. We hung a bunch of them, I remember.

We left the dead ones lie there, and she couldn't figure out what had happened when she found them. She checked for holes in the henhouse and looked all around to see how something got in there and killed them like that. She had my dad check and count them chickens for weeks after that. We only had trials and hung them that once, but we did steal some for picnic-frying another time. Cooked them down by the lake.

Well, we hadn't been home very long before my mother decided she couldn't handle us. She didn't want us. She sent us away to some Catholic school down by Petoskey. And, boy, I'm telling you! I was raised Catholic. Now I haven't been in the church for years unless it's a funeral or something. I'm not putting down the whole Catholic religion, but the parts I went through was mostly awful. When you're a psychiatrist or principal or whatever to a school, you got an important job because you're shaping a kid's future. Now, to some people, that might not be much, because they've did their job with their kids, which I'm doing now. But it's the people that don't do their jobs, and the kids end up in home schools like the one I did. I seen cruelty in that place but never no love. Them nuns never had kids of their own, so how could they know about love?

In that school you had to be a quarter Indian to get in there. I never thought much about it before I went there. I had seen that in public school I was darker-skinned than lots of the other kids, but I never paid no attention. I knew I was Indian and I didn't know it, if you can figure that. Being Indian wasn't important, anyhow, because I felt so bad about being poor and raggedy.

Everybody in that school was Indian, but you'd see a wild mix. Some looked completely white, and others looked mostly Indian. I'm pretty dark, so that's when I knew for sure I had Indian in me. I liked the idea of being Indian. I mean, we played cowboys and Indians, and I really was one. But that was about the extent of it. I had no idea about my heritage as an American Indian at that time, and I never learned much about it till years after when I'm talking about now.

In there, you heard the word *Indian* all the time—not *Chippewa* or *Ottawa*, just *Indian*. Sometimes they'd mix you up, though. That one black-robed bitch what hated me, she'd say, "You're a bad boy,

Ronny. You're not an Indian!" Well, I didn't know who or what I was anyhow, so this was no help. Donny and I talked about it. "What are we doing here if we're not Indian?" we'd say. A big confusion it was, something more to worry about.

It cost our old lady forty dollars a month to keep Donny and me there. Hell, she wasn't spending that on us at home. She'd been better off to keep us. Well, anyway, a sense of insecurity is growing for my twin brother and I. She sent my brother Tommy there too. I couldn't figure it out, but my younger brother Tom kind of followed us around.

Well, we got there, and everything was "You guys are going to toe the line; you guys are going to do this or else; do this; do that." It scared me. I wasn't there three days and I run away. And the reason why I run was for fighting with this kid I hung around with on the streets, Tommy, an Indian kid. I whipped him, but I got a beating from Sister Mary Arnold. Both of us should've been punished, because both started calling one another names and then we had it out. She beat me. God, she beat me. "Well, goddamn," I said, "where am I going to go where I won't get beaten?" So I took off. I got caught within a few hours after I run. Got another beating when I come back.

Sister Casiano, a mean-looking bitch, used a Ping-Pong paddle on us. She had a pine board about a foot and a half long, and she'd smack us with that. I'm telling you, she would get so enthused in

Donny LEFT *and me. When we went to Groscap elementary school, we met this guy, Floyd, there. He said he was our brother, and we found out then who our real parents were. We decided we didn't want to stay at our aunt's no more. They sent us back to our parents like we asked. . . . The house was a log cabin with four rooms in it. There was Donny and I, six brothers and sisters, and my mother and dad living there.*

this beating. She did this not only on our butt but on our arms, our face, and head. Once in a while she'd catch you with the edge of it, and her face, her forehead, would break out in a sweat—all flushed she was, excited. Her eyes blazed, and she'd yell, "Cry, you little so-and-so!" I wouldn't. Only time I cried was when I felt bad, not when I was in pain.

They did things other than beat us. I wet the bed; they made us sleep in it for several nights. But every morning we had to take the sheets off the bed and go outside. We stood there with them stinking sheets over our heads where the girls could see that we peed the bed. I'm half gagging on that smell and feeling ashamed, but I could hear them girls laughing at me. I don't know which ones, because I couldn't see and you didn't dare lift that sheet up till the sister said. Here was them nuns, religious people, and they figured the way to cure us from bed-wetting is to make us sleep in it. They seen that it wasn't working. I'd do it again every night and every night. I'd go to sleep dreading, praying that I wouldn't wet the bed. They sent us out in front of the girls to embarrass us and have them make fun of us.

Those people have got your life right in their hands. They can make you or break you, help you or drive you down, a kid like I was then—scared, dying for lack of love. I'm nearly fifty years old, and I'm talking about more than forty years ago, but I ain't forgot one backhander, I ain't forgot one vicious thing that was said to me, I ain't forgot none of the poking fun that was made of me, I ain't forgot the dirty names that kids called me in school. I ain't forgot any of that. It stuck with me all these years. I ain't ever going to do that to my son. I would never do that to my child or anybody else's. Cruelty never solved nothing, not a damn thing. All the pain I've carried through the years—it's hard to see how people can do that to each other. A little love would've gone a long way.

Sister Casiano liked hitting kids. I didn't know nothing about sex back then, but she was sure getting something out of whacking us. One time I run away, and when we was brought back, she started with that paddle. I kicked at her. Well, one of the priests lost his head and swung a backhander on me. I still got the scar on my face. He hit me with a set of keys in his hand, and it cut in and drew blood. I kicked for his nuts, but I missed. It took three nuns and him to calm me down.

We run away from there thirteen times before they got the message we didn't want to stay.

My mother come to see us just one time. She come four times; three times she didn't even ask to see Donny and I. One time she did call us out. I don't know why. She was messing around with this guy from Fowlerville—shacking up with him. Well, she brought my brother Tommy a pair of sneakers. We needed shoes too, but she didn't bring none for us. That bitch sat there and asked Sister Casiano how Tommy was doing in school: "I want to see Tommy get an education, but I don't care about them other two." I tried to hit her. Sister Casiano grabbed me, slapped me for going after my mom.

What a cruel thing my mother did, to sit there and talk about me like that! Parents make the mistakes, but the kids suffer for them. They got sick of me and Donny at the school and sent us home. It didn't work out there either. My mother's jaw dropped when she seen us come back.

Nothing worked out at home. The beatings got worse. One time my dad threw a double-bitted ax at Donny, and if he'd nailed him, he would've killed him. My dad was constantly throwing things. I give him credit; he worked hard, but he didn't have enough intelligence or opportunities to get good jobs, I guess. He had a drinking problem too.

My father was a big man, tough, strong, real old-school, and a damn hard worker. But you'll get some more history on him later on—like he was in the penitentiary. He stayed with and supported his mother and his family for quite a few years, so he had made some effort toward being a good man. He was too old to start raising a family, I think. I can't tell you much about my mother, other than what my aunt told me. She was greedy, always hoarded stuff. Never thought of nobody but herself. As a kid, I hated my mom and dad. I hated them fierce. At times, I hated my uncle and aunt. I hated lots of people back then. I don't hate my mother anymore. I don't respect her. I don't feel anything now. Nothing—just empty. I did like my dad. Of course, sons usually look up to their father more than they do their mother. But I couldn't get close to my dad.

My dad was mostly Chippewa, I found out later. But when I was young, he would always curse Indians like he hated them. It's odd how it come about, and in lots of ways it don't make sense. Seems like I don't know the whole story, but I'll tell it anyway.

My aunt Agnes is full-blood Chippewa. She married my dad's brother, Bill. Well, every time my dad would see her, he'd curse her: "There's that goddamn worthless Indian, that no-good squaw." He'd rage on and on against her. We wondered—me and my brothers—why he talked like that and why he hated Indians so much. Maybe, we thought, he got mistreated for being Indian, but that's not the story Aunt Agnes told about it, which is a little hard to believe.

Years later, after I was married, my aunt Agnes told me that

right after I was born, my ma took real sick. My uncle Bill and aunt Agnes lived next door in a little shack. When my ma went to the hospital, Agnes and Bill took us kids, and all my dad give for support was a few oranges, a little food. But my dad had money enough to booze it up. He was always drunk, but he had just a couple of oranges for his kids. He never come to see us — nothing.

When my mother got out of the hospital, they never even picked us kids up. She and my dad forgot about us. Agnes and Bill talked it over. They had their own family to raise. They told my mother and dad, "Please, come get your kids." They did. Now, up to this time there was no talk about worthless Indians. But after that,

Alec Paquin, my father, FAR LEFT *was a big man, tough, strong, real old-school, and a damn hard worker. He stayed with and supported his mother and his family for quite a few years, so he had made some effort toward being a good man. He was too old to start raising a family, I think. . . . I did like my dad. Of course, sons usually look up to their father more than they do their mother. But I couldn't get close to my dad.*

My grandmother, Rose St. Onge Paquin LEFT, *and my great-grandmother, Suzanne Lavake Paquin. I had never thought much . . . about being an Indian. I didn't know nothing, not even who my grandparents was. But in 1972, when I was about thirty, I got the drift that Indian rights was real. . . . I got interested in my Indian heritage.*

my dad cursed Indians. He hated her, and so he hated Indians. I know that don't make good sense, but it's true, I guess. Ever since then when we was growing up, we heard bad talk about Indians.

Back in 1959, I think it was, they was signing Indians up in the courthouse, putting them on the roll, maybe a countywide thing. I don't know what roll, just that it was Indians. My mother said, "Alec, you go sign them kids up." Well, he yelled, "Them kids don't have no damn Indian!" A foul-mouth he was sometimes. He never signed us up. Now, we wondered about this. What was we? How could we go to Indian school if we wasn't Indian?

My dad used to walk downtown, and I'd walk with him. I didn't know how to talk them, but I knew he was speaking different languages. He would talk to Antoine Moses in Chippewa. I can tell, now that I can lingo the dialect some. Georgie Pond would come along, and they'd be going in French and Indian both. Seems odd that he'd talk Indian and deny being Indian at the same time. A stubborn old man he was, or maybe there was other reasons for what he done that I was never told about.

Indians got a raw deal around here back then, but nobody talked about it. It was hid pretty good, so they didn't know how bad off they was or how they was being cheated on the sly. It's only now, looking back on it, that I can see these things. In the days what I'm talking about now, no one admitted being Indian. You was looking for trouble if you did. Maybe that's what was bothering my dad. I don't know.

I got some records here that was put together before I went to reform school. Here's what it says about my mother and dad, a little parental history:

> Alec Paquin, seventy-one years of age, was incarcerated at the Ionia State Prison for the criminally insane for arson. At the time of his admission, he was suffering from a mental condition. His sentence was from six months to ten years. This was on account of a drunken idea of revenge towards a man who put them out of their house they had lived in for sixteen years—the man had bought the house. The only other criminal history was sixty days in jail for public intoxication eight years prior to this. He is a Roman Catholic and his education is fifth grade. He began school at thirteen. He began work when eight years old. Always went to church. He helped his father until he was seventeen years old and stayed at home and supported his family until he was fifty. His recreation was an occasional dance, carnivals, but no shows, hunting or fishing—played cards for fun. At present he seems a hearty person with no apparent malice. He is of French and Indian extraction.

Well, there you go—he didn't start school until he was thirteen. Talk about backing a kid up. He did go to church—I remember that. He went every Sunday. And he was a hard worker, a very hard worker, but didn't get good jobs—just handyman work around town, nothing substantial. For as good a worker as he was, he should've got better jobs. People must have known that he was a hard worker.

And then it says here:

> The mother is a large dull-appearing person. She is a Roman Catholic, thirty-nine years old. Her education is not known. [Well,

"Well, Here Goes"

it says the eighth grade someplace.] She is of Dutch-German extraction [actually it's Dutch, German, and Indian, I think]. She has had no major illnesses. She has had corrective surgery but nothing serious following it. Her concerns seem more with her imaginary aches and pains rather than her family and their delinquency. She does not have good feelings towards her relatives. Mrs. Paquin is much younger than Mr. Paquin. She was keeping house in his mother's home and became illegitimately pregnant by Mr. Paquin and he married her. They have lived on public assistance most of their married life. Their home situation is not good and Mrs. Paquin is now resenting . . .

Something's missing here, but I'll read a bit more. It says my mother would like us out of the home, and she would like my father out too:

When he tries to kiss her or pat her, she says, "Go away, don't touch me. My back aches. My stomach hurts."

And she never loved nobody, I guess.

So they sent Donny and me home from that school anyway. We started wandering, really wandering, then. We was never home. We run around till twelve, one o'clock at night. In summertime we'd sleep out in a little lean-to or on the ground—anything to stay away from home. We started stealing—breaking into houses, warehouses, stores, and taking just whatever we needed. We did things that was uncalled for, but a lot of the stuff we stole was what we was getting deprived of. I'm not saying it was right. It wasn't. I know that. But if you leave a kid nothing, mistreat him and beat him and starve him and don't clothe him, he's going to try to get them things for himself.

When I come out of that home school, I was confused. I had an awful temper. Didn't take much to get me riled up. My feelings was hurt easy if somebody razzed me.

About that same time, my brother Floyd got me a job at a fishery. Mainly the fish that went through was smelt and herring. We got four cents a pound for cleaning smelt and a cent a pound for pan-readying herring. Well, it took me from six in the morning till six at night to get my hundred pounds of smelts. But it gave me some spending money, and I bought some clothes—not too many clothes. Mostly, I bought hamburgers and french fries and pop and peanuts and potato chips. I remember when it come time to buy clothes that year for school my mother said, "Well, youse worked all summer. You should've bought your own clothes." I was nine years old.

Now, my brother Floyd helped me more than anyone did through the years, but he hindered me, too. I shouldn't say "hindered"—taught me the wrong things, maybe. He taught me how to fight. He'd put on the gloves and beat on me without pity. I stood and fought till I couldn't fight no more. He taught me to be tough, and when he told me to hit some guy, I would, because he was there to protect me. I don't think he did it to turn me bad or anything like that. He probably figured I needed to know how to defend myself.

Here's a story to tell you what kind of temper I had. Bobby Gray is a good friend of mine. I spent time in the penitentiary with him the last bit I did. Well, I was nine, and he was three or four years older—quite a difference at that age. I was cleaning smelt. I had about thirty pounds cleaned. The bucket we put them in held about forty pounds. He kept putting fish with heads in my bucket, and I told him to cut it out. He laughed, but he could see I was in a rage. Well, I'm right-handed, so my left hand is full of fish guts, and when he did it again, I swatted him across the face with that gutty hand, and now he turned mad. I run, and he tore after me. He caught me and slammed me against the freezer door. He pinned me there and began laughing. I had my fish knife in my hand yet, and I stabbed him in the shoulder. He screamed. I smacked him in the eye now—I could see it turning color. He let me go. Then I cracked him in the face with a Pepsi bottle. Floyd pulled me away. He said, "Cool down, Ron." Bobby Gray was bleeding, but I still wanted to hurt him, so I grabbed a padlock off the freezer door and I threw it at him. He left me alone after that. Here I was a nine-year-old, violent as hell. I was going bad, and nobody was helping me. And I didn't have no idea at all why my life was turning sour.

I got in trouble in school. Kids can be awful cruel, like if you're not dressed right or if you smell from not being clean. The name still embarrasses me—they called me "stinky Paquin," them kids did. I pissed the bed; I imagine I did smell. One time—I forget what year it was but around when I'm talking about—I only had one pair of pants, old Levi's that Randy Becker gave me. They had holes in them. I had one pair of shoes and no stockings and I forget what kind of shirt, but the shoes was Hush Puppies. Pierson kid gave them to me. Actually they was his mother's. They was women's shoes, but I was proud of them.

But things happened fast in school. This girl called me stinky Paquin, screwing her mouth up. I sat behind her. She kept it up till I couldn't stand no more. I grabbed her by the hair and jerked her back, punched her in the mouth, and down she went, her mouth bleeding. I was sick of her making fun of me, so I put her on her ass.

I didn't feel bad about that. Today I still don't. If that's the way I had to shut her up, that's the way it had to be, if the nuns didn't know enough to make me leave the room and tell them people, "It's not right to call names. After all, Ron's from a poor family, and he can't afford nice clothes or anything like that." That would've been their job, I would say, to tell them kids that. But if I hit somebody or did this or did that, they called me antisocial. Hey, I would've welcomed a friend in them days. But the nuns aren't hurting, I'll tell you. They're well fed and have nice clean places to live. They'd give us the leftovers off their table. We'd go home on the bus, and we'd have packages—sacks of food—and the kids knew that it was the leftovers from the nuns' table. Well, we needed that food. Mother always picked the best out of the deal and ate it herself.

I worked at the convent. They fed me and gave me fifty cents a day for stoking the furnace with coal. So I did try to earn a living for myself. But it just got worse as it went on. If we had got some kind of halfway attention at home, I think it would've been better. In fact, I know it would've been, if you did get a decent grade in school or you did something, and you got some attention. Like my boy brings home papers, and I compliment him, make him feel proud. He's doing a good job in school. Well, there was nothing like that in our house. If she had just looked at the paper and said, "Oh, is that ever nice!" or something like that, but she never did. You couldn't get no help if you needed it for stuff that you was having trouble with in school. It wasn't long before we started constantly skipping school. This was in the fifth grade.

I went to church quite a bit then, and I worked at the fishery. One time I went in the church when I was all fish-smelly. Oh, boy, one of the priests gave me heck. "Oh, you don't come this way," he said. And I said, "What do you mean, I don't come this way? It's all I got to wear." Well, I suppose it made for confusion when I come in smelling like a dead herring. That's all I had to wear, the same clothes I worked at the fishery with. I told the priest, "What's the difference? You say our Lord more or less catered to the raggedy people and the poor people and created food for them and miracles to that effect, and so what's wrong with me coming like I am? I'd come different if I had something else to wear." He told me to stay out of church if I couldn't dress right.

We lived in the woods more than home. We was constantly in the woods and stealing. Oh, we broke into everything within three or four miles of St. Ignace—everything. You keep wandering like that and keep stealing and pretty soon the authorities are going to bust you. Now, one bust they made, but we didn't get sent up yet.

We robbed old man Albright's. He never put his money in the bank. I remember going in there, and he had a drawer full of nickels and dimes and quarters and half-dollars. We took three bags of the silver, and we took rolls of money—several thousand dollars. There was a bunch of it. I remember seeing hundred-dollar bills. I think so, anyway. We'd go in the stores with this money. We bought one store completely out of watermelons and peanut butter. These storekeepers took the money from us little ragbags. Well, what I'm building up to is, I know damn well that money wasn't returned. We hid most of it, which the police had to have found because we told them where to look. But the money was never returned, just a few hundred dollars. Now, you can figure where the money went. I won't mention names.

We didn't get sent up that time, but it wasn't long. The gang wars was before we went to reform school. Let me tell you about them. We was in the fifth grade—in Mother Mary McCalo's class. Anyway there was wars between the country boys and the town gang. They was the Wilson gang. We was the Little Acres. The lake we lived by was Chain Lake, but they called us Little Acres. Things was violent. Guys got cut. One was slashed across the nose, and another one got an arrow in his shoulder. They had BB guns too. We caught this one guy, a traitor. He used to be with our gang. Danny was his name. We tied him to a tree and whipped him with willow sticks. We shot him with BB guns, and we pissed in a bucket and poured it on his head and beat the can. Man, he was hurting. Then we tied him up in a swamp and left him. One of the gang cut him loose. It's a good thing they did, because it was summer and he would've got sick from mosquito bites.

White and Indian come out in them gang wars. The Little Acres was mostly Indians, and the Wilsons mostly was not. It amounted to a sort of race war, but we didn't see it that way at the time.

Well, anyway, building up to the story, we was in the fifth grade, and there was something about the French and Indian War or something about Indian culture, and Mother Mary McCalo said, "I wish somebody knew how to make tomahawks and spears." I jumped up and said, "Well, I know how. Donny and I do." We got Floyd to help us make some spears and arrows. We used sea gull feathers and hawk feathers—real nice work. When we brought them to school, somebody said, "That's like my brother got shot with." I run out of the class. The police was called to the school, and they asked lots of questions. That put an end to the gang wars.

The stealing heated up now. We broke into the Alpine Construction Company one time and took dynamite caps. I remember we didn't know what they was. We stuck them in the fire, and they blew up. I caught some pieces in the throat, and my brother got hit in the face. Others was hit too, with little pieces of stuff. We was lucky we didn't lose an eye.

One day this other guy and I broke into Tamlyn's Warehouse, and the guy didn't press charges. The same day, we broke into a clothing store. We fitted ourselves out in stockings and shirts and pants and everything, really suited ourself up. First good clothes I had in a long time.

Then we broke into a cabin. Took everything out of there: the gas range, the gas tanks outside, couches, chairs. And we stole a big canvas from someplace. We had our own shack in the woods. I remember the cop, when he busted us, said, "Boy, I'm going to move out of my house and come on up here."

Well, we had everything. We'd take turns stealing food out of grocery stores. We never did get caught, so we stole lots of stuff. We'd raid gardens, and we broke into the Wishing Well Motel. Now, I'm telling stuff that we've never been caught for here too. I'm not proud of it, but I want to say what really did happen. We stole everything. We stole at random sometimes, but like I said, the food we stole because we was hungry. The clothes was stole because I didn't have any.

After we got busted, we went to court. There was sixteen kids taking stuff, as I remember, but the other kids had good homes. They got good home reports. Anyway, all the mothers was at court crying about their kids—every mother but ours. Hearings was held for each kid. My twin brother and I didn't know at the time, but we was hanging ourselves when we told them about the cruelty at our house. It didn't help us a bit. I can see that now. They had to send us away, since our home life was so bad. Well, out of the whole bunch of us, sixteen to twenty of us, the only ones sent away was Donny and I. I remember saying to my probation officer, "How come them guys did just as much if not more than us and they're getting off?" He shrugged his shoulders and stared at me without answering.

And so we was sent to reform school.

Reform School

The trip to reform school took a long time. I felt lonely, and I was afraid. We had heard stories about cruelty and about big kids picking on the little ones like we was, so I figured we was headed for trouble. I've got to pay for my crimes and for the fact that my parents didn't want me. I just wasn't wanted by nobody but the authorities—they'd take me. And for them it's just "Hep, hep, do this, do that. We got you now, and we're going to break you, make you suffer the consequences." Your parents beat you and backhand you, hit you with belts, and throw axes at you. They don't feed you, don't clothe you, don't give you blankets to keep warm at night, don't wash the bed sheets if you have any. This ain't no crime for them. I was the one getting locked up. I had to suffer for how my parents was. So it was a bad trip, sitting in that car, thinking all this stuff. I caught myself sniffling, but I didn't let nobody see me.

It's a shame at that age to be so bitter. Is there any justice for a kid that's trying to grow up with bad parents? I wonder about that. Even at that young age, I knew something was wrong. You go downtown and you see a kid and his parents holding hands, walking down the street. I never had little things like that. Never had my parents hold my hand when we walked downtown and did a little shopping for Christmas or whatever. I never had that privilege. It seems odd, but I never did.

At the reform school there was cottages named for the states—Rhode Island, California, Texas, Colorado, like that. And they had a dormitory. You ate in a cafeteria. They didn't feed too bad; I don't remember going hungry. And the sheets was changed once a week. Us boys did that, which I didn't mind. It would more or less be almost on the basis of keeping your own bedroom clean. And the cottages was always locked up. They was a brick outfit. They had these square steel windows in them about five by eight inches, with thick glass, so there was no way you could crawl out a window.

Us boys kept our cottage clean. That was our job, to mop up and stuff. They had recreation for us, a big gymnasium, a great big field house. You could lift weights and play basketball, Ping-Pong, and tennis in there, and swim. We had our swimming classes and our wrestling classes and boxing—just everything athletic.

But it's the stuff that happen outside the cottage—like when cottage parents aren't around. Things happened between the schools and the details where you'd walk around. Lots of times they'd say, "Well, the boys are doing good," but, truth is, they were scrapping with each other and doing stuff that the authorities wouldn't like.

In reform school there I learned quite a bit, I really did: how to fight, and fight dirty. I learned how to masturbate. I mean that's real education. An older guy showed me how to do it. I was taught first off that nobody was supposed to lay a hand on my ass. Even at my age I played the tough guy so they'd leave me alone.

Well, the first thing that happened to me was I was damn near raped. I was in the hospital with a swelled-up jaw from a toothache, and these two guys come up to me and was trying to put their hands on my ass. They asked me if I knew what *punking out* meant, and *bun boy* and all that. I knew it was wrong, what they was doing, but I didn't know quite what to do. I remember slapping that guy's hands away. Well, there was this one guy. They called him Beak, a big guy, big to me, probably eighteen or nineteen years old. I remember he wasn't around long after I got there. He was in the hospital for measles. He jumped up and said, "Cut the boy loose. Leave him alone." Anyway, he knocked hell out of both them guys. I remember that. And he sat on the bed, and he explained to me the facts of life. He said, "If anybody puts their hand on your ass or tries anything, you pick up everything imaginable and you hit him."

At that time I only weighed about fifty pounds. I wasn't very big, but real wiry. Several times I had to pick up weapons or kick guys. In other words, I was getting taught quite a bit that I really shouldn't have had to be taught at that age, or at any age in fact. And now, God, the big guys scared me after what happened in the hospital there.

I learned about fighting from the other inmates: Kick a guy in the nuts, kick him in the face, kick him in the throat if he's down— that's a good place to kick a man. I learned how to use my fingers in somebody's eyes. Now, I'm talking about twelve years old and learning this stuff. And I learned well. So when I brought this stuff out on the streets and some kid mouthed off, if they got in a fight with me, they was in trouble. Because them kids outside wasn't learning like I was. I knew about every way of dirty fighting there is. Well, to me, if you're going to fight, I don't think no way is clean. You go at it any way you can.

Lots of times they called me "breed" in there, marking me for being Indian. Sometimes they'd say "half-breed." They was trying to ride me, I guess, but I didn't care. Mostly I just worried about being funny-looking, real skinny, and about the niggers. Black against white is how things split up in there.

I had my first pencil fight in reform school. Still got the scar off of that. Lots of stuff in them places aren't on record, like the little scraps you get into. But once in a while they'll catch you fighting, and you'll be in real trouble.

I remember I traded a kid a pair of beat-up shoes for a pair of loafers. I thought them loafers was really something, because I never had any. He snitched on me for having them loafers. But, hell, to me he come out good. He got his loafers back, and I got my raggedy shoes back. He started laughing at me, so I punched him and I bloodied his nose. Mr. Williams—my cottage parent, the guy who looked after us—stood me in the corner for about three hours, from shortly after dinner until suppertime. Well, I'll tell you how fair the man was. He said, "All right, scarecrow, you can come out of the corner now." The kids began laughing. That blew my cool. "You bald-headed son of a bitch," I said. I popped him in the mouth. He grabbed me and tried to hold me back, half laughing and half trying to get me under control. When he got me calmed down, in front of all them boys he said, "I'm going to apologize to Ronny, because I had no right to call him a scarecrow. That's what made him punch me." He used that as a lesson to the boys not to make fun of each other. The man was really fair.

One time I opened my mouth the wrong time, I'll tell you. There was this other cottage parent named Becker. The day before this happened I got in a fight with this kid named McCleary. And I beat him bad. I blackened his eye and split his lip. Mr. Becker broke it up. He grabbed me so hard, he put bruise marks on my arm from his fingers. And I opened my big mouth that next day.

Two guys in our cottage group was coming back from the Laundromat, and they got in a tussle. We had to line up in formation in threes and march. One kid tripped another one from behind—kicked his heel. They got in a scrap, and Becker broke it up. So he said, "If you don't straighten up, you're going to Colorado," the disciplinary

Reform School

cottage. Ohio was for the older guys, and for us younger guys it was Colorado. Now, you could get thrown in there anywhere from thirty days up, whatever it took to straighten you out. And Becker said, "Packquin." That's the way they pronounced my name. They couldn't even do that right. It's pronounced "Paw-kan" actually. Anyway, Becker said to me, "If you don't straighten up, you're going too." And I said, "I don't give a fuck"—my exact words. Why I said that, I don't know. I was being tough, I guess. He said, "All right. You asked for it." So in I went.

The proprietors of that place, Mr. Danby and some other guy—I forget his name—they knew their business. Mr. Becker must have told them about what happened, because Mr. Danby lined us up and said, "I see we got a bunch of bad attitudes here which need straightening up." He turned to me and said, "Paquin, you got a big mouth, I heard." I said, "Yeah, so what?" and he smacked me across the face, knocked me down. I learned right then to keep my mouth shut in that place. Should've kept it shut before.

Here's what they did for our disciplinary. Most of the time all you did was march around, but the rest of that day we beat the mops to get them clean. And I remember a little song everybody sang when you was beating them mops: "If you are tired and cannot sleep, drop your mops and beat your meat." We all sang it. We beat them mops real clean.

Next day, we had breakfast and went back to the dorm. We moved the beds to one side and blocked the doorway with a rug. There was these big silver garbage cans full of soap. Mr. Danby had us strip our clothes off just to our undershorts. He handed each of us a toothbrush—us three that got thrown in and a couple other guys that had some disciplinary coming before that, I guess. We scrubbed that place spotless with them toothbrushes. Then he gave us each a hanky, and we sopped up the water with a hanky.

All this time you had to stay on your knees. You couldn't get up. If you did, you got smacked. I didn't try to get up. Another guy did and got slapped down. His knees hurt. After a while, kneeling in that soap and water rubbed them raw. And you soaked all that up with a hanky. Then you filled both garbage cans full of rinse water, poured them on the floor, and started with them hankies again. They'd stand there, and the one guy would say, "Well, what do you think, Mr. Danby? Don't look very clean to me, eh?" So on come the soapy water again and the toothbrushes. This went on for more than a week—I think it was eight days. I could barely walk.

We'd go to the field house. We'd march. It was steady disciplinary. We'd have to beat the mops and mop in the cottages—the stairways and the basement and the dining room. I was in disciplinary for about a month. It curbed me. I shut my mouth after that—for a while, anyway.

My twin brother and I never got along. You'd think that being together all the time, we'd be close, but we wasn't. We argued and fought like brothers do, but we got quite physical with each other. If there was some new underwear that come out when we'd go to the laundry, I'd try to pick the pile with the new stuff in it. Them others was so cheap that after one washing they was no good—wouldn't even stay up. There wasn't much elastic in them, I think. So one time I got that pile of new underwear, and he grabbed it from me. I punched him. Him and I fought it out right there. Mr. Williams give me punishment.

Another time we was getting confirmed. We had our chaperons, sponsors, and the day of confirming come. We was in the church. I hated to be called skinny. Donny kept doing that; him and Joseph Lynon had a thing going on me that day. I got so mad, I couldn't stand it no more, so I punched Donny. The priest was up there talking about the nice fellows what was getting confirmed, and we was scrapping it out right in front of him.

I had a few good times in there along with the bad, but not many. I learned to do handicraft, and I got experience with my temper. I learned in sports about sportsmanship and keeping cool while I was playing. A man don't have sportsmanship, I don't care how good he is, he's not going to do his team good. No way can he perform if he don't have good sportsmanship. And I found this out in individual sports too, like golfing. That is one of the most frustrating sports I've ever went through. You can't get mad, because you'll never do good. And I can see that works on the same basis as when you're on a team. If you get mad at yourself or somebody else, you're going to screw up.

In sports, I done good. I won a swimming championship. I remember when I went to swimming class, I was so skinny, Mr. Olgum didn't know what to do with me. But I learned everything real well, like lifeguarding. Later, cottage went against cottage in intramural competition. I won a twenty-five-yard freestyle race. I felt proud because they was bigger than we was. So we had to compete against bigger fellows in basketball and other sports. I did all right in sports. The wrestling team I enjoyed most, I think, because I learned to handle myself.

They had a place in that reform school for the real bad ones, and they called it Cell 5 and Cell 6. It was completely dark. Now,

Reform School

they threatened to shut me in there one time, but I think Mr. Williams stopped them. I told them I didn't care. I did see kids come out of there, and I heard them yelling, "Let me out of here! Let me out of here!" One guy took a knife, a table knife, and slashed his leg to get out of there—needed seventy-some stitches. They couldn't leave him in there cut up and bleeding.

Here's the thing. We were always locked up at night, and the cottage was locked till we went outside to play softball or whatever or went to dinner. When we came back, it was lockup time again. It worked at me. I felt uneasy all the time, real anxious. I didn't like being closed in. And I couldn't figure out why they put me in there. Sure, we stole stuff to get in there, but always on my mind was, what about them other guys that got off? How come they were free and I was locked up?

If you had a good report at Christmastime, you could go home for the holidays. I remember the first time we was there, which I'm talking about now, I think seven of us was left in the cottage. There was thirty-some boys other than that. Seven stayed, and the rest went home to mom and dad. I can't remember what excuse they gave us for not being able to go home, but later on, I got these reports which said that there was no way that we should go home. At that time my mother was supposed to have an operation—I guess that was it. But when I was in reform school the second time, the same excuse applied. Actually my parents didn't want us.

There was always physical stuff going on. Oh, God, it's no place for a young fellow. I know that. You got a few dedicated people in there, but you got more who don't care. Even Mr. Williams. He was good to me, and he helped me, but I also seen what happened when he didn't like a kid. He beat one guy nearly every day. There was always something—that kid couldn't do nothing right. From what I seen, the kid wasn't that bad. He was more timid than anything else. But he steady caught hell from Mr. Williams. Mr. Williams just didn't like the kid, so you can see what happens if they don't like you. I don't know what happened to that kid. I met lots of guys later on in the penitentiary that was in reform school with me.

We went to school, but I didn't learn anything. They should've had more sincere people teaching, because we damn sure never had no what I would call qualified teachers there. I mean something was wrong when I had a third-grade reading capacity at age fifteen. I spent some of 1954, 1955, and some of 1956 and 1957 in that place. And I was supposed to be getting so-called schooling. I learned to sew a sheet and a pillowcase, and I learned shop and to weed a garden and put the weights back up after everybody used them. I did learn how to lifeguard. That was constructive. I learned how to wrestle and box. And I learned how to fight.

But I learned nothing in school. When I left there, I was backed up so far that I could barely read and write, and I couldn't do numbers. If they wasn't going to teach us the academic part of what we should have, at least they should've went more into a trade deal. In other words, you're just locked up. They forget that you got to go back to the outside world.

They had women teachers and men teachers. I don't know that if they would put older women in there, whether they'd have a motherly relation with the kids or not, but it was far from that. Now, this one teacher—I forget what class she taught. She was a nice enough woman, but she ignored stuff that went on. Like these older guys would come behind the desk, and they'd rub against her ass. They'd come behind her, and she let them do it, and they'd look under her dress. They'd be on the floor and looking under her dress while she was walking or standing by them. She must have seen that going on. I did it a couple times.

We had another one like that in the linen shop where I first worked when I went down there. They was hiring just whoever they could get. Like that night man, that queer son of a bitch. I'm still vindictive about him. I took lots of beatings from that bastard. To me, you can't beat a kid and straighten him out. You might scare him. After all, you being the authority, you got the upper hand. He's stuck there, but you can leave, go home at night with your family. But as far as doing any good, it don't. Ain't nobody ever beat me that gained my respect or done me good. Let's put it this way: Anybody that ever did me some small favor, I appreciated it, remembered it. Somebody did me a good turn, even if it was through me doing them a good turn first, I respected them, and anybody helped me out later on in life, I did good by them too.

Well, we finally got released. I don't know how they could've let us go back home to that place, but it did say in the report that it seemed like the mother and dad wanted Ronny and Donny home. It *seemed* like it. But as far as the home being favorable, I don't know how they found that, because it was an old log cabin—a shack. It wasn't insulated, it had no electricity, no indoor facilities, and it was filthy, real filthy, and there was bedbugs in that place so bad. But we did go back home. Same old thing.

I remember when we left reform school, Mr. Williams told us, "Boys, you'll be back in four months." Well, by God, he knew what he was talking about, because it was about four months, and we was back. When we got home, things was bad like before. A week of novelty—here's the twins—but that was it. And they was constantly saying, "Why, you little sons of bitches, you're going to get sent away. You're going back to reform school. Ain't you learned yet?" Constantly going to send us away.

I've been religious at times in my life, like when I'm talking about now. Mother Angela was strict, didn't show much leniency. But of all the things that I learned in school—which wasn't much—she taught me the most, I'd say. Anyway, there was a prize for the most rosaries said and the most masses and communions. I won a Bible—I still got it someplace—for going to the most communions. Real religious. Nice pious young fellow.

But everything blew to hell on that. You tell people something when you're a kid, and they're going to believe the authorities, not you. It all amounts to authority. Well, I feared authority, was evasive to them, and didn't respect them. Anyway, to get on with the story, when you go into the pew in the Catholic church, you should move to the center so people don't have to climb over you. One time I went over to the pew, and Gerald, a state cop's son, new kid in school, was in the pew first, and I had to climb over him to get to the center. OK, fine. And I knew damn well I did this. Somebody else climbed over him too. So here comes the priest. He said, "Mr. Paquin, don't you believe in doing what you were told to do?"

I said, "What are you talking about, Father?"

"You didn't move over in the pew."

I said, "What do you mean? I didn't have to move over, because Gerald was there first."

"No, he wasn't," he said. "I was watching."

That damn Gerald just sat there. I said, "I didn't do anything wrong, Father."

"Yes, you did. When you get back to the school, I want you to tell Mother Angela that you did this."

I said, "You want me to tell her the truth then, eh, Father?"

"That's right."

So I told her the exact truth. I told her what happened, and I told her that Father was accusing me of doing it. A little while later there was a phone call. She left, and when she came back, she said, "Ronald, you come here."

Her face was red. Her face would get flaming when she was mad. She brought me in the back room. She said, "You lied to me."

I said, "No, I didn't, Mother. I told you exactly what happened. How come Gerald was never asked? How come I was the only one accused?"

"Hold out your hand," she said. "I'm not going to talk to you any more about this." She took this little ruler and started slapping my hands.

I took the ruler and busted it. Then she took her board, got carried away. I grabbed it, and I said, "Look, I'm tired of this. Father is a liar. I don't care who you believe anymore. Why won't you question Gerald? Maybe he'll tell you the truth. Maybe you don't want to accuse him because his father gives more money in the collection than mine. You're all hypocrites." I turned on her like a snake.

A week later she found out that Gerald done the same thing again. I hadn't gone to church that week—piss on them. She said to me, "Ronald, we found that you weren't the one who did it."

I said, "Oh, you found out. Oh, Gerald's word is better than mine, eh, and Father's is too?"

"Well, why don't you come to church again?"

"I don't get nothing out of it," I said.

I was in trouble all over the place, but it was doings at home what sent us back. And, God, she wouldn't give us blankets. We was freezing. Of course, we had to report to our probation officer. I respected our probation officer and Bert Taylor, the probate judge. I liked both men. They got complaints on us from the neighbors and the schools and just everybody—anonymous calls. And all we heard at home was "You're going back to reform school." We wanted blankets one time. My mother said she didn't have none. She left the house, and we looked under one of them couches that come into a bed, and there was all kinds of blankets under there. Why she wasn't giving them to us I don't know. Something is awful wrong to treat your kids like that. She wouldn't feed us.

My dad drank a lot and let his family go hungry. He was drunk all the time, even in the morning. He was drunk, I think, that time me and my brothers tried to kill him. That was one of the climaxes to getting sent away again. I told my brother Floyd the day before it happened, "I am not taking another backhander across the face or a beating from that bitch. Neither one of them. I'm fighting back." He said, "I won't interfere, Ron," sort of giving me the OK.

Well, my twin brother and I wasn't allowed to have the whole milk, the homogenized milk. We had to use canned milk. I figured to show her different. Next morning, I had my oatmeal, and I went right in there and got the whole milk. I poured it on, and my mother hit me across the face with a belt. I wrapped it around my arm and pushed her into the wood stove. She had a nightgown on; she got burned bad. And I punched her, all the time hanging on to that belt.

My dad tried to grab me, but my brother Floyd pushed him and said, "If one of youse can't handle him, two of youse ain't going to jump on him."

I had to figure out how to let that belt go and get out of there without being killed. I let loose of the belt and tore out of the house, but I tripped. This is no lie: My dad grabbed a poker and swung at me. I ducked. We had some masonite over the door, and that poker busted through. If he had hit me, he'd have splattered my brains, killed me. I kicked him and run out the door.

I threw a rock through the window by the phone. Donny helped me now. I knew she would call the cops. And so my twin brother and I kept throwing rocks; Tommy got with us too. My dad opened the door. He swore at us and shook his fist. He still had the poker. Donny picked up a rock and fired it at him. It spun off the door and caught him on the side of the face near the ear. He fell. I run up and slammed him in the head with that rock. He was bleeding hard when we left.

You know, I still get riled when I think about this stuff, even though it happened years ago. What went on that morning was real ugly—a near tragedy. What makes a kid want to hurt so bad? When my brother hit my dad with that rock, I didn't feel sorry for him laying there and moaning, not at all. I went up and smacked him again. I wanted to kill him. When my mother headed for the phone, we flung rocks at her too. If she had got in the way, she'd have got hit too. We was that mad.

The Mackinac Bridge was being built then. All them sections to the towers was about a half mile from the house. We hid there. We broke into some boxcars and got something to eat. We hid near a week, I think, before they found us and tossed us in jail.

There was this fat turnkey in jail named Walter. When people come to see us, which wasn't often, he'd say, "Oh, they're bad ones, real wicked." My sister Donna come down with a woman—I don't know her name—who bought us a jacket, underwear and stockings, and a coat and shirt so we'd have something to wear back to reform school. Them was the best clothes we ever had. Walter said to my sister, "They ought to lock them up and throw the key away or else gas them. Useless little bastards." I remember one time we was talking loud, laughing, and giggling. "I'm going to come in there and whip both of youse guys' asses," Walter said. We said, "Come on in, you fat son of a bitch." We tore this chair apart. Walter threatened to beat us, which I think he might've did if we hadn't scared him.

So they had a hearing. It come down to Ronny being afraid of the big guys at the school. I never told them why. Maybe I should've told, but they ought to know what's going on: kids getting raped. I can't understand why they didn't send me to that school in Marquette like they said they would. They said that I could be worked with, that reform school was no place for me. But we was going back to reform school.

We was reform-school toughs. We'd brag about it, making out we was real bad, which we was—little Al Capones, you might say. See, even now, after I was in prison and come out, it fascinates people. They wonder what you went through. "I'll bet you he's really tough," they figure. Anyway, we stuck our chests out. We'd been in jail and reform school. And when I went back to reform school, I was seasoned, so nobody messed with me. But I got in lots of fights. In other words, I was getting institutionalized. That's bad. Later on in prison, I met guys that was so institutionalized that they had got to the point that they couldn't adjust to living in society. They're better off in the pen—they get along in there. *Con-wise* and *institution-wise* is the words for it.

Nothing much went on in reform school. I learned nothing in school, but I enjoyed working with my hands. There's not much more to tell, other than fights and wrestling. I joined wrestling again and basketball. Didn't play no football. But it wasn't much different than the first time, other than I learned how to smoke there and, like I said, to masturbate. But I never played the dog-type kid, like the big guys doing it to the little ones like I didn't want done to me. To me a kid learns the wrong things when he sees kids getting busted out and pissed on and beat up and cruelty by the cottage parents. You don't gain nothing.

Something good almost happened on that second trip. They check your home report. This time the home report was so bad, it looked like we'd have to stay in reform school till we was nineteen. If you're an older kid, they get you a job in a bowling alley or someplace so you can have some money when you get out. Well, the Lions Club women would come. They'd bring box lunches and stuff like that, and you'd do things together for an evening or a few hours in the afternoon.

Well, this Mrs. Carnady picked us twins, and we really got attached to her because, boy, she seemed to care about us. I liked her. In fact, sometimes I think about her even now. I wonder how my life would've been if I'd went with her. At that time I was scared of big cities. The niggers scared me in reform school, and I knew they lived in Lansing and in the big cities. So I was afraid of big cities. It come to where she wanted to adopt us. They left it up to us boys. Maybe they shouldn't have. I believe somebody could've talked us into not being afraid of the big city. Well, Mrs. Carnady wanted to adopt us. She asked us boys, and she said, "I love both of you." She meant it. You could tell. She said, "You will be well clothed and well treated, but you have to go to school." And she said, "How would you boys like to come and live with me?" We turned her down. She started crying, bawled her eyes out, begged us. I look back now, and it was a sad ordeal.

I run away from there one last time after I come back the second time. That was a ill deal, though. It was wintertime, just getting winter. The puddles was froze with ice on top and water underneath. When we jumped the fence to the East Lansing High School there, we got our feet wet. Was it cold! We busted into a car and got an army blanket and some cigarette butts and matches and a box of .30-30 shells. We couldn't keep warm. We finished smoking the cigarette butts, and I said, "Why don't we give ourselves up? We won't get nothing for running off if we do." We turned ourselves in and never got punished.

In there they start you out with a hundred points, and you get so many points taken off for doing bad and so many gained by doing something right. If you lost more than half your points, you was in trouble. A lot of times I didn't have no points at all. If you run away, you got ten days' disciplinary for that. If you got caught smoking, you got thirty days for that. If you got caught fighting, that was thirty days too. Well, Donny was ready to go home, and I wasn't. He put on like he was waiting for me because he didn't want to leave without Ronny. Well, that wasn't the case. He had to stay because our home report was so bad.

One day we were in line at the cafeteria. We was getting our food, and Mr. Williams called us aside. He said, "Boys, I got a surprise for you. You're going home."

I said, "Aw, come on, don't bullshit us."

Now, Ron, you are," he said. "Your uncle Francis is here, and he's going to take you home."

I didn't believe him till I seen my uncle's car. They took us to dress up and put new khakis on us, and home we went. We didn't even want to finish eating. He asked us if we wanted to eat. I said no. I couldn't wait to leave there.

High School Days

They let us out of reform school, and we went to my aunt and uncle's. I suppose between the two choices, that was the better one. But really I think they should've found us another home like they did with Mrs. Carnady, but not in the city, where all the niggers was. We feared them, but we'd have gone to a small town someplace.

I liked my aunt. She swung the strap too much when I was young, but she was a better mom to me than my mother ever was. I remember in reform school they did what you call scoring, like they'd say, "Hey! Your mom's a whore, and I'll be at her door," stuff like that. Always scoring on your momma. If you didn't like somebody and you wanted to sass them, you'd say something gross about their mother. I'd tell them guys, "You can call my mother anything you want, but don't call my aunt nothing." They'd look at me like I was crazy. I'd tell them, "Call my aunt something and I'll smash your face."

Well, our uncle made all sorts of promises. "One thing," he said, "you boys are going to school. We're going to build a nice new home. You boys are going to help us." Fine! "But one definite thing is you're going through school," he said. What bullshit! He worked us from daylight till dark, from dark till daylight, no rest, just worked us steady. We weren't experienced carpenters, but we pounded lots of nails building that house. The bedroom made for us was barely longer than the bunk beds that was in there; that was our twins' bedroom. They made my cousin a nice big bedroom.

Then Donny got a job at Belle Isle Restaurant. When Donny got that job, I had to do all the work around the house, like go after wood. My uncle cut pulpwood. Them sticks is eight feet two inches

High School Days

long and pretty big around, so they was heavy. It was damn hard work, but cutting fireplace wood was worse. Uncle Francis sold that, so when Donny got the job, then I had to do it all.

Uncle Francis is huge—six feet one inch tall and about 270 pounds, a great big man. And my aunt was a pleasant-looking, heavyset woman. She favored me, and Francis favored Donny, so Francis worked my ass off. But when Donny come home, he didn't do nothing. He did his shift in the restaurant; that was the extent of it. But I worked all the time, it seemed like.

Well, one week I split fifty cords of newly cut beech, plus hauled all the water, plus went out and helped get that fifty cords. I mean, it was work, work, work. And so I said to myself, "Piss on this. I'll fix it. I'll get a job too." I heard about an opening at the same restaurant Donny worked at. So I got work washing dishes. My uncle was mad at first, but he calmed down, and I can see why, which I'll explain later.

I stayed with my aunt and uncle through the ninth grade. Donny and I worked at Belle Isle Restaurant that summer. After I went to work, we both helped with the chores, like hauling water. There still wasn't no electricity or indoor facilities, but we had an outdoor toilet, and the house was clean. My aunt was a good housekeeper. And later on they got gas mantle lights, which gave better light than the kerosene lamps we'd been using.

We went to school that year. I was one of two guys in their freshman year that got their letter in football—made first string. I made B-team basketball and was quite a star on that. And I run track. My uncle come to one basketball game. You know, when a kid plays sports—I know how I felt—you want to show not only the fans that you can help the team, but if you got somebody there personally thinking about you and watching the game, it helps. I know if my son ever becomes good at sports, or even if he's not so good at sports but likes to play them, I'll go see him. I'll make darn sure to let him know I'll be there too. It helps him, lets him know I care about him. But nobody come to but one basketball game for me.

I didn't go out at first for track, and there was only a few weeks left in the season. Bud Tascillio, the track coach, come up to me in study hall and said, "Ron, you went out for football and basketball. How come you haven't been out for track?"

I said, "Aw, I can't run."

"Aw, come on," he said. "We got a meet today. Why don't you come with us? We got a meet with Cheboygan."

"What do you want me to run?"

"The mile," he said.

I never smoked while I was playing football and basketball, but I started smoking again as soon as the basketball season was over, and I was out of shape. So I said, "No, I can't. I can't." But he talked me into it, and, Jesus, out of sixteen guys, I come in third.

That felt good, so I started working out, and within a few weeks I was running good times—good for a tiny school like I went to. I come in first in the regional trials in Marquette and third in the finals, but I got a bit of an excuse there. I think I could've beat the top man. In the trials the coach told me to pace the fastest guy. So I stuck with him for three-quarters of a mile, and the coach said, "Get going finally!" He yelled out, "Get going, stork!" And I beat the guy. So he told me to do the same thing in the finals. In high school track you got to be two steps ahead of a man before you can cut in front of him. When I tried to make my move, they had me what you call boxed in. It's an old trick, but it worked. I couldn't get by them.

I did real good in sports. I liked that, but I hated school. I never learned much. I had D's and D-minuses—just passing and no more. But I tried to keep passing in three of four classes, even with D's, to keep me eligible for sports. So one thing worked for the other.

Sports was good for me. I drank some on weekends, but when I played sports, there was no way that I could get drunk and fight, or even smoke. When I was in the athletic program, I didn't get in trouble. But I didn't have the concentration I needed in school. I was backed up so far that I never knew what was going on, so I felt stupid. When I was fifteen, my reading capacity was third-grade level. Christ, third-graders, even smart ones, can't read much.

So there wasn't much going for me in school. I could always get up in front of a crowd and talk. If I'd write a composition, I'd flunk right off because I couldn't spell. I guess a kid's got to be comfortable when he's going to school. If he's got any brains, he can learn something with help from his parents. If he's having trouble in school, well, help him out. Don't treat him like a dummy, because that's exactly what he's going to be. If a kid loses confidence, he don't do good. I know I didn't.

I never dated then. I was scared of girls. In my sophomore year I went out once, but I never messed with girls in ninth grade. I was always afraid they'd say no to me, which one did when I was a freshman. She didn't say no; her mother did. She was a real prominent girl, and she sat next to me in a lot of classes. Catherine was her name. It was the homecoming dance, and I was a bit of a football star. Everybody was asking a girl to go, and I kind of had a crush on her even in grade school, so I asked her for a date.

High School Days

"I'll be glad to go with you, Ron," she said.

Next day, she came and said, "Ron, I can't go."

I said, "What do you mean?"

"Well," she said, "I've got to be honest. My mother won't let me." I knew who her mother was, and this really pissed me off. Her mother worked in an office in St. Ignace.

I went to the office building and waited till Catherine's mother come out of work. I held the door open for her. She said, "Thank you, young man."

I said, "Well, that's OK, you slut, you two-faced bastard. Every one of them like you are sons of bitches."

She stood there, her mouth hanging open, her hand up by her throat. She couldn't figure out what was going on—this nice young man calling her a slut. So I told her, "You didn't even know me, yet you go by what you hear. You think I'm no good for your daughter. Go to hell! Go pure to hell! People like you stink!"

She started yelling then. She was going to throw me in jail.

I said, "You can't throw me in jail for nothing. You're the one that ought to be in jail."

People like her piss me off. They think just like her. They're against guys that have had a rough time. Spend time in reform school or in the joint and—I tell you, I went through it—you don't never get through paying interest on your debt to society. Those kind of people are your worst enemies after you've went and done your time. They are prolonging your sentence. It makes me sick.

I stumbled through school my freshman year and got advanced to being a sophomore somehow. Of course, now the coaches was really looking me over. I was first string on all the sports coming up.

Donny and I was working at Shores Restaurant that summer before my sophomore year, and, ill luck, we fell in love with this girl, Liz. We was infatuated with her. Both of us liked her at the same time, and she played us for suckers. We never come in much physical contact with her. I don't know if Donny did, but I doubt if he knew any more about girls than me. I kissed her and don't remember feeling anything special. I mean, it was different, but I never petted her. I didn't know nothing about them aspects of girls yet. Donny and me wore out a patch of grass behind the restaurant fighting over that girl, but she was soon forgotten in the fall.

My uncle was making his move that summer. He kept asking, "Are you boys going to draw unemployment this year?" I said, "I can't draw unemployment and go to school." Summer slid by, and football practice began in August. I went to practice. I was looking forward to the season. Well, somebody gave my aunt and uncle a little cabin, and they moved it down. My uncle stuck it behind the house we built. It's still there. They put a bed in the cabin, and Donny and I slept there. Fine. Then they were going to get a little stove, a wood stove for us to cook on.

It come time to go to school. Donny got kicked out first. My uncle kicked Donny out. Donny come up and seen me. He didn't give a damn if he went to school. He said, "I'm kicked out."

I asked, "I'm kicked out too?"

"You can't draw unemployment and go to school too," Donny said. "You got to pay room and board."

My uncle, that son of a bitch! We were giving him money, and he was getting welfare all the time we was staying there. He was putting it like he wasn't getting a cent to help feed us and that. I called my uncle on the phone. He said, "If you're going to school, get out!"

"What happened to all them promises you promised us?" I asked. I was in a rage. I am again right now, just thinking about it. "What happened to all them promises that we were darn sure going to finish school?"

"I can't support youse if you ain't going to bring no money in," he said.

"I see your game, you fat bastard. We build your house, clear your land, put your ass on easy street, and now we got to get out. You get all that free work and then throw us out." He was denying all that, and I said, "I'll come down there, and I'll cut your fucking head off with an ax."

I hung up the phone and zoomed out the door. I took off running, and the owner of the restaurant jumped in his car. He stopped me, caught me about a quarter of a mile down the road. He said, "Jesus, Ron, calm down. You cut that man and you'll end up in prison." He grabbed hold of me and talked me out of it.

Next day, I went to the probate court and asked them if there was any way we could hold him to his promise. I thought maybe there was guardianship papers signed on us or adoption papers—something written down. But there was nothing. I was crying and really upset. The judge told me that he couldn't help me, and I thanked him. I said, "Jesus Christ, thanks a lot. I really got protection from the courts."

He said, "I'm sorry, Ron."

"Yeah," I said, "not half as sorry as I am."

So there I was, out in the cold. Well, they had a little cabin back of the restaurant where they stored things. The owner fixed up a place for me to live there. Pretty decent guy, huh? Then my sister

High School Days

Donna heard about my troubles and offered me a place to stay. I accepted. Donny went in the service then, but I had a chance to go to tenth grade. I'd wanted to enlist in the Navy like Donny did. Talk about disappointed! I really wanted to join. But my academics was so low, I couldn't pass the mental test. Probably now I could, but then I couldn't. I tried hard, but they wouldn't take me.

My sister Donna married a guy named Don Corp. I didn't stay at their place long. Don Corp is smart. I remember I'd come home from school, and he would try to teach me, but he would be ridiculing me at the same time because I was so backed up. I wasn't learning. I don't even know how I was passing anything, to tell you the truth. I wasn't learning, and I was confused, emotionally confused. I didn't know what was going on.

Sports held me together more than anything else. I'd play basketball or football, and Don Corp would come to all the games. He really liked sports. I got some damn good compliments from him and his friends, and it built me up. I thought, "Well, somebody cares." But then he'd go drinking, and I'd be with him—I don't want to tell much of this. Well, I just couldn't get along at their place. I like Donna. She's my favorite sister, and I don't want to hurt her feelings, so let's just say I felt uncomfortable in that house for reasons I'd rather not say. When I left there, I started living in a junked car. That's where I slept.

That goddamn old lady of mine, my mother! I slept in that car. My brother Floyd junked a few cars around the house, and I used to sleep in an old Ford, only it didn't have no wheels on it. She knew I was there. I'd drink to keep warm; it was wintertime going into spring. I'd get pretty drunk. You could always find somebody to drink with. I washed up in a gas station—I forget where. And I'd go down and do my clothes at the Laundromat, get them pressed, so I went to school pretty decent—dressed, clean, I mean.

But she let me sleep out in that cold car. She knew what was going on with me, her flesh and blood, but she left me out there. She never offered me to come in at all. So I drank quite a lot, and I started fighting, getting in fights all the time. I got a reputation as a tough guy. Nobody could whip me, and lots of them tried.

I turned eighteen years old in my sophomore year, 1960. My grades in English made me ineligible for track. I could beat everybody in track. I'd practice with them, pace them, but I could never run in meets because I was ineligible. Bud Tassillio, the football coach, took an interest in me. He tried to teach me to spell, which I can't do even now. Spelling takes a lot of concentration if you're an average student.

I had one date, and I didn't even ask for it. Susie and I rode the school bus together. She went to Brevort, and I went to Groscap. I was staying with my sister Donna then. Susie asked me for a date, and the way she went about it was, she said, "You going to the show tonight?"

I said, "Yeah."

"Well, I'm going to the show too," she said. "Who are you going with?" Then she laughed and said, "I'm going with Ronny."

I looked at her. I did kind of like her. She said, "Aren't we, Ronny?" And I said yes.

"Why don't you ask me?" she said.

"Are you serious?"

"Yes."

So I said, "OK. How'd you like to go to the show with me?"

She said, "I'd love to."

So her friend Patty said, "You don't have a car, so we'll double-date if it's OK with you and Ron."

I said, "Sure." I don't know how else we could have did it, because I didn't have a car.

Well, I took her to the show. I did kind of like her. I kissed her once in the show, and it was quite a long kiss, and I enjoyed it. She was a nice-looking girl, and I did have some feeling for her. I kissed her a couple times on the way home and once good-night. That was it.

That was Friday night. On Saturday I went to Hessel Dance Hall and got in a fight. Susie heard about it and said, "What's the idea of going there? How come you didn't call me?"

I said to myself, "What is she trying to prove? I take her out once, and she's bossing me around." I told her, "Forget it. I'm not going steady with you." She got mad and walked away. I didn't ask her out no more, and no other girls for a while.

I did go out with this one girl, Sue Thomas from Trout Lake. She was working in St. Ignace. I don't guess it was love, but it was big stuff to me. I didn't know what love was, but I liked her a lot. I didn't get in her pants or anything like that, but we got pretty heated up. We used to dry-screw, if you know what I mean. That sounds funny to me now. I'd lay on top of her, and we'd rub together. Sometimes I'd come doing that, but mostly it was just frustrating. I'd slide my hands inside her shirt and her pants and touch her. But we never took our clothes off. And I put my hands between her legs. She never said no or tried to stop me. She moved her hips like she wanted more than I was giving her. I knew she'd had it with other

High School Days

guys. I wanted her, but I didn't know what to do. I was afraid of making a fool of myself, that she'd slap me or laugh at me. So we never got it on together. I couldn't get my nerve up to try it with no other girls neither. I'd still never been laid.

I got in one hell of a scrape when I was eighteen—near killed my buddy. I'd drink too much and go crazy. I'd be the life of the party for a while, cracking jokes and dancing to beat hell, clowning, but then I'd turn violent. I'd think somebody crossed me or something like that, and I'd fly into a rage. I lost friends that way, and kids my age feared me. I'd go to the dances, and I'd have a good time, but at intermission there was always a fight, and I'd get right into them. I was making a bad life for myself, in other words.

I got drunk with whiskey. Hermie Montry bought it for me. I was with Murray Stanley—he ended up in the penitentiary—and Pete Ogle, which he got locked in the pen too, more than once. Between the three of us, we probably done about fifteen years behind bars.

I got really stumbling drunk that day. It started out OK, but I started thinking about my brother-in-law, and I got real mad. We bought more whiskey and drank it. About eight o'clock that night I decided I was going after my brother-in-law Don Corp. Murray and Pete and the girl with them steady tried to talk me out of it, but I said, "I'm going to get an ax and kill that son of a bitch." I was riled.

We got rid of that girl somewhere, and we rode around the boulevard down by the lake towards where the bridge is now. We was riding down there, and I said, "Turn this goddamn car around"— I boiled over—"because I'm going back." Corp lived in Groscap, and we was going the wrong way. And they said, "No, Ron, we can't do it." I burst into a rage, grabbed the rearview mirror, broke it off, and slammed Murray in the face with it. I hurt him bad, cut him. He still carries an awful scar on his face.

They stopped the car. Pete grabbed the wheel. We was heading for the lake. We got out, and Pete said, "Come on, Ron. Calm down." I punched him, really hit him hard, knocked him out. I drove the car into the lake and drug Murray into the woods. Pete woke up, and then I got scared. I said, "Now, I'm telling you two"—Murray was still out—"stay here! I'm going to my brother-in-law's." I meant my other brother-in-law, Sonny Huyck, not the one I was after. I told them guys I'd get help, so I went up to Sonny's.

I looked awful. I had bloodstains on me from Murray; blood sprayed all over the car. I told Sonny, "I've been drinking whiskey. I think I killed my buddy."

Sonny got serious. He said, "Ron, what happened?" and I told him. And he said, "I can't close the store till ten o'clock." He owned a gas station and a grocery store.

Just then, Sholey Smith walked in, and he looked to me like the guy I told to stay down below the hill. I picked him off his feet and smashed his head against the door casing. Then Sonny was shook up because that was his customer. Sonny grabbed me. I don't know where a man gets his strength when he's drunk, but I had strength left over. It was frightening strength I had. I threw Sonny around the store. He yelled for my sister to call the cops.

Well, there was Sonny throwing canned goods at me, and I broke off a Coke bottle to keep him away. In walked Murray and Pete. I had the Coke bottle in my hand, and I hit poor Murray. He stumbled and fell. Pete, not wanting to die, run out the door.

The cops come and drug my ass to jail. Two of them brought me there. Their names was Barclay and Riker, state cops, good-sized fellows. I got a crying jag, and they said, "Well, Ron, you going to calm down now?"

I said, "Yeah," but in my mind I said to myself, "Wait till them sons of bitches get them handcuffs off me."

They took them cuffs off. Riker was standing near me, and I slammed him. Barclay grabbed a blackjack and smacked me with it. I staggered back, but I didn't go down. And I said, "Come on, big boy. You're going to need more than that." I headed toward him, and he hit me again. I passed out.

When I woke up next morning, I said, "Boy, am I hurting!" I was swelled up and sick too. I said, "Those guys beat me up. They hit me, and I got witnesses." Sonny didn't press charges for the destruction in the store. All I got out of that deal was a drunk-and-disorderly and ten days' lockup time. That was my first real jail time except for when I went back to reform school.

When I come out of jail, I went to Trout Lake to see Sue, and, dumb me, I had wrote and told her I was locked up. I asked her not to tell, but her mother and dad found out. I went with my buddy to date her. Her parents was polite to me but real evasive. I knew when somebody didn't want me around. Her parents figured I was a jailbird.

Sue and I dated a few times after that, and then she went out with somebody else. That tore me up. I didn't care that much about her when I think back on it, but at the time I felt bad, was jealous. It was my first halfway serious encounter with a girl. I heard she went out with a guy named Tony Lee, so I hitchhiked all the way up there

High School Days

to Trout Lake. School year was going on then. I waited till noon hour and called him out. He come out, and there must have been fifty kids that followed us down by the baseball field to watch the fight. I knocked him down a few times, and he said he quit, so I didn't press things.

Sue and I went out a couple more times after that, but she kept dating this other guy too. And I finally said, "Hell, I'm too jealous, and I don't even know why."

I don't know, maybe it was wrong what I did. I told this buddy of mine, "I'm going to talk to her about it, and then I'm going to slap her." So I hit her, but not real hard, just enough to sting her. I didn't hurt her, but I could see the red hand mark on her cheek. She called me a son of a bitch and walked away. You can see how violent I was—settling stuff with my fists, slapping a girl.

I quit school in the spring of my sophomore year. I had no place to live and no money. That summer I had a hard time getting a job. I bummed around, half-starving to death. I figured that I had better, next fall, get a job. My brother Floyd told me about it. Floyd is a raw-boned fellow like me. He and his wife, Catherine, and their kids was in a cabin in the woods, cutting pulpwood, so that's where I went. Wasn't long before Floyd cut his leg real bad and couldn't work out there no more, so I drove the family into town. I couldn't drive very good, but I got it home for them and I give them my paycheck that week to help his family and buy groceries. But talk about bad luck running with bad luck! He was using a drawknife, and it cut above his kneecap all the way to the bone. It really screwed him up, laid him up for better than eight weeks. Then his house burnt down, so I give them that check to buy food for the kids. I liked his kids. Always did like kids.

After Floyd cut himself, I went back to the woods and stayed by myself for a couple weeks. Then Big Boy Curry—Leroy Curry—heard I was out there. He was about my size, a little heavier, a few years older. He asked if he could stay with me, and I said, "Sure. I'd enjoy the company." Which I did. I enjoyed it immensely because you'd get talking to yourself out there after a while. No radio, no nothing.

And so that winter of 1961–62, I batched out in the woods. Me and Big Boy cut pulpwood all that winter. We snared all our rabbits, our deer, and we'd make nine cents a stick cutting pulpwood. We did it with a bucksaw and a double-bitted ax. And I didn't give a damn how much money I made. I'd cut my 100 sticks for one day's work, and after I got 100 sticks, I'd quit. Once in a while I'd cut maybe 120 if I felt like it, but I usually just cut 100 sticks. I worked six and a half days. And then I'd usually cut 50 sticks Sunday morning. Well, that was my paycheck.

We'd pitch in for groceries—cost us five bucks apiece. We'd buy some bread and butter and flour. After you did that a few times, you didn't need to buy much more. Sometimes we'd get to splurging and buy some pork chops or bacon maybe. We didn't have a refrigerator. Of course, in wintertime you didn't need it because we had a big silver garbage can where we froze stuff up. And that one room in the cabin had a dirt floor, so that's where we hung our deer. Deer's damn good when it's hanging like that. If we needed a chunk, we'd go cut her off. Rabbit's the same way. Of course, you got to take the guts out of rabbits. You do your deer too, but when you hang them up, boy, they taste real good.

We'd run our snare line every evening after we finished cutting sticks. We tried all sorts of snares. I set spring poles and the snares for rabbits and deer—deadfalls for rabbits. I used one of them number-four triggers. They go off, you got a little pile of logs there, and it catches the rabbit. The rabbits look funny when they're caught. They're on their hands praying almost, and it catches them in the back of the neck, and it's a sure thing.

We tried an experiment too. It worked good. We took rattraps, drilled a hole through them, and put on an extra spring. We put them upside down on a tree and put cinnamon, salt, and sugar strings on it. When the rabbit come up, he'd set the trigger off when he started nibbling on that string, and that wire would smack him in the head. He'd stagger off, and you'd find him ten, twelve feet away. Sometimes they'd die instantly.

One time we come down and checked our traps, and there was a weasel. They'll attack a full-grown rabbit and suck the blood out of the jugular vein. Anyway, he was sucking the blood out of this rabbit we caught. Damn, if a weasel was three feet tall, I wouldn't go into the woods. I studied up on them, and they got what they call a constant migraine headache. They're mean. They'll have as many as fifty mice in their den—they're killing constantly. Anyway, that weasel come at me. I thought he had rabies and was going to bite me, but he stopped and stared at me. I grabbed some rattraps off the tree, and I set them around there. The weasel come at me again, and I caught him. I mounted him and got eighteen bucks for him next time I went into town.

But the extent of my life that winter was cutting pulpwood, getting drunk, and going into Hessel Dance Hall on Saturday nights and knocking hell out of a few out-of-town guys, and going back to

High School Days

the woods. Ain't no girl come near me or Big Boy. Christ, we smelled like a goddamn cedar tree. We just went to the dance hall to brawl. We got what we was looking for too. Then we'd go heal our wounds for the rest of the week.

After a while Big Boy and I been out there too long. We were bullshitting together, and pretty soon we knew everything about each other, and we were trying to catch each other in a lie, just looking for a fight. The last two months we spent out there, we couldn't get along for nothing. We were always fighting. We'd get fighting among ourselves when we'd go to these dances. Every once in a while somebody would come to see us, and we'd go shoot a deer with them or ride into town and get drunk. I'm surprised I didn't do no jail time that winter. We was constantly drinking something out there. We made home brew and wine, plus the stuff we bought. We'd stock up on the weekend for all week.

In that cabin where Big Boy and I was staying, we didn't have no toilet or anything. We shit and went to the bathroom out there in an old 1937 Chevy truck. I remember we put rabbit fur around the seat there so we wouldn't freeze our buns off. But we'd bring the fur out with us, because if you left it out at night, it would get frosty. We each had one. In that cabin you could stand in and piss out if you wanted to, or stand out and piss in if you wanted to. It didn't really make much difference. Usually, if we had to piss at night, we would just stand in the doorway and piss out. There was about a foot drop to some pine boards. At night you could hear porcupines chewing them boards—getting salt, I guess.

One night Big Boy had to take a shit. He had to walk out to the truck. He was drunk. Normally he would've heard them porcupines. He stepped out the door in his stocking feet. Why he didn't put some boots on, I don't know. He stepped right on that porcupine and let out a scream. Scared me. Big Boy was a sight for having pain. I said, "Take it easy. I'll take you inside and fix you up."

When you get a dog with quills in him, you soak their foot in vinegar and milk—warm vinegar and milk. If them quills stay in there, they'll keep drawing and pull themselves in. Big Boy's foot looked like a pincushion, and his ribs was sore from a fight he got in. He was in bad shape, and I was half drunk myself. I was pulling them quills out with a pair of pliers. God, did he yell! I got most of them out, and the rest I clipped right off. Then I soaked his foot in vinegar and milk for about two hours. I imagine that hurt. We had some drawing salve. I had halfway sobered up, and he damn sure sobered up, so I took and bandaged him up good with that drawing salve and put him to bed.

The next day, his foot was swelled up but not as bad as I thought it would be, and that drawing salve really worked. He had some infection, so the next weekend when we went into town, he got a shot for infection—I guess he got it for tetanus. But in four days he was walking around good anyway. He even went to work the next day; we each got our hundred sticks.

That was the extent of my life in the woods—cut our sticks, get drunk, and a lot of fights. I stayed out there all that fall and winter. I come out in the spring, and I remember saying to myself, "Christ, there's got to be a better way to make a living than this."

On the Skids

My life was on the skids. I had tried to go back to school one last time. I was nineteen, but I got hemorrhoids and had to quit. That was the end of me and school.

Most of my time was just drinking and fighting after that, and running after women. I hung out with some crazy guys. Don—now, there was a wild son of a bitch. His sister was a nice-looking girl, but she was pretty rank too. Anyway, he said he boxed in Chicago. He said he was good, and I said I didn't think he was that good. So we were friends, and we had a boxing match. I found out he might've boxed, but he was a slugger.

I put his lights out three times in one little scrimmage. His sister watched from the balcony or above it on the stairway to the upper apartment. We was on the ground. We had the car lights on— that's what we boxed with—so I beat him, no big thing. His sister walked up to him and said, "I thought you could box." She spit in his face. He swiped at her and missed, and she run.

I'll tell you the type of guy Don was. He's dead now; I still haven't figured out how that happened. The day he died, I was walking down the street. I was married then. I seen Don, and he waved a beer at me. "Ron," he yelled, "want to have some beers?" And I said no. He was in a strange car. Then come to find out later that he fell out of the car, they said. He got killed. Killed himself, I think. He did some crazy things, so I think he probably jumped out of the car and people kept it quiet.

One night he was up to the same apartment where I'm talking about now. I'm just telling you this so you'll understand the company I was hanging around with. He had a hunting knife with a six-inch blade on it. He was picking his fingernails, and his sister, making trouble again, said, "You big sissy, quit picking your fingernails. You want a manicure, go down and get one."

"You call me a sissy?"

"Yeah, that's all you are."

He was drinking. He put his leg up on the chair and stabbed that knife right through the calf of his leg, right through. Fool! I pulled it out.

Another time when we was drinking, he held his eyelid down or up and showed everybody how close he could put a cigarette. I knocked him out that night—he'd have blinded himself. He had a crooked finger, like where the tendons were all goofed up on it. And how he got that was he bent a beer can in half and showed everybody how tough he was by slamming his hand down on it. He cut hell out of it. He did weird things when he was drinking. But like I said, he killed himself.

There's a thousand stories I could tell you, mostly about fighting, but by now you get the idea of what my life was like, so I'll just skip all them brawls I got into.

A lot of times when I'd get drunk, I'd want to hurt myself. This is a bad thing for somebody, though—feeling sorry for yourself. Sure, I got kicked around. I never had a chance, no chance at all of making a decent start in life. But the worst thing a man or woman can do is feel sorry for themselves, because self-pity is the most lethal weapon there is against yourself. Believe me, I know. If somebody's feeling sorry for himself, he's never going to get on the right street toward becoming a man, or woman either. Self-pity is a lethal weapon. Self-lethal is what it is.

I got drunk one time, and I got to cutting myself in the arm. I was more or less looking for attention. This woman used to run a restaurant down there, kind of a kids' hangout. Northern Pines, it was called. She and her husband watched me like a father and mother. She took the knife away from me. And she was a nice woman, real likable. She liked us kids, you know, and everybody hung out at Northern Pines. She took good care of us. We'd get rowdy, but she only called the cops when things really got out of hand. Eileen Gay was her name, and Andy was an ironworker, a big burly fellow. Him and I was friends. In fact, Eileen and Andy would take in babies that girls had out of wedlock and couldn't keep. Eileen and Andy was raising three of them. They were real good people.

Another time that I got drunk, me and another guy held our arms together and let cigarettes burn between them to see who could take the most pain. This was on a dare. I got three big scars on my left arm now from those cigarette burns. I've carried these scars for a long time, and they'll probably be there for the rest of my life. Then I carved my initials in my arm one night with a knife. I've tried to kill myself too, but I'll talk about that later.

Other than drinking and fighting, one thing I did do a lot of is violating — for deer, you know. I can't see how the state owns the wild animals, deer in this case. I believe in regulation, but if a man's hungry, he should have the right to shoot a deer to feed himself. And heck with these seasons! That's politics. People won't go out and just shoot deer for the fun of killing.

I'm an Indian, and I don't have to buy a license, which I never did get one. But I didn't senselessly slaughter deer. If I shot three or four deer in a night, I gave them to my relations that I knew needed meat. Once in a while I'd sell some. But when I busted my hand fighting one time, all I could do was pull a trigger. I shot deer then. That's the way I made my living.

Same way when I worked on a fish tug. We'd get a few trout we was meant to put back, but I'd sell them. They was dead. Why throw them back and waste the meat? And you're selling these deer to the very people that won't go out and dirty their hands to shoot one for themselves. But they'd buy it from you if it's hush-hush. I've sold deer to prominent people in this town, and to me if it's wrong to shoot them like that, you're just as guilty buying it. I'd snare deer and rabbits. I was always selling rabbits in wintertime. I did a lot of violating, but none of the meat went to waste, unless I sold it to some fancy son of a bitch, and he didn't eat it.

My friend Roger and I went violating one night. He had a 1953 Chrysler. It was a heavy car and went down the back roads real good. We was at the airport there by Engadine, with a deer in the trunk. We left the airport, and here came the game wardens. "Well," Rog said, "if they search this car, we're in trouble." So I put my head on his shoulder, and he put his arm around me, and we made like we were a guy and a girl. Them wardens followed us for a while, and I told Roger that if they stopped us, I'd have to shoot — they'd think we were a couple of queers. But that trick worked good.

When there weren't no deer, we'd steal cedar boughs. In fall you'd start cutting them, and then you'd sell them by the twenty-five-pound bale. We'd get permits; you needed a permit to cut this stuff. On the permit for Roger's property we'd say we got a hundred bales off that. There wasn't two bales to be cut on his property. Then we'd steal them boughs from state land. One night it cost us eight dollars in gas to get seven dollars' worth of boughs, but we had fun sneaking around. We'd sell boughs to this Lawton guy, a crooked son of a bitch. Then we'd steal them back from him and sell them somewhere else. We had bales going all over for a while.

So I did a lot of violating. I'd get them deer ready just before the season opened. I'd hang them up; they'd be all gutted out. I'd have eight-pointers and ten-pointers and some spikehorns. One time we had a fourteen-pointer. Now, these hunters from down below, some of them are avid hunters, but most of them come up here to drink and whore around. I'd go into the bars and start talking to these hunters, and one night I sold eight deer. I can imagine the stories they brought down to Detroit and Chicago and all over about how they shot this deer. The most money we ever got for a deer was 150 bucks for that fourteen-pointer. Usually it averaged about 75 bucks for a deer. I did that for two years, and I never had trouble getting rid of them. Some hunter would always buy them.

My friend Larry was cherry yet, never been laid. Man, this is embarrassing. We had Al Davenport's car, a Mercury, red and white wreck. I think Mike's Pontiac was in the garage getting fixed. Al went to jail that night for something—I don't remember what—so we ended up with his car, said we'd take it home for him. He said it was OK when he went to jail. So we were going to bring Mike home out to Point aux Chenes. Larry and I was going to bring the car back; he was staying at the trailer with me.

So we were on our way to bring Mike home. Be goddamned if there wasn't a girl hitchhiking! The brakes went on. I got in the back seat, and we stopped and asked her where she was going. She said, "I'm going to Wakefield." And we said, "Jump in, ma'am." She did.

We thought then that she wasn't worried when she got in with three strange men—we was drunk too. And so she said, "Will you bring me to Wakefield? I'll buy you a case of beer and some wine." Well, I mention the wine. That's what we drank. That's what I drank mostly. "We'll go some place and drink it," she said. This told us a whole bunch. I pretended I didn't know anything about girls, which I didn't know a hell of a lot other than what I learned from Sharon, which I'll tell you about in a bit.

So we went to a parking place in the woods. This girl told us that we could have all we wanted. Well, I took her, Mike took her, and it was Larry's turn. We was telling him, "This is how you do it." So he got on her, and we said, "For Christ's sake, Larry, move your ass back and forth. Do something!" Mike and I had Larry by the ass, pushing him back and forth and moving him up and down, just having one hell of a time. I think Mike took seconds. I didn't want no more.

She got dressed, and we said to ourselves, "We ain't going to bring her home way up to Wakefield, that's for sure." Isn't that rotten? The car stalled out all the time—you had to get out and give it a shove. It stalled when we were just about to the highway. So Ida—all we knew her by was Ida—got dressed, but we had her underpants. Well, anyway, we got Ida out to help push, and when the car started, we bugged out and left her standing there. She yelled at us, so we drove down the highway and waited.

She walked about a hundred yards to the highway. We got to where we could see her, and, Jesus, she was hitchhiking cars going both ways. I said, "Mike, we're in for it. That bitch is going to go to town and snitch on us." But she didn't. A truck, a big semi, stopped. He picked her up, and we said, "Boy, is he going to be one disappointed son of a bitch!" And Larry said to us, "If that's all I've been missing, I haven't missed a damn thing," and that's how he lost his cherry.

Mike got to talking, "What if she's got the syph or the clap or something?"

I said, "Oh, jeez."

And now Mike mentioned this: "I heard if you take lye soap or just soap, and wash yourself in your own urine, you'd never get nothing."

"Aw, come on," I said. "You're bullshitting."

Boy, I think that back then we must have been out of our minds. We went to the trailer. Mike come with us, didn't go home. I went in the shower and did exactly that, and Larry did too. We hung our pants outside the trailer. They looked awful. One of our buddies came up afterwards, and he said, "What do you got hanging on the fence there?" We told him, and he just split a gut laughing.

Them guys pulled another thing one night. I was in on this a little, but I was going with Sharon, my first love. I brought Sharon up to Trout Lake, and I come back. This trailer I had was a flop-out for just everybody that wanted to flop in it. Well, I come home sober that night. I started drinking. There was a few guys there. And I got drunk pretty quick. I had maybe a couple of quarts of that muscatel and some beer. I slugged Al Davenport that night. He started getting shitty with Mike, and between the two of them, I liked Mike better. Mike and Al left for a while and come back with this girl. She went in the bedroom with my brother Tom. We got in there, turned on the light, and there she was, bare-assed. She wanted it from everybody. I didn't have nothing to do with her, but they plowed her all night long, taking turns. I slept on the floor in the next room. Nice life, eh? Absolutely zero!

But with girls, I got ahead of my story. I better back up and tell you about Sharon. I went with this girl named Sharon Riley. I lost my cherry with her. She was from Trout Lake, about thirty miles west of here. Sharon and Kitty, a girl from Wisconsin, stayed in an apartment in St. Ignace, working summer jobs. A friend of mine, Bob Allsworth, lived in the apartment above them. He welded for Alpine Construction.

Well, I got to know Bob. Him and I was in his apartment, and here was two good-looking chicks staying below him. I knew Sharon before this. I met her when I was dating Sue Thomas, who was from Trout Lake too. Sharon waitressed at one of the restaurants — Shores, I think. I went down to see her one night. Well, that damn Bob Allsworth, he gave me two bennies. I took them, and did them things screw me up! I never shut my mouth. I don't even think I slept that night. So I was cruising high, and I went down to see them girls. I talked to them most of the night. After that, I'd go down and visit them regular. And one time Kitty said to Sharon, "Why don't you give him a kiss?" Sharon did. We started going together after that.

With Sharon, things happened fast. She'd been around some and knew how to bring me along. She never told me, but she let me know that she wanted it, if you know what I mean. So the third night we went out, we were petting hot and heavy. She slid her hand inside my pants and grabbed my cock, which was just hard as a rock. I knew this was the night I was going to become a man.

We started taking our clothes off. I took off most of hers, and she took off most of mine. I was pretty excited by now, fumbling with buttons, trying to unhook her bra. My heart was pounding. It was going too fast, and I couldn't hardly stand the excitement.

We was naked. I put my hand between her legs, and she was wet. She took her hand and played with me for a few minutes and then rolled over on her back. She told me with her eyes it was time — we weren't talking. I got on top of her, half laying on her and half on my hands and knees. She reached down and grabbed my cock, and I went soft as a noodle.

Thinking back on that night now, it seems kind of funny. But there wasn't no humor in it at the time, no humor at all. I had no idea what was wrong with me. I never heard of this happening to any guys I knew. I had no warning, so I was worried. "What's wrong here?" I thought. One minute I was going to be a man; next minute I wasn't no man at all.

Sharon said, "Why don't you take it easy, Ron? Just lie here beside me. It's OK." She was being real good about it, in other words. She could've laughed or something and made things bad for me, but she tried to help me out, which I'm damn glad of, considering how bad I felt. We lay there for a while, and then she took hold of me again. I was still soft, but in about two seconds I came. It was all over, and I wasn't a man yet.

I was thinking about myself and worried about going soft like that. I never thought about Sharon having no pleasure or that I could still make her feel good. Being inexperienced, I had no clue about pleasing a woman.

I wish I'd had someone to talk to. I felt like something was wrong with me being half a man like that. I didn't tell nobody. And it would've helped to know that lots of guys have this happen to them. But I had to work it out alone. I couldn't even talk with Sharon.

Every night Sharon and I would try, but it was always the same. I'd think about making myself hard, but it never worked. Thinking was probably the worst thing I could've done. Thinking and fucking don't mix, if you get what I mean. During the day I'd think about sex all the time and I'd be stiff, but when I got ready to climb aboard Sharon—soft again.

This went on for a long time. It seemed like forever, but I think it was only two or three weeks. All this time, Sharon was being real patient with me for as horny as she must have been. Stupid me. She wasn't getting no sex at all while this was going on. Well, one night things was different—I don't know what, but I wasn't soft. God, that felt good, and it made me happy. It didn't last long, a minute or so, but I came inside her. "I did it," I said. She smiled and nodded yes.

A little while later, we tried again, and things went good. I lasted a pretty long time, and she enjoyed herself. Wasn't long before we had a regular sexual relationship, and I stopped worrying. By now, my nose was wide open all over her. I had a crush on her, you know.

I worked fish tugs then and had a room at the Okie Hotel. Mostly, though, I slept at Sharon's and left in time to change clothes and go to work. I liked the girl a lot. Suddenly it came to I loved her and she loved me, but then who would've married a wild one like me? I was wild. And I drank a lot when I was going with her. She did too. And her mom hated me.

Sharon was engaged to a guy named Roger James. He was in the service. They was engaged to be married. I remember one night I said, "Well, if you love me, why are you carrying Roger's ring around?" She threw it outside the apartments somewhere. I remember we looked for it later and found it in the bushes. Anyway, her mother didn't like it that her and I went together. Christ, I wondered if maybe the mom was in the hots for Roger herself.

Well, during deer season, in November, Sharon had gone back to live with her mother in Trout Lake. And I didn't have no car, so I'd find rides when I could or I'd hitchhike up there. Mike, George, my brother Tom, and I went to Trout Lake. They hunted as they drove, looking for deer along the side of the road. I said, "Let's go see Sharon."

It was about ten o'clock in the morning. I knocked on the door, and her mother answered. I said, "Is Sharon here?"

Her mother said, "No, she isn't. She's baby-sitting."

I seen Sharon's jacket in the front room, so I yelled "Sharon!" as loud as I could.

That woman said, "I'll shoot you, you son of a bitch."

I didn't take her serious. Sharon heard me and come out of the bedroom in her nightgown. She said, "Ronny, you better go. She's loading that gun."

I said, "Aw, come on." But I looked in the kitchen, and she had a shotgun. The kitchen was in back of the house, and the driveway run along side of the house. We had parked on the street across the driveway. I ran off the porch and was halfway to the car when she busted out the door, shouting, "You son of a bitch, I'll shoot you! You no-good son of a bitch!"

She pointed that shotgun at me, and I froze, not knowing what to do. She was shaking so much, she could've pulled that trigger without meaning to. Mike — he was crazy. He stuck his deer rifle out the car window. He yelled, "You old bitch, pull the trigger and you're dead." Her concentration broke, and she looked his way. I dove in the car. She was still holding that gun, though, and swearing. George started his car, but he couldn't get it in gear, he was so scared.

Sharon yelled, "I'll be down at Sam's Restaurant." So we went to Sam's and waited. She walked in a few minutes later and come back to St. Ignace with me. We shacked up again. I told her, "Jesus, maybe you love your mother, but she's crazy."

Sharon said, "Yeah, I know Mom really likes Roger, but I didn't think she hated you that much." But it was worth getting scared, I guess, because Sharon and me had a real hot time.

A couple weeks later I hitchhiked to Trout Lake, and when I seen Sharon, she said, "Ma wants to see you."

I said, "Not likely. She didn't get me the first time, so she's probably planning something else." I wasn't going in the house.

Sharon said, "No. Honest, Ron. She wants to apologize."

I went in the house after a while, and Sharon's mom said, "Ron, I'm sorry. Will you forgive me?"

I said yes right away, half afraid she'd get that gun again.

Sharon sure had me messed up. We went to a drive-in movie up to the Soo [Sault Ste. Marie]. Sharon and I started arguing. We argued all the time, usually about Roger. You know, I felt sorry for him. He must have loved her a lot to put up with knowing that while he was in the service, she was running around with me. So we were arguing, and I jumped out of the car when it was going maybe fifty miles an hour. It was wintertime, and luckily I lit in the snow and slid on my ass and my back till I smacked into a snowbank. I wasn't hurt at all. But that girl, I'll tell you, had me confused with "I love you, Ron" and "I don't know, Ron—Roger and I . . ."

Sharon and I had a hot thing going. I loved her ass, but I liked her too and was thinking along the lines of marriage. Was that ever lucky for her and me that we didn't! But I'll tell you what a rank thing I pulled. Maybe I could say it was love. I thought so, I guess. Let's put it this way: I wanted her bad. I could have her sexually anytime I wanted. One time Sharon and I borrowed a car and drove out in a cornfield. We got stuck. It was wintertime, but the ground hadn't froze. I laid one on her, and a little while later I laid another one on her. She did the damnedest thing to get rid of that stuff—she wasn't taking birth control, but she was a well-versed girl. We did it the third time, and I had a climax but she didn't know. I said, "Whop"—I tricked her. I said, "Oh, I'm wore out." So she did nothing to get rid of nothing, and that's why she got pregnant.

I'm getting toward the end of her and I's life together. I went with her about a year. I was going to go down to Ludington, get a job, and send for her. And we talked it over—this was going to be the deal, see. But after a while she didn't answer my letters, didn't write me at all. I said, "Goddamn. What's the matter here?" Then I found out from her friend Susie that Sharon really was going to marry Roger.

I got drunk, and, boy, this was a stupid thing to do. I was smashed on Thunderbird, out of my mind, and my intentions was to kill myself. The more I drank, the more I thought about it. I called Mrs. Count's, where we met when Sharon was baby-sitting, just this side of Trout Lake. Mrs. Count didn't know where Sharon was, and I felt sorry for myself, very sorry, and I explained to Mrs. Count what I was going to do. "Oh, no, Ron, you don't do that," she said. And you know, when you feel that way, the worst thing somebody can do is talk too much pity, because the more pity they give you, the more you're going to feel sorry for yourself. You'll work right into the climax of what you're going to do.

I look back on it now, and if you want to commit suicide, all you got to do is hold a gun to your head or a quick slash with a razor on your throat, and it'll be over. But I didn't do that. There was a bottle of Bufferins and a bottle of aspirins. I took them all and sat there for a while. Nothing happened, so I figured the pills wouldn't do it. I slid down, getting more and more depressed, crying. I took a double-edged razor blade to my wrist. The scar's about five inches long. I stuck that razor blade to the bone and slit right through. I didn't feel anything, but it opened up and blood flew all over. I said, "There, that'll do it." And I sat there.

Somebody got my brother Floyd. He said, "What'd you do?"

I was bawling. I said, "She's going to marry that rich son of a bitch." I was carrying on.

He said, "I got to bring you to the doctor."

I went to the doctor, and then I decided they wasn't going to stitch me up. And I said, "Naw, forget it."

The doctor got mad, but the nurse said, "Now, look, he's depressed. He had a rough time, and he's depressed." She tried to get me in a good state where I'd get stitched.

By that time I was getting a little sober and very sick. Oh, I was sick. The doctor said, "How many pills did you take?"

"A couple bottles full."

"How long ago?" he asked.

"A few hours," I said. It was too late to pump my stomach. I was puking it up anyhow. So he stitched me: nineteen inside stitches and twenty-four on the outside.

A couple weeks later I went to Trout Lake and talked to Sharon. We both cried, and I just said, "If I ever make it before you marry him—" and she said, "Maybe we'll have something together yet." I left there brokenhearted, and she was still crying when she left the car.

Her mother come out, "I hear you're going to go down below, eh, Ronny? Make something out of yourself?" Was she ever smiling! Good-bye, Ronny.

I left, and that's how I ended up in Ludington, running from a broken heart.

Busted

I wanted a job, and I needed to get out of St. Ignace. I called the boss of the crew I had mason-tended for on Mackinac Island. I'd worked there the spring after I cut pulpwood with Big Boy Curry. I got along good with that crew, and John MacCumber, the boss, told me to let him know if I ever needed work. So I called him down at Ludington, where he lived. "Sure," he said, "come on down. We got a job for you."

I was pretty broke, but I had enough money for a bus ticket to Ludington. It's a small town about two hundred miles south. After I bought the ticket, I had just forty-five cents left over, my total life savings. When I got to Ludington, I headed right to South James Street, where they was building a clothing store. I had my work uniform on, so when I found them guys, I dropped my suitcase and went to work.

Down at Ludington, I stayed at John's house — what it amounted to. I did the morning chores on the farm. Then I'd do the evening chores and help Mrs. MacCumber, John's mother. She was a sweet old lady, seventy-four years old, but sharp. She had her ways, but if I live that long and get around half as good as she did, I'll be happy. What I was getting at was my room and board. I paid her twenty-five dollars a week, and if I wanted extra food or anything, I could get it myself.

I worked hard, but my temper soon got me in trouble on the job, like it always did. We had another Indian fellow with us, a full-blood. Ossageesee was his name. He had a booze problem. He'd tend for a few days, and then he'd get loaded and disappear. He had the same job as me, so when he didn't show, I worked my ass off. Well, Ossageesee was gone, and we were building this sixty-foot wall—quite a few blocks. We had three masons, and then they brought in a new one, Elmer Rummer. Ossageesee was drunk someplace, and we were working two scaffolds high, with an extra mason.

I mixed the mud outside at the stockpile and wheeled it into the building. Then I'd hoist the stuff to the first scaffold, climb up, lift it to the second scaffold, and distribute it. Well, damn, on a straight wall like that a mason can flat lay block, I'll tell you. I carried the mud in five-gallon buckets. I don't know if you ever lifted a five-gallon bucket of mud, but it's heavy. I'd hoist them up and carry them along. I kept up for a while, but I was dragging.

Lots of times the mud dries out from the sun or from just sitting, so you temper it. Usually that's the tender's job, but a mason can temper his own mud too. In a case like we was in there, he damn sure could've tempered his own. The guys knew how hotheaded I was. They laughed at first. But Elmer Rummer, the new one, said, "Hey, slim"—or something like that—"jump up and temper my mud."

I looked at him, and I said, "What are you saying? Jump and temper your mud?"

He said, "That's right. That's your job."

"Well, if I come up there," I said, "I'll ram that trowel up your goddamn ass." Them other masons started snickering; they knew something was going to happen. I said, "Temper your own goddamn mud. I ain't going to do it. I got to go make mud, let alone temper yours. If you'd work instead of mouthing off, you wouldn't have to have it tempered."

Now, Elmer was an experienced mason, and he must have known I was already doing two men's jobs, but he kept at it. I had two eight-inch blocks in my hand. I was ready to put them on the supply scaffold when he said, "Come on and temper my mud." I had already lost my temper, and when I look back on it now, he was just razzing me, but I was too mad to realize it. I grabbed them blocks and flung them at Elmer. "I quit," I said. "Go to hell! You want me to do four guys' work, you got to pay me for it."

So I went into a bar and started drinking. After work, they come into the bar. Elmer Rummer said, "Buy that man a drink."

I said, "I don't want none of your beer."

Bob Freeland, one of the masons, said, "Ron, did you really quit?"

"Goddamn it, I said I quit, and I mean it," I said. "I can work for Gibbs Construction for three and a quarter an hour—they're union. I don't have to take this crap. If you want me to do four men's work, pay me for it."

Well, they gave me a raise, a good one, three-something an hour, better than union wages. I had started out working for a buck and a half an hour. So I went back to work. In a way, my temper done me good there. I was doing OK till I got broken up in a fight.

We was in the Town Tavern one night, my favorite spot in Ludington. It was Thursday night. I went to the bar while most of the guys went to a union meeting. I didn't belong to the union. I could get served in the Town Tavern even though I was underage. I drank a few beers and was having a good time. I met this fellow who said he was German. We was bullshitting with this young guy, Kenny — I can't remember his last name. He worked for Gibbs Construction. We had just met. He was about my age, a little older, I think, because he had no trouble getting served, and he thought it was cool that I was. We did some heavy drinking.

The boys come back from the union meeting, and this big Swede walked in with them. I remember him blabbing earlier, but I didn't pay no attention. John MacCumber, the Scotch-Irish fellow I stayed with, drank a lot and was one hell of a nice guy. This big Swede said to John, "Who's the young fellow?"

John introduced me as his friend from up north, and he said, "Can this boy ever hod-carry!"

The Swede said, "He looks pretty weak for that."

I was drunk, and I said, "Just because you're so goddamn big don't mean I can't hod-carry." John told me to shut up, and I said, "Go stick it," and stuff like that. Everybody laughed because I mouthed off to this big guy. Nothing happened yet. I left that table, and Kenny and I went over and started talking to this German. I got a little loud. Little loud, hell! I was louder than loud. That's the way it was when I got drinking. I didn't have no sense. I would just yell and carry on.

The bartender, Big George, told me to calm down. I said he could go screw himself. Kenny laughed.

The bartender said, "What'd you say?"

"Go screw yourself!"

He said, "Aw, come on, man."

"I'm not any louder than anybody else in here," I said. He was trying to get John to help him, but John was too drunk to know what was going on, I think. Big George said he was going to throw me out.

"Like hell you will," I said. He started around the bar, and I hit him. He stumbled backward into the whiskey bottles. It happened so quick, I don't think anybody seen it, other than Kenny and that German fellow.

So I got rooted out of there. Outside, in the parking lot, John told me to go home and sleep it off. Don't get me wrong. I liked John, but he drank heavy and wasn't beyond getting on the muscle. When I look back on it, he tried to help me. John told me to get in the car, and I said, "Hell with you. You ain't big enough to put me in that car." I was on the muscle then.

Well, the German said, "Come on, man." Drunk as I was, I forgot who he was, so I punched him.

That's when John tackled me. Did he have a grip on me! I tried to get loose, but then I seen it was John. I yelled at him, "You Irish foreign bastard, let me up!" But I didn't swing—I never did swing on John.

He let me up and told me to go to hell. "You going to act like that," he said, "hell with you."

I got mad at him when he said that. Then I said, "All right, you Irish sucker, you go to hell then." He left.

Kenny and I thought it was all a big joke, so we went to the Sand Bar, next door to the clothing store where we was working. We had a few drinks and rolled back into the Town Tavern. Common sense would tell you we wasn't wanted there after what just happened. I don't think George, the bartender, seen us come in, because that place was packed with farmers and a few tourists. I went in there, and I challenged the big Swede that I was half-ass arguing with earlier. I said, "You ain't so tough when John's around or when John's not around."

He didn't know where I was coming from. I shoved him. First thing I knew, I was on my ass. He pushed me, and I fell into a couple bar tables. Chairs flew, and glasses and beer bottles. A woman screamed. He said he was going to take me outside and pound me. I said, "I'll go outside with you. Come on." Then everybody knew there was going to be a fight. We went outside, and a crowd followed. When a fight starts, everybody wants to see.

He was strong but slow. We went round and round, and I punched him—not hitting hard, just getting in and getting out. Somebody said, "You're doing all right, son." I remember that. I turned around and thought he said something else. Here I was, fighting this goddamned gorilla, and I slammed this other guy.

Well, that was a mistake. The Swede nailed me. They told me later that he hit me so hard, he tore me off my feet. I couldn't breathe. He'd hit me in the chest; that's when he broke my ribs. I fell. I kicked at him, but he was on me, smashing me, and nobody stopped him. I figured I had to get away before he killed me. I reached in my pocket for a beer can opener. I slit him down the face with it.

He got up. He held his face with both hands, blood streaming through his fingers. I kicked him. I ripped his face open. He was screaming and yelling. He had both hands over his face, and I kicked him again—this happened fast. But the cops came and broke it up. They said, "You, you get in the car."

I got in. The Swede got in too. They set him on one side of the back seat and me on the other. My ribs hurt. I could barely get my breath, but I slugged him again while we was sitting in the cop car. When the cops calmed that down, they brought us to the hospital. In the hospital, I hit that big bastard again.

That Swede could've pressed charges, but he didn't. Nothing happened. But I was guilty as hell—ripping him with a can opener like that. At the hospital they x-rayed my ribs and taped me up. I had three busted ribs. I hurt. Kenny had followed us to the hospital in his car. We went into town to the Grand Hotel and got a room.

Next morning, I was crippled. Talk about regrets! I didn't know exactly what had happened. Most of it I knew, and Kenny filled me in on the rest. What a fool! I had a good job, and I blew it. Kenny asked if I could work. "No," I said. "I can hardly move my arm." I went downtown and found out a little more of what I had done. I met that German fellow I hit. He was all smiles, a big bruise on his face. I apologized.

I went to see my boss, John. When I was at the hospital, I'd called him. I had really screwed up. I don't know how much truth there was to it, but they'd been talking about getting me my own mortar machine and scaffolding. They said, "You can contract your own work. We'll get the job, and you can contract from us." And on small jobs like basements I could scaffold and do the work myself, or I guess I could. But I lost all that when I got in that brawl.

I caught the bus north to St. Ignace. Before I left, I told John, "When my ribs heal, I'll be back."

He said, "Ron, I'll tell you something. You've got a job here anytime you want it. Remember that."

"Thanks," I said. "I'm sorry this happened. I'm going to go up there and get healed." I jumped on the bus for home.

So I come back to St. Ignace. What a mistake! I remember telling John—and this is my exact words—"If I go back to that town, I'll go to prison." Why I thought about that I don't know. I had told my fortune and didn't know it. I got into town. I was glad to see my buddies. My brother Tom and some other guys stayed on Spring

Street—he had an apartment up above. Bob Henry, a friend of mine, stayed there, and anybody else who wanted to flop.

Right off we get drunk. I drank sloe gin and a bottle of muscatel, some beers. Not much beer. I drank it with my wine as a chaser. We rode around, and I was looking for trouble, drunk as hell. We went to the drive-in to get something to eat. Carol Alex was there. I knew her from way back and always liked her. She waved to me and said, "When you going to take me out, Ron?"

I said, "Well, I don't know. How about Sunday?" This was Friday night. I didn't have no car, but I guess she had one. So the date was set.

Carol left, and everybody said, "Boy, are you lucky!" We joked about it, and I felt happy. I never kept that date after what I done the next night.

On Saturday we went out. I know I drank the sloe gin then, and some wine and beer. I was very drunk when we landed in Miller's Camp, a bar just west of town. We went in, and this guy from New York had just come from the quarterfinals Golden Gloves in Chicago or something like that, or maybe he was just bragging on himself. But they was talking about boxing, and somebody said to this fellow from New York, "See that skinny kid over there? He's good with his fists." They pointed at me. I was taped up from that brawl in Ludington, but the way I was, I had to take him on.

I knocked him down once. I hit him with my right—I cracked him a good one. Everybody was screaming. Maybe I was wrong, but my boozed-up mind thought he drew a knife. He went in some kind of crouch. It didn't look right to me.

I made a quick decision. I grabbed a cue stick off the pool table and stabbed him. I remember grabbing the stick when I seen it in his hand. My friends just stood there—I can't blame them—but I wish they had grabbed me or yelled at me. I stabbed him with that stick, and I saw blood gushing out of his eye. I dropped the stick, and we run.

I knew I was in trouble. I was scared and didn't know what to do. We went back to the apartment, and they talked me into giving myself up. About an hour later, I guess, we walked into the police station, and the cop said, "We been looking for you, you son of a bitch."

"Kiss my ass, then," I said. "I come to give myself up. Here I am. I give myself up." I don't remember who went to the police post with me, but they brought me up there. A lot of this I was told later. I know I saw a knife. That's why I did it. I thought he would cut me.

So there I was, locked up. They handcuffed me behind my back and threw me in jail. I told them my ribs hurt. Here's the way it is with the cops. I was guilty as hell, but they didn't know that. Why should I be handcuffed behind my back while I'm locked in a cell?

I woke up the next morning, and I could barely breathe. I needed medical help. I yelled that I needed a doctor. They took me, but the doctor pressed my ribs and said, "There's nothing wrong with him."

I said, "What's your problem? Check the hospital in Ludington. They have my X rays. They said my ribs was broke, so they taped me up." I had pulled that tape off, and they wouldn't believe me. Back to jail for me.

I got some towels, and the boys in jail with me tied it up the best they could. As far as I know, them ribs was healing all right, but they hurt for a long time. I stayed in jail forty-some days before I went to the wacky farm.

Things go through a man's mind when he's locked up — regrets mostly. If I could only have went back three days and done what I should've did, but now I'm busted — busted good. The ex-cons in jail told me, "Ron, we're sorry, but you're going up."

"Then what's all this about sending me to the funny farm?" I said.

They said, "They got to see if anything's wrong with your head."

Your food in jail ain't good, and talk about meeting some characters! You meet crazier ones in the penitentiary, but in jail they brought a guy in one night, a big fellow, a Canadian. They picked him up for vagrancy. He said, "How you guys doing?" He looked a little dim.

I said, "Oh, we're all right."

"I really didn't do anything wrong," he said. "I was sent here by the Lord to do my good deed for him."

I said to myself, "This man's out of it."

He said, "I was sent here by the good Lord to help you repent."

Well, Jesus," I said, "looks like you're too late." Them fellows in the jail roared.

Another guy come in, a redheaded fellow with shorts on. It was about chow time. All you got to eat in the morning was four slices of toast and some coffee. So you were hungry by noon. This guy kept saying, "I missed my boat." I thought he was talking about going to Mackinac Island. He said, "Goddamn it, I wish I wouldn't have missed that boat." I asked him what boat he had missed. He said,

"Slow boat to China." Now, you always heard that goddamn joke, slow boat to China. Well, this guy actually thought he missed it, I guess. But them goofball guys help you pull your lockup time.

So it come noon, and dinner was hardly better than breakfast. Usually you got like a sandwich and a bowl of soup. They had a little door in the back—there was a slot in it about eight inches deep and about a foot and a half wide. They slid the trays in there, stainless steel trays. We'd stand in line and get our chow. That crazy slow-boat guy took his tray and dumped it. I grabbed for it, and Bobby Gray did too. That guy was throwing his lunch away. We saved the sandwich but not the soup.

We found out that he had run away from Ypsilanti Mental Hospital. That afternoon one of the guys was looking out the window, and a big Cadillac drove up. A bunch of mink got out, really decked out. It was his parents. I guess they was rich, but he was a sick boy. And so they just come and got him.

There was a heavy screen outside the window, and there was a hole in there. A kid come by there one afternoon, and he had a little dart. He stuck it through, and we grabbed it. Boy, did that dart help us pull time! We had books—well, *Post* magazine. Somebody had a pen. We drew a picture of a woman and her beaver. We threw the dart at that for hours. We had a distance of about fifteen feet. You'd walk back, throw that dart, walk up and get it, give it to the other guy, and he'd throw it. We played for toast and other food mostly. Son of a bitch, you didn't want to lose or you'd be hurting food-wise. But then, guys would be locked up, and people would bring them goodies. We played for cigarettes too.

I spent a lot of jail time back then, and it seemed like everybody in there was Indian or hung out with Indians. I don't know why. The cops? The courts? It's hard to say. But I'll tell you, in a small town like this, if an Indian's drunk, people notice it. They call the cops, and he goes to jail. When a white man's drunk, people look the other way. If the cops come, they take the white man home. He don't go to jail. So the jail showed stuff the town was trying to hide. One time I was in jail, it was all Indians. Cops done that, I figure.

Indians got a raw deal in the courts too. But I think the courts screw everybody that don't have money to back them up, to hire a sharp lawyer. In St. Ignace that would be Indians and the poor ones like them.

Jail time went slow. We'd look out the window. It was depressing; you were looking at freedom out there. Sometimes a band would march by and practice when you were in jail, or you'd get a little hawkeye at the girls. Certain cars would go by, and they'd honk; they knew I was in there. One night somebody brought us some beer through that little hole in the screen I told you about. The bars was spread apart. Somebody did that trying to get out, I guess. You'd never get out of there unless you had lots of help. They had bars on the outside and steel windows with that funny-looking glass you couldn't quite see through. Most of them windows was punched out.

We had cups in there; you could make instant coffee. When they brought us that beer, they made a little trough out of paper and poured the beer in it. We caught it in our cups. But goddamn, they only had a six-pack. That didn't go far. Nobody got drunk that night. But it was something to do.

I went to my hearing, my arraignment. I stood mute. If I know about the law, if you stand mute, they can enter a plea for you, usually not guilty. But if you stand "no contender," then you're saying "no contest" in other words, I guess. Well, I stood mute, and the plea of not guilty was put in for me. But I was guilty as hell.

My family stuck with me for a while, a little leery maybe, but all right. Nobody went over backwards to get a lawyer, but I was on my own for quite a while then. Piss on them if they wasn't getting me a lawyer. It wasn't up to them, I guess. I got myself in the mess, so I was supposed to get myself out of it.

The Loony House

The time came to send me to the state mental hospital in Newberry, Michigan. Going there worried me. I know what small-town people think when you go into a mental institution: You've been in a nuthouse, so you're nuts regardless of what you went up for. I was afraid of that when I come back to St. Ignace.

They explained to me, "Ron, you're going to go up there, and here's the deal. You're getting a diagnostic. They're going to take brain scans of you and try to get your head together a bit, see what's the matter with you. How does that sound?"

I said, "OK, I guess. You never know. There might be something wrong with me, because I'm sure not acting like a rational young man." So off I went.

I remember looking at that place when I first arrived. Scary. They brought me into a place called ITM—Intensive Treatment, Male. When you went up there, all your records from prior arrests, anything to do with court or juvenile problems, was sent to be evaluated by these doctors and psychiatrists. I went to ITM. It was on the bottom of the Ferguson Building at the state hospital. "Hello, Ron. This is your home for a while," they said.

You walked in. I'll never forget when I first seen them people, you know, people that you know from the way they look that things wasn't right with them. I was scared, but there was a nice-looking girl sitting there crying. I wondered what was the matter with her. She got up out of her chair and run into a little room.

Nothing happened the first day I was there. Dr. Cameron was the ward doctor. He wasn't very distinguished-looking. He was humpbacked, but he did have the appearance of authority anyway. He checked me over. I stripped to the waist, and he took my pulse

The Loony House

and blood pressure and put that thing, whatever you call it, on my chest. And he said, "You're pretty healthy."

I stayed there two days, I think, and then got shifted upstairs. That's Intensive Treatment, Male, too. Down the hall, across the hall, behind locked doors, there was the girls. Here I was on that ward, and quite a few slept there. There was a dormitory with maybe ten beds and some private rooms: two dormitories and five or six private rooms. I was new to this place and kind of lost. There was attendants, male attendants for us and female attendants for the girls. Nurses came in, ward nurses. There was another dayroom where you walked down the hall from the dormitories, a pill room, pill line, and a office for the attendants.

Off to the right, just before you hit the dayroom, there was something they called short haul. If somebody went real loony, they'd wrestle them in there and give them a shot, a hypo to calm them down. I remember when I saw it, I said to myself, "That's one place they're not getting me into."

I didn't know what was going on, but I'll tell you, go to Newberry if you want to see weird people that are out of it. I lived with them strange ones. I figured out later that some of them wasn't as bad as they looked, and some others was worse than they looked.

I was a court case. I was supposed to get no freedom other than taking a walk to the canteen, where they had goodies you could buy if you had money. For the first few weeks, I was stuck in that ward. Never went to the dances or nothing like that.

I took tests. To this day I can't figure them out. I'm not a doctor, but they had pictures of ugly people, like missing an ear and all sorts of defects. They told me to pick out the one I liked the best. I didn't like none of them. I don't know if you're getting what I'm trying to explain. You looked at pictures of ugly people. "Which one do you like the best?" they asked. I didn't like none of them, but I picked one out. The man kept insisting for me to choose one, so I did. I pointed to it. "Is that the one you want?" I didn't know if it was or not. I just said, "Yeah, that one."

They had a thing that looked like a target and spun around. What I was supposed to do with that, I don't know. I forgot. That was one of the tests. Then they had me draw a picture of a man and a woman. I said OK. I can draw fairly good if I'm looking at something, but I just drew freehand there, a man and woman standing side by side. And the guy said to me, "Oh, Ron, that's pretty good drawing." I didn't say nothing. He said, "Well, well, what do you think they're doing?"

I said to myself, "This is unbelievable." Then I said to him,

"Them are two people, imaginary people on that piece of paper. You asked me to draw a man and a woman, and I did. Now you're asking me, what do I think they're doing?" I swear I wasn't trying to screw the man up. I was confused. Then I said, "I can't see anything possible that they could be doing, when I just drew them standing there." I said, "There's your answer. They're standing up." So he accepted that, I guess.

We had to put blocks together. They were checking for dexterity and mechanical-mindedness. I look at a puzzle now, and my son can put one together faster than I can. I never was worth much at puzzles. Some of these puzzles was triangle blocks to see how fast you could put them into the holes. Now, I could see sense in that, because you got to figure out where they go and how fast to put them in.

For the brain test, they hooked wires to me with paste. He said, "It's not going to hurt," and I told him it better not. I asked, "Is that electricity you're—"

He said, "Ron, it don't hurt you a bit," and I said, "All right." But I was scared.

"Now, don't roll your eyes," he said. "Lay still, and don't roll your eyes."

He asked me questions. I can't think of them now. I remember seeing a little thing like's on lie detector tests. They make lines. This was the test to see if you had any brain convulsion. Well, nobody ever told me the answer as far as the brain test went.

Now, there was a couple of nice-looking social workers. You talked to them. But the one I had wasn't nice-looking, because he was a guy. He asked me, "What do you think your problem is?"

I told him, "My problem is drinking and fighting."

"What do you think causes this?"

"I don't know for sure why I'm drinking," I told him, "but I think it's because half the time I'm depressed about something. I never got no good work. Well, I did in Ludington. I screwed that up, but I mean before that. I didn't have no place to stay, no home, and if you don't have nothing—don't feel right—it's easy to hide in a quart of wine."

He said, "What made you start fighting?"

"In reform school I learned how to fight," I said. "I knew some before that, but I learned to fight mostly in reform school."

"Well, how did you feel when you were in reform school?"

"Pretty bad. I don't like being locked up."

"What did you do to get in reform school?"

I told him, but you already got the story on that.

"Well, you were a bad boy."

I said, "OK, I was a bad boy, but I don't like being kicked around all over—this house and that house, like garbage nobody wants." I turned vindictive when I talked to these people about my childhood.

The social worker said, "Are you blaming all this on your childhood?"

"I don't know," I said. "I burn up so quick—my temper, you know. I get mad. Goddamn it, I don't want to be this way. But I just get so mad. I don't even think when I get mad."

I had some fun while all this head-shrinking was going on. We had dances on Saturday nights, other nights too. One of my favorite songs back then was "Sugar Shack." It come out around 1963, I think. But one time at a dance in the gym we had a dancing contest. Dorine, my girlfriend in there, and I did the twist to "Sugar Shack" and won. Well, that ain't much, I guess, winning a dance contest in a nuthouse, but we did win it.

I enjoyed roller skating too. It's like ice skating. I could only go to the left. But roller skating with Dorine, she was good. I'd try to go backwards, and I'd flop on my ass or smash into the wall. But it was fun. We'd skate and talk and try to figure out where we'd go to diddle a little.

One time—this was close—I got the key to a room down the hall from the hobby craft room. Nobody ever went into this room. I told Dorine, "I got the key." So we waited for the right time, and I opened the door and watched close till she slipped inside. I waited, and then I went in too. We was just getting down to where we could have a little natural fun, and somebody was unlocking the door. The door opened, and there was this old nurse, real nice woman. So there she was, and here we was. I got my pants up just in time. I don't know if she knew what was going on, but we grabbed a table and carried it out of there, and she didn't say nothing.

Now, there's so much to tell about this institution. If anybody in this world is feeling sorry for themselves, they should take a walk through a mental institution—just right through it—and then sit down and think about what they seen. There's lots of people with problems—believe me, I know that—but if anybody is ever feeling sorry for themselves, they'd change their mind after seeing the people in there. It is pitiful.

We walked in the children's ward. That's off to the left of the cloister, to the east of it. The cloister was a big square thing of units where they kept patients. We went in the children's ward. They got mongoloids, girls and boys. One baby had a head about the size of a football. And it was alive. And then there was this other little girl, a pretty little thing, probably seven or eight years old. Off her spine above her butt was a tail about ten inches long. They couldn't remove it, because it was hooked to her spine. There was something mentally wrong with her too, I guess. And then you see a crib, a kid laying in it staring into space. God! Deformities and ugliness of every kind. I never went back to that section.

On the ward, we played cards with the attendants and kept busy that way. And I met guys. I got so I knew what was going on. I got used to it a bit.

I mentioned about this pretty-looking girl that was crying downstairs at the ITM, in the admittance room. Her name was Mary Kay. She had a nervous breakdown. And later on, when I was in the penitentiary, I met a guy from the same town she was from, and I slipped up. They always thought that she was on vacation; her parents lied about where she was. Anyway, she had a nervous breakdown. I walked by, and she was laying in her bed without a stitch of clothes on. She went, "*Pssst!* Come here." Damn, I wasn't going in there, much as I wanted to. She had a body on her, and there she was naked. Well, it's a good thing I didn't mess with that, because nervous breakdowns are unpredictable. I could've maybe walked in there, and she'd scream. But she sure looked good — real tempting.

There was a diabetic, Sheldon, a bus driver. I didn't know nothing about no diabetic. I heard it was something about sugar in the blood. I went to the canteen; you could order hamburgers or french fries, Cokes, and what-all. Sheldon gave me money to buy candy bars for him. I bought them and give them to him. That night we was going to bed. I was sleeping in that dormitory. Sheldon slept next to me against the wall. I lay there, half-asleep. Suddenly he screamed. I rolled out of bed and scrambled away.

The attendants run in and grabbed Sheldon. He was having a seizure. One attendant said, "Who gave him candy?" It didn't dawn on me yet. It's funny how they have a seizure like that, and they pull them out with orange juice and sugar. The attendant said, "I don't know who did it, but somebody's been giving him candy or some kind of sweets. He's not supposed to have them." I never bought him any more after that. But I didn't know. And he was a real nice guy. He was in there for an overdose of insulin, tried to hang it up.

Another guy was Gary. I seen him on the streets since then. His favorite TV program was "Captain Kangaroo." He was an overintelligent guy. He had an awful drinking problem, signed himself in. He kept telling me, "I'm going to sue the government, the Army." They gave him cobalt treatments. He said that he was a conscientious objector, didn't like violence. He lectured me on violence. "Never use your fists," he'd say. "Use your brain, Ron." I told him that if I could ever get my brain straightened out, I would do like he said. The Army goofed him up. And he won his case. He gets a pension of five hundred and some dollars a month.

Well, I started to know what was what, and I was trying to figure these people out. One kid—I never did find out what he was in there for—wouldn't open up to them, but he'd talk to me. One day, I was outside, and when I come upstairs, they said there was an accident. "Ron," they said, "the kid wants to talk to you." The attendant told me, "He cut his wrists bad, both of them. Really bad! He wants to talk to you."

I said, "All right."

I went in, and he was bandaged, laying there crying. He said, "Ron, I, I—"

I don't know what made me think of this, but I know pity is the worst thing a person can have for himself. I told him, "What's the matter with you? You should be ashamed of yourself!"

He said, "I know, Ron." He was crying. I remember with me it was nice to have somebody to talk to, but if they laid too much pity on you, you felt sorrier for yourself. I think I'm explaining that right. He got stitched up and was all right, but he meant business. He put them deep, clear through the tendons in his wrist. I seen the scars later on.

One time I went into the bathroom. There was stalls, some sinks, and mirrors. I walked in, and this inmate had smeared toothpaste in his hair. I looked at him. I said, "Charlie, what are you doing?"

"I'm going to comb my hair, Ron."

"Charlie," I said, "you better wash your head first. It's always smart to wash your hair before you comb it." Here he had that whole tube of state toothpaste in his hair.

There was a guy named Stuart in there. He ended up in the penitentiary. I walked in the bathroom, and there he was with a razor blade in his hand. He was cutting himself lightly across the wrist and the arm. He said, "I'm going to hang it up, Ron."

I said, "Well, if you're going to hang it up, you ain't going to do it like that. Put the blade right across your throat."

"Oh, no," he said. "I don't want to do that."

I said, "Well, how are you going to commit suicide then?" I

watched him real close. I knew what he was going through, because I did it two times, not in there but on the streets. He relaxed after a while, and I grabbed that blade from him.

Then there was the epileptics. We had four or five of them on our ward, I think. Usually when epileptics have a fit, they'd drain their strength, but one guy—he had scars on his face, head, all over—he'd fall on his head most every time. He'd have a fit. That's pitiful to see. They shake, and saliva runs out of their mouth. You got to work fast, stick something in their mouth and cock their head to the side so they don't swallow their tongue. One time I was in the medicine line when a guy had an epileptic fit. He fell, and his head hit my foot. Good thing it did, because he black-and-blued my toenail. Would've done more damage if he'd hit the floor directly. Right there in the pill line, he done that.

One guy would pace the floor and change expressions on his face so fast. He had a big nose. John, they called him. He didn't never say nothing. He'd stand there. His mouth was moving, but no sound come out. And another guy, a Finlander, never said nothing either. He sat without talking. He sat there and sat there day after day in that same chair and wouldn't say a word. The one who paced the floor, I swear he hit the same spot every time. He started early in the morning, and he'd go till night. You couldn't get him to sit down. We had to move the TV when we watched. Otherwise he'd walk in front of us.

I worried that if they didn't get me out of there, I would go nuts. Being around weird people does strange things to you. They sent me to Newberry for a ninety-day diagnostic, but I spent nearly eight months in that place. But I don't want to get ahead of myself, because so much happened there.

There was a guy called Lappy. I wondered why they called him that. He had freedom of the grounds. He stayed in some cottage. Well, Lappy would get on the grounds and slurp up puddles like a dog. A funny thing happened one time. You was allowed to go to Hopula's Store near the mental institution. I headed to the store one day and saw Lappy standing there talking. He said, "I ain't going to do it." I looked. Nobody else was around, and he wasn't talking to me. He said, "I ain't going to do it, now, I'm telling you. You son of a bitch, I ain't going to tell you again." He kept saying this. Finally he walked over to a tin can laying on the ground and said, "I told you I ain't going to do it. You're going to dig your own worms." He walked away, and I burst out laughing. I couldn't help it. You have to hear him to understand what I'm saying, but he told that can to dig his own goddamn worms.

The Loony House

The scaredest I got in there was when I saw this one guy for the first time. We had a softball team. The attendants played, and I did too. I always did like softball. Teams come from all around to play us. We was called the Nuthouse Gang — I called us that. Anyway, I was on deck to go to bat. I stood there, and I heard a noise behind me — *ah, ah, ah,* like that. I turned around, and there was the ugliest man I ever seen, uglier than any of them pictures the shrinker showed me. His mouth curved up almost to his left eye. His eyes was crooked. God, was that guy ugly!

But he was harmless, I found out later. He was born ugly that way, and his mother kept him hidden in the house for thirty-four years where people wouldn't find him. She must have loved him a lot. Somebody found out. They put him in a mental institution. But he was in charge in the kids' unit. They had to mop the floor as part of their therapy. We did it in the ward too. We'd mop and buff the floor every morning. Anyway, I was there one day when he was foreman. They'd slow up when they mopped, and he'd point at a kid and go, *"Ah, ah, ah, ah, ah,"* like that. You ought to seen them mops go; they really moved. It was funny, yet it wasn't, if you know what I mean.

They pushed drugs on us in there. Like if you couldn't sleep, you could go get these pills — high-powered things, they was. I'd enjoy a cigarette just before I fell asleep, and when I took those pills, I was high by the time I finished that smoke.

Lights usually went out at ten o'clock, except when Friday-night fights come on. We was allowed to watch them. A few of us boxing fans talked some of the attendants into letting us stay up. One night the attendants was poking this guy with cue sticks. I walked by the office, and I said, "What are you doing to that guy?" He said, "He took a handful of them sleeping pills." He should've been dead. They was trying to keep him awake, because if he didn't, he'd be a goner. They did that all night, kept him awake.

They gave us what they called vitamins. Sometimes I went as long as nine days without eating. I was so wound up, no way could I eat anything. They was giving me some kind of pills. I felt frazzled, and I couldn't eat. The slop they fed you wasn't much anyhow — rice and hot dogs.

I'd stay in the kitchen and help clean up. I volunteered. This old fellow was in the loony house there for quite a while, fifteen years or so. He never talked. He washed the glasses, and I rinsed them and put them on the rack. One night he decided he'd kill himself. There was one place where you could get up on the roof. He meant business, poor old fellow. He had half a stomach and other problems. He climbed on the roof and dove headfirst onto the cement. His brains and skull—everything—splattered. It was quite a drop—two stories. I thought he was a nice old fellow. He wouldn't talk to me, just nod and smile.

A guy came in with the d.t.'s. They strapped him down to give him blood transfusions. He hallucinated that gangsters was after him. Before they brought him in, when he was at home, he busted out the windows, got shotguns and rifles, and posted them at the windows like he was having a war. His wife was scared. She didn't know what was going on. Anyway, he imagined these guys was after him. When it come to the final scene, he said "They ain't going to get me! I'll get myself!" He took a boning knife with a long, thin blade and jammed it into his chest. He come out of it, though. He was with us later and said, "God, I didn't want to die." I heard through the grapevine a few years back that he quit his drinking. I would think so, after an experience like he had.

I'm getting lost for words. That place tore me up inside. I feared the shock room. You'd see them take people there. It was between Intensive Treatment, Male, and Intensive Treatment, Female. When they come out of there, they'd be drained of strength, passed out. I wondered about that place. I asked one of the attendants one time, "Does that do any good?" He looked funny like and said, "Well, Ron, sometimes." He paused. I said, "What do you mean, 'sometimes'?" I figured it was just an experimental thing or for punishment. Some of them people had been there more than ten years. But they come out completely drained—just done for.

It's a pitiful thing to see, I'll tell you. I never seen the actual shock treatment, but I was told by one of the attendants there. I don't know if he was supposed to tell me about what they go through. Mucus comes out of their nose and everything. There's no control. Shit their pants and piss and everything else, some of them do. I don't think I'd want to witness it, and I sure wouldn't want it to happen to me.

At night I'd lie in bed and think. I couldn't fall asleep. Goddamn, that bothered me. I'd lay there, thinking, worrying: "What is this anyway? Here I am taking tests, living with strange people I know are not like me. What's going on? What's going to happen to me?"

Days went by, months. I was supposed to be there for a ninety-day diagnostic, but ninety days was long gone. I asked about it, and they said, "Be patient, Ron. We got to run more tests."

I said, "What tests? You stuck them wires on my head. You made me look at funny-looking people and talk to these shrinkers.

The Loony House

The only one in here that knows anything is Dr. Collier. These social workers is hardly out of college, and they don't know nothing."

And we'd sit in a circle, and you'd talk about your problems. Some of the guys with us could barely talk, let alone tell what their problems was. I could see how they tried to get them to cut loose, but I wondered what I was doing with people like that. It didn't make sense. I cooperated, but I felt embarrassed to talk. I hope I'm making myself clear. I felt depressed. You feel like you're in the same category with these other people, and you're getting treated as such most of the time, because they won't tell you nothing.

They brought me into conference. This was right before I went back to jail. They said quite a few things, but what the whole thing amounted to was, they asked me, "Would you like to be convalescent status for a year?" I asked them what that was, and they said, "It'd be like an outpatient for a year." It was like probation. When I felt something bothering me, I'd go to a psychiatrist or social worker and talk about it. I'd go regularly. That sounded better than prison, and I was getting my thinking around right. I thought so, anyway. So they recommended convalescent status to the court in St. Ignace. And they said how I did good work around there.

The psychiatrist I had was Dr. Collier. Of all the experiences I had on that funny farm, he did me the most good. He'd listen, and I'd tell him about my frustrations, about things I didn't understand. I didn't know what to do about my temper. I'd get mad and go crazy. He'd sit there listening, not saying much. I remember one time he told me some stuff that stood by me, but I'll tell you about that a little later.

There was a guy in there that owned a bar in Escanaba. He had a drinking problem. I'd sit and talk with him and his friends. They was older than me. They'd tell me what might happen—you know, about me hurting that guy. They'd say, "Be rational, Ron. Keep your cool, no matter what. Something good will happen in your life yet."

I said, "I don't know, really. I hope so. I wish I knew what's going to happen to me."

They said, "You seem like a nice fellow. Maybe nothing will. Maybe you'll just get released with no lockup time."

I got straightened around in there. My thinking started to get better. I was understanding some of what I was doing with my life. About a month before I left Newberry, I was with Dr. Collier, and he asked me, "What do you need, Ron? What do you figure you need?"

I remember saying, "Well, to get out of this place, I can tell you that. I better get out of here soon, before I go nuts too."

"I understand your feelings, Ron." He asked again, "What do

you think you need?" I couldn't answer him. He said, "I'm going to tell you what you need. You need love." And he said, "It's too late to get it from your mother."

When he mentioned my mother, I said, "Keep that bitch out of this."

He calmed me down and said, "You need love. You've got to get it from a woman, and you're going to fall in love easily. I hope when you find a woman and get married that you make a good choice, because it will be your whole life from then on." Strange how he could know so much. He went on. "It's too late to get love from your parents. You've got to get it someplace else. And you need something to work for, to have responsibilities. That's what you need."

I didn't understand all of what he meant, but I knew something important had gone on. I tried to remember everything he told me that day.

About a month before I left the state mental hospital at Newberry, the doctor told me, "You need love. . . . It's too late to get love from your parents. You've got to get it someplace else. And you need something to work for, to have responsibilities. That's what you need." I didn't understand all of what he meant, but I knew something important had gone on. I tried to remember everything he told me that day.

Later, when I was in prison for the second time, Bobby Gray and I talked about reforming ourselves on the streets and keeping out of trouble. I'd tell him, "I'm going to find me a good woman and get married. . . . I want to get married and have some kids. I want to buy a nice home and find a decent job." We talked like this all the time, and I began to work out a plan for myself.

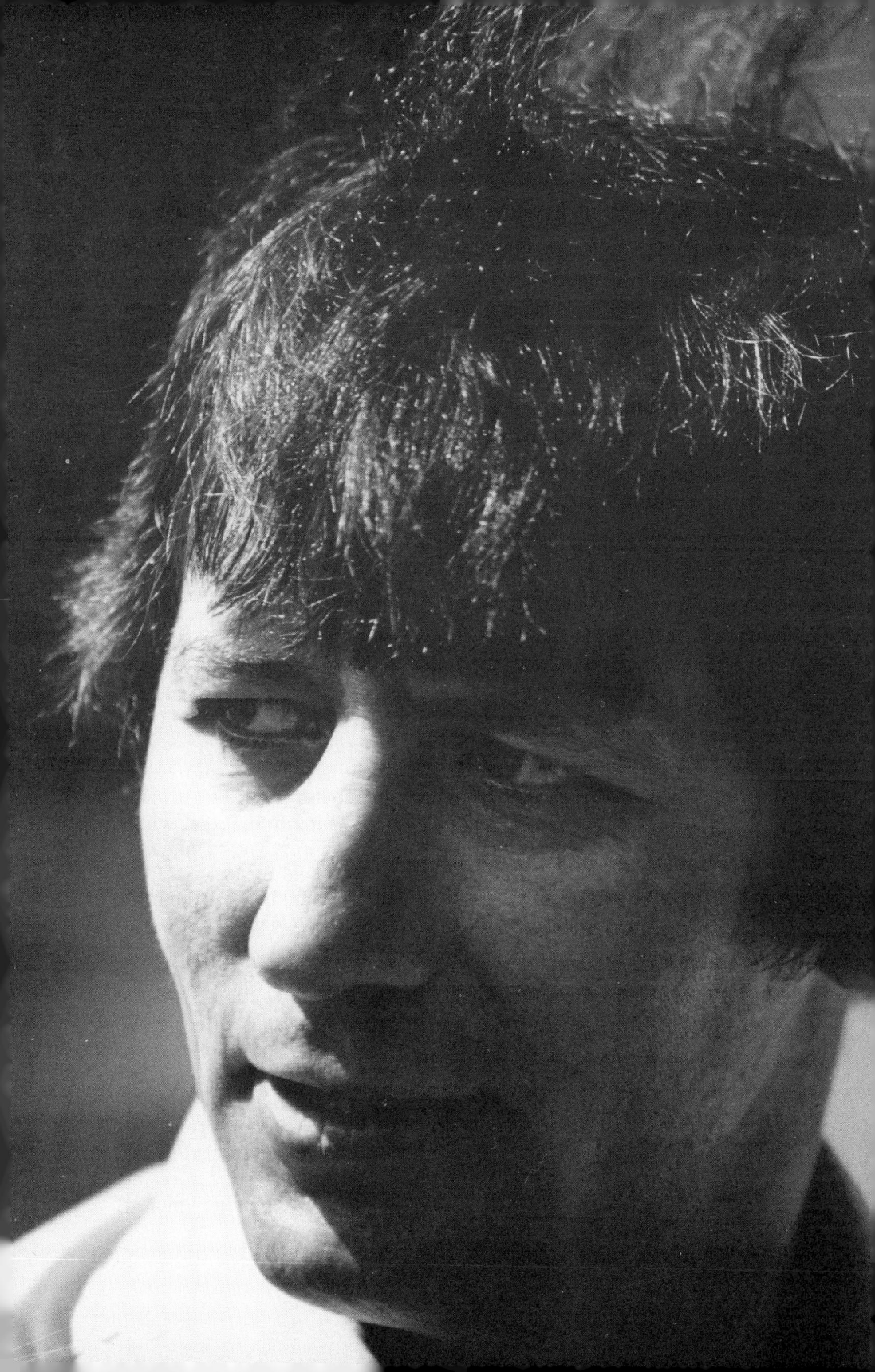

Moving Up the Line

I left the loonies on the fourteenth of January 1964. I went into the chambers to see the judge. I didn't find this out till I left the nuthouse and got back to the jail in St. Ignace, but the guy I blasted with that cue stick drifted in and out of critical condition all these months. He nearly died. I thought he was all right. In fact, I remember asking about how the guy was and if anybody knew about him. And I think they kept me waiting in the loony house to see if he was going to die. I don't know that for sure, but I do believe that's why they kept me there so long, because once they sentenced me, they couldn't bring new charges.

So we went in the chambers, and Judge Finland said hello. Parker, the parole officer, was there. He wrote up the pre-sentencing report. I didn't know it then, but you're going to the joint when Parker starts writing reports. The judge said, "Ron, you're no hardened criminal, but you like to use these." He held up his fists. He said, "You like to use them. I'll tell you, the hospital bills for the man you injured are very high, and he's still getting treatments. Insurance will cover most of it, but they can sue you to recover their costs. They can bleed you—sue you and bleed you for the rest of your life."

I stood there quiet-like, listening. I was going to do time. The judge was telling me I was going to get time. He said, "I've got to give you at least a year." My heart sunk. I was going up the creek.

This was close to noon when the judge said I was going to get a year; that was my impression. But he didn't sentence me yet. So I went back to jail, and I ate my dinner. I told the fellows that I was getting a year. I was depressed. I thought about the time I spent at Newberry and the recommendations from them. The judge ignored them. "They're going to drop it in court, Ron"—that's what those guys told me. Hah! Drop the hammer on my ass is what they did.

I went to get sentenced. When I was first arraigned, I pled mute. They entered a plea of not guilty. But I pled guilty before the judge that morning. There never was a trial. I was guilty, guilty as hell. So I was standing in that courtroom, thinking that I was going to get a year, and then he dropped it on me. He sentenced me from two to four years.

I don't know what happened. They went out for dinner and brought back a lot of time behind bars for me. I remember in the morning Parker said, "You want to go to the Flame and eat, Ron?" I remember joking around. I said, "How about if I go with you?" They got a big laugh out of that. They went to dinner and come back with two years.

I stood there. I couldn't believe it. One year was bad enough, but two years—God! I told the judge, "I'll do my best to get straightened out." Shit, I wanted to kick that bastard's teeth in.

The fourteenth of January I got back from the funny farm, and on the seventeenth they sent me up the line to Marquette Prison. The family was there. Well, Gerry, my sister Geraldine, was, and Floyd and my mother. I wonder who talked her into showing up. She didn't come to the jail or the mental institution to see me. But they came to see me, and they said, "Ron, we'll write. We'll do this. We'll do that."

I said, "Thanks." I was half crying. Gerry hugged me, and I hugged her back.

How did I get to the prison? The sheriff drove me. Up I went. When you got to the prison, there was a big office. The cons could visit people there. Jesus, my heart sunk. You know it's over when they strip you of your old life, take everything away from you: wallet, identification, everything. They just took it, and them bars opened. In the hall office there was bars, and they were opened and closed electrically. When that barred door closes behind you, it's good-bye, streets. It's all over. I remember looking out. I couldn't see much, but there went my freedom.

They brought you in, and you got showered. And they took you in and you got your mug shot, and you got fingerprinted. Then you stripped. Goodbye street clothes. They took them and put them in a bag. You had prison clothes now. They even took my underwear, shorts and T-shirt. You didn't get no underwear in prison. They just put us in coveralls.

Now, the cell that I got was in A wing; it's condemned now. Should've been condemned then. You walked in, and there was a big block, big square emptiness, but inside there was solid concrete two galleries high. Not many cells, maybe a hundred. And at the end of that emptiness was a big wheel. I looked at that and thought we were back in the days of Sir Lancelot, in a dungeon.

They took a key and unlocked that big wheel. I could hear them cons saying, "Here come a fish. Is he a fish? What is he?" A fish is a first-timer. "Yeah, he's a fish," the hall boy said. I didn't know what was going on. I never heard of a man being a fish. Well, that's what it meant: a first-timer.

They took this chain off of that big wheel. It stood about five feet in the air; that was the distance across it. They cranked that thing, and you could hear it clanking. They had these old-time keys, big ones, and they unlocked your cell. There it was. In you went, and they locked you up. You heard that big wheel clanking again, and you figured you were never going to get out.

The bed took up the length of the cell. There was a table in there where you ate. And you got a wash basin and a dipper. There was no toilet facilities. Welcome home, like where I lived as a kid. They had these buckets—homemade, you could see that. That's what you shit and pissed in. And that disinfectant they had—I'd rather smell my own shit than that. You opened that thing up, and it smelled awful, made you sick. Once a week you could go up and take a shower; otherwise the hall boy would give you water every day to wash with. I thought to myself, "My God, is this what it's going to be like all the way through?" The first night, I cried myself to sleep.

I didn't have no smoking stuff, but next day they come by with what they called silver packets, uncut Chippewa. It wasn't bad. But that other Chippewa was like powder. I rolled a smoke one time and forgot to twist the end of it. I leaned back in my rack, and the tobacco went right in my mouth. I spit and spit.

The meals wasn't bad. No quality to the food, but there was plenty of it.

I looked forward to that once-a-week shower. I couldn't keep myself clean without running water. In the back room where we took showers was more cells, six of them, where they kept troublemakers. You could hear them back there: "Let me out of here! Let me out!" Well, they screwed up out in population—that's what they call where you're not locked up. The ones in them troublemaker cells was mostly niggers.

We went to take a shower, and the troublemakers was saying, "We got any sissies in this bunch?" I looked in there and gave them the finger.

Moving Up the Line

"Say, boy, you wouldn't do that if I catch you on population."

I said, "Anytime." I started getting back to the old tough ways. Well, you had to be tough in a place like that to survive.

I wondered why all that headshrinking stuff and then end up in a place like this? I slid back like I was. And damn, you looked out, and all you saw was wall. Marquette is a small prison. That was the only thing you'd see was that wall. Talk about depressing! And you'd think about women.

I wanted something to read, a comic book maybe. They give me raggedy *Post* magazines. I was glad to get them; they passed the time. But what a way to keep a man! They had one kind of recreation that I enjoyed. They had closed-circuit radio, and they had earphones. You could plug in and listen to TV. That was quite a trick. When "Perry Mason" was on, that was pretty cool; you could understand what was happening.

One night I was listening to the "Twilight Zone." All of a sudden there was something wrong with our earphones, and I yelled to the guy in the next cell, "Anything wrong with your earphones?" He said no, but I couldn't hear nothing. There was different channels you could plug into. All I could hear was music, nothing but weird music. No way I could figure out what was going on. We was in suspense quite a while. We wanted to find out what happened in that program. Well, what was happening was this guy on TV was getting hung, and pictures flashed through his mind just before he got strung up. He was thinking back on his lifetime, but there wasn't no talking. You try to listen to the TV. It's quite a trick. "Bonanza" was easy. You could almost always figure out what went on there.

I was worried. I wondered if I'd make it. I said to myself, "I ain't going to be able to do it. I can't handle two years of this." I talked to the hall boy, and he said, "You'll go to diagnostic. You'll get transferred. At diagnostic they'll run tests to figure out where to send you. Hit for the camp program if you can." I thanked him.

I was going to Jacktown—Jackson Prison in Jackson, Michigan—to take tests. We waited for the transfer bus to come to bring us there. They chained you up with one long chain. They handcuffed you to another guy and to the chain, eighteen guys to a chain. The capacity of the bus was thirty-six convicts. You backed into the bus so you got in right. We left Marquette at four in the morning.

There was bars on the bus windows, and big screen mesh in the back. The guards had shotguns and pistols too. When you went on the bus, you were chained up, and these goddamn guards stood there with all them guns. Here you were, another human being, and they had to do this. I looked at that bus, all caged in. They pushed you in and locked them cages, and I worried. What if the bus tipped over into a lake or river or got in a wreck?

I was chained to a little fellow, a murderer, been in prison fifteen years. And he told me he done time in Ionia, Jackson, and Marquette. He was a refrigeration man, and he'd been fixing refrigerators in the prison camps around Marquette, but now he was headed back to Jackson. He told me a story.

Now, they say that a murderer never admits that he did it. Well, he didn't either. He was a little guy, quite old. He told me that there was a party, and he was quite a scrapper, little as he was. He said he remembered getting in an argument with this big fellow and then passing out. He woke up, and that big fellow was lying on the floor nearby. He went over and looked at him—now, this is his story anyway—and the guy was beat to death. He said he didn't do it, but they accused him of beating that guy to death. He got a lawyer and everything. But he got sent up anyway.

I looked at all these other hard cases. He wasn't no hard case, but there was some chained up. One guy, a colored guy, had seventeen years in and was getting transferred to Jackson for release. They was going to release him out of Jackson because he lived in Detroit. I guess it saved the state a bus ticket that way, or maybe they was giving him a last taste of the chain.

But you know what tore me up when we was going down to Jackson? They pulled into St. Ignace at the Pure Oil Station, the truck stop, to have something to eat. Did that make me feel lonely, being in my hometown! I looked for somebody I knew, as if it would've did me any good. I felt like nobody cared.

On the bus, you'd look at the people's faces, the other cons, and some of them would look real sad, but a lot of them would be watching the cars to see if they could get a peek at a woman, especially when a car passed us. We was up above, and you could look down into the cars. Everybody was watching to see if they could get a look at a woman's leg. A sad affair, really.

What a ride! We didn't get to Jackson till five-thirty that night. The bus had stopped for breakfast, and they stopped down south for dinner—bologna sandwiches and coffee. If you had to go to the bathroom, you pissed in a duct. In the back there was a bucket like what was in the cells. If you had to take a shit, you could use that.

We got to Jacktown—Jackson Prison—and it was fingerprinting time again, fingerprints and mug shots real quick like. They fed us and brought us where we took showers. They sprayed you with disinfectant. They sprayed us after we took our showers. You couldn't see the cells yet.

Moving Up the Line

When they throw your ass in prison, they give you a number. Mine is A111382. I'm the 111,382nd guy that got in trouble. They said, "This is your number, 111382. Memorize it." There went your name. They'd say, "111382, report here; 111382, report there."

I was memorizing my number. They gave you some clothing: a pair of coveralls, another pair of pants, and a shirt—or pullover shirts, like. They had your prison number on them clothes. And of course you got blankets and sheets—the first thing you had to do was make your rack.

I walked into where the cells was. There was five hundred of them in that block. I looked at that and wondered what I'd got myself into. There was long galleries, stacked up four stories high on each side. My cell was sixty-eight, first gallery. But them cells was better than Marquette. They had a toilet in them. There was a catwalk behind them—bars to the front and bars to the back.

I went into the cell, and the guy locked up next door said, "Say, man, where you from?"

"St. Ignace," I said.

And he said, "Do you know Ron Paquin?"

I didn't answer right away. Then I said, "Jesus Christ, that's me." And here it was Kenny Alesandro, a buddy from home. He'd been in the joint a couple weeks already and knew the ropes. He was a fish too, though.

I got a job in the kitchen. That's what Kenny told me to do. He said, "Hit for the kitchen. See if you can get a hitch there." Wasn't long before I was in trouble. The cook, Kowalski, was an old-timer. He had been in about fifteen years. And there was Parchet, a colored guy, real strong he was. He had over fifteen years in too. Them two run the kitchen. We wasn't supposed to talk while we worked. Kenny and I's job was putting trays into the wooden racks, running them through the dishwasher, then go back to the other end and take them out.

We was yakking and joking around. Kowalski said, "I'm telling you guys, no fat-mouthing when you're in the line."

I said, "Why don't you go to hell? Who the hell are you? You ain't nothing but a convict. I'll do what I want."

He grabbed one of them big spatulas. They're stainless steel, with a big handle to stir the potatoes with, mashed potatoes and that. He swung at me.

I leaned away and grabbed one of them wooden trays. He swung at me again, but I blocked him with the tray. I worked myself around to where I could grab a spatula too. When I got hold of it, I said, "All right. Come on. I'll tear your face off."

Parchet walked in. He looked at Kowalski and said, "Drop it." Kowalski dropped his spatula. Then Parchet turned to me and said, "Drop her, Slim!"

I held on for a minute, but then I got thinking. Kowalski was tough as hell with that spatula till Parchet came in, and then he dropped it like a little kid. Parchet said, "I'm going to tell you something, Slim." He walked within reach of that spatula, and he said, "I'm going to give you one swing. Then I'm going to take that away from you and beat the shit out of you. How does that sound, huh?"

I dropped the spatula. "OK," he said, "everything's cool." That was the end of it.

I couldn't stay out of trouble, with that temper of mine. I got in fight after fight, damn near every day. One time the basketball come over on the volleyball court where we was playing. There was about fifty niggers by the basketball court, some playing and the rest standing around. So when that basketball come over, I put a little mound of dirt up and set the basketball on there. And a nigger over there said, "Don't you kick that, boy. Don't you kick that."

I gave them the finger and kicked the ball. It curved, went sideways. This nigger was standing there with his arms folded. He wasn't looking, and, wham, it smacked him on the side of his face. Holy crap!

"Who did that? Who did that?" he said.

I stood there laughing. I said, "I did. What you going to do about it?"

"I'm going to get you, man," he said. There was no use explaining that it was an accident that he got hit.

Bobby Gray, my old friend from home, told me I was in trouble. He and I done a lot of time together. He said, "I'll tell you, Ron, don't stay in your cell, whatever you do. You got to get it over with." Show them some heart, in other words.

I said, "Yeah, all right."

Well, that was during morning yard, so we had noon meal. I got in the chow hall, and this nigger stopped. He had four or five of them with him. He said, "I'll see you out in the yard, boy."

"Don't bring no more than twenty of you black bastards," I said.

He said, "I'm going to get you."

"Get on with it, punk," I said.

You didn't dare start nothing in the chow hall, because up above—way up above where all the offices were—there was little openings. It was all steel, and there was little openings about two feet long and eight or nine inches wide. There was guards looking through there, and they had guns. If you started a fight in the chow hall, they'd get you for inciting a riot. That nigger wasn't no fool. He wasn't going to do nothing in there.

Right after dinner you got a yard break. I said to myself, "Goddamn, I got to have a weapon. I ain't got nothing." I did learn a few tricks in there. You can take a razor blade and put it in a match cover so you won't cut yourself. Well, I made that. You can make another weapon with them Schick razor blades they give you that come apart. You tie string around the razor handle so you can grip it good. You don't have to put the string on, but it works better if you do. You carry that in your hand. That makes a good weapon.

I brought a razor blade in the yard with me. Nine niggers stood waiting. I walked right over to them. I was scared, but I walked right up to that nigger and said, "Say, man, what about dropping this? I didn't mean to kick that ball into your face."

Well, that held. In other words, I didn't walk up like I was going to start swinging, see? I got them off guard. When I got close to him, I quick jammed that razor in his throat. "Move and you're dead!" I told him.

This other nigger standing to the left said, "Don't move! The man be crazy! Don't move!"

I said, "Anybody moves and I'll cut him. I'm going to tell you, and this ain't no cop-out: I didn't mean for no ball to hit you in your face. But if you want to make something out of it, make your move."

I showed them heart all right, but I shook inside. If he'd moved, I don't know what I would've did. But he said everything was cool, and there wouldn't be no more trouble. I let him go, and them niggers walked off.

In the kitchen, we'd steal rolls and Polish sausage and other food and sell it down the block for cigarettes and stuff. Kenny and I did, and some other guys too. Well, one night, damn, here came the shakedown. You ought to seen the weapons. All you heard was *clang, cling, clang*—guys throwing stuff out. The screws caught them in the first cell, but after that everybody knew the shakedown was coming. Them screws had big laundry bags. They had three of them damn near full of contraband by the time they got through all the cells.

Well, Kenny and I had rolls we had swiped from the kitchen, and I said, "Christ, Kenny, what are we going to do with them?" We ate all we could and flushed the rest down the toilet. One screw—we called him Galloping Ghost—was a skinny gray-haired bastard with pale skin. He snuck around trying to bust everybody. Kenny was laying on his rack talking to me. He couldn't see in my cell, and he said, "Hey, Ron, good thing we ate them rolls."

He was talking, and there was that Galloping Ghost in back of my cell. Kenny was blabbing about them rolls. I let him rattle on for a while. Finally I said, "Good evening, officer."

Kenny shut up. All the Ghost said to him was, "If you wouldn't have stoled all them rolls, you wouldn't have to worry about eating them and getting sick."

At Jacktown you took your tests, like aptitude tests, I guess. Then your counselor would talk to you. I went to see my counselor—a nigger, wouldn't you know? I'll tell you, with your screws and your counselors, there was lots of prejudice. So I went into this counselor. He was looking through my folder, and he said, "You haven't got a very good label on you."

"What do you mean?"

He said, "When you were in Newberry State Hospital, their diagnostic on you wasn't good."

"What do you mean, 'wasn't good'?"

He said, "When you get mad, when you lose your temper, you're likely to do just about anything."

I said, "Well, so—"

He broke in, "This means that you'd kill somebody and wouldn't regret it till later."

I said, "Aw, come on."

"Look what you're in here for."

I said, "I'm sorry for what I did there. I didn't say, 'Well, good enough for the guy,' or anything like that."

"I'll tell you, young man," he said, "we'll straighten you out in here."

"Oh, yeah, rule by the rod. You're going to straighten me out. Back of the hand to you. What do you mean, you'll straighten me out?"

He looked at me and said, "We can take care of tough guys like you." Then he said, "You got the rabbit out of you yet?"

"Rabbit out of me? What are you saying?"

"I see here that you ran away from reform school several times."

I said, "Yeah, I did."

"Why did you run?"

Because I didn't want to be there. Wouldn't you? Put yourself in my position. If you was getting mistreated, if you was lonely, wouldn't you run too?"

He glanced away. "That's been quite a while. Where would you like to go?"

"I'd like to get a camp program."

"OK. You got a good possibility of getting a camp program,

Moving Up the Line

because it's been a while since you run away. You're going to learn a trade in here."

I said, "A trade would be good, but I'd like to get some schooling."

"I'll recommend schooling," he said.

The conversation calmed down from tough guy and getting radical to talking with each other. I don't know if that was their way to try to find out your attitude, but I didn't like the hothead label that he said I had on me from the mental institution.

I took my tests and was around average IQ or a little above average IQ. I'm not sure which. You got a blood test. You went to the hospital, and they took a physical of you, for what it was worth. Not much, as far as I could see. I'd had something wrong with my arm since I'd been in reform school, and I wanted it fixed. They didn't even figure out something was wrong, let alone fix it.

A week or so later, they told me I was going to Cassidy Lake. All the cons, the old ones, said, "That's a resort area, Ron. The warden there is a freak for flowers and he's big on AA." So because of my age, they sent me to a camp. There was older guys there, but only first-timers could go to Cassidy Lake.

Cassidy Lake

The camp at Cassidy Lake did look like a resort. What you stayed in was cabins. There was a cabin by itself; you slept there the first night. Some guys came and got you. Other cons showed you the ropes as far as where the chow hall was and the rec hall. Then you got into classification. They decided what your duties was and what group you'd be assigned to.

When you walked into your cabin, you'd have a oil stove there. Straight ahead was the center room, where the head of the shack stayed. And to the right and the left was rooms with tables. There was four beds on each side—nine men to a cabin. Between the cabins was a building with a big bathroom—toilets, sinks, and showers. Not a bad place, really.

They had a screw there named Selby, a guard. He was a smart ass. I think he did stuff just to rile us. Every Saturday we had inspection in our shacks. Well, it'd be about ten o'clock. And these cabins were just wood. They created dust. Friday night we'd straightened her up, and then Saturday morning we'd mop and do things good. There was a beam going across on each side of it. We'd get up there and wipe that clean. We'd really deck her out. They'd have inspection. Here came Selby with white gloves on. What an asshole! He'd get up on a chair and check the rafter with his white gloves. Then the ignorant bastard would get down off the chair and say that the chair was dirty. Of course, it was dirty. He'd just stepped on it. He'd pull shit like that.

Well, they'd gig you. You'd have to fix whatever they told you was wrong—really get working on it. But I'm telling you we went through our shack good. If he found anything wrong, it was Mother Nature's fault, not ours. Your beds had to be all taut made up, with square corners, everything. I learned in reform school how to make beds, and to this day I don't like to do it. Reminds me of bad times.

They put me in school for a while. I wanted to finish high school, so I needed help in so many things. They put me in remedial classes where I worked on math and language. And while I was there, I knew my figures good in my head, but I remember we had simple fractions. I did them, and I come to class with all the answers. The teacher wanted to know how I figured them out. I said, "I got them in my head, but I don't know how—" I had to learn how to put them on paper. By God, I really tried. I got A's and B's in math and in language use.

But you know what them dirty sons of bitches did? They called me into classification and said, "We got a job for you, Ron."

I said, "I want to go to school."

"You'll have time," they said.

I wanted to go to school and take that test that's equivalent to a high school education. They said, "You'll have time for that," but they was lying.

They made me foreman of the rec hall. I had my own crew. I'd assign guys to mop the floors—the gym floor and the library and the TV room. I'd tell guys to clean the weight room and assign them to watch the boats. Guys could check boats out and row around the lake. We got paid fifteen cents a day. If you worked in the rec hall, that was a seven-day job from nine in the morning till nine-thirty at night, when the doors was locked. The foreman locked the doors. That was me. It was long hours for fifteen cents, and you didn't get no overtime. I made thirty cents more a week than everybody else except the kitchen help, because they had to work seven days a week too.

I was in the yard one day, and this guy kept staring at me. Finally I walked over and said, "Say, man, what are you staring at?"

He said, "Don't get mad. I know you. Aren't you a Packquin?" That's how they said my name in reform school. He did time in reform school with me. I met several of them like that while I was in prison. Shows you how much good reform school does.

He said, "Aren't you Ronny or Donny, one of the twins?" I looked close at him. I knew the face but couldn't remember his name. I met a colored guy from reform school named Woods. He was in prison, and James Berger and Bruce and others—I can't remember their names. And they knew other reform schoolers what was in different camps. So there was a lot of them that never made it. Like I always said, reform school is a training ground for prison.

I'll go into a few things that happened while I ran the rec hall.

Whew! There's a lot of them. Tree Williams—his first name was Larry—was a colored guy, and he studied two years at Michigan State. He was well educated, anyway. He was in for armed robbery, and he did time in Old Ionia, then got shifted to the camp towards the end of his bit. I don't know, he had five years left, I think. I heard through the grapevine from another con that Tree's dead now. He got shot.

I got into it with him one time. Tree's job in the rec hall was to do the TV room. He'd sweep it, mop and buff it. He decided that he wasn't going to do it. We had a good understanding, the fellows I worked with, so Tree had put me in a spot. If he wasn't going to do his work, I sure wasn't. And I couldn't snitch on the guy. Actually, they'd find out even if I didn't tell on him. Fay or Heinke would come—they were screws—and they'd ask why the TV room wasn't done. They knew it was Tree's job.

Tree was by the fireplace. There was never any wood burning in that thing. He sat there and said, "I ain't going to do it, Chief."

"You better do it," I said.

He said, "I ain't going to."

I said, "Get on it. Goddamn it, get up and do it."

"Ain't no hick be bossing me around," he said.

I picked up an iron-back chair, and I could see he was mad, in one of them moods. He said, "You wouldn't hit me with that, would you, Chief?"

I said, "You're goddamn right, I will."

He lunged at me, and I bashed him over the head. He rolled onto the floor. I run.

I carried a baseball bat with me after that for a while and watched him close, but he never did nothing. He joked around later. He said, "I figured you wouldn't hit me with that, Chief, but, goddamn, you sure did." I cut him across his head there. But, damn, was he tough!

Tree never stopped teasing. There was this guy named Wally in there, a French-Indian fellow. I remember he was odd, stuck to himself mostly. We'd talk sometimes. He pulled his time pretty straight. Tree was always messing with him because he was a goofy little guy.

Tree said to me one day, "Hey, Chief, the Indians are after me. They're out to get me."

I said, "Man, I don't know where you're coming from, Tree."

Tree and Wally was in the same shack. Tree would be taking a nap or sleeping, and Wally would whisper in his ear, "Going to get you. The Indians are going to get you." He kept doing this, but one time he was saying that and Tree woke up. Wally stood there with a hammer in his hand. Tree woke up, and there was little Wally standing over him with that hammer.

Tree rolled away, but he had no place to go. Wally smiled and said, "No matter how big you are, you can be had. I didn't have to wake you up."

So that's what Tree meant when he said the Indians was going to get him. Wally told me later he was psyching Tree out. Tree left Wally alone after that.

Every bit that went down, most of it happened around that rec hall. If guys had a score to settle, it was back of the rec hall, in the weight room, someplace around there. Sexual stuff went on there too. One time I bent over to take a drink, and Fears, a nigger, that son of a bitch, put his hand on my ass. I whirled around. It was just a reflex, me coming around. I said, "Man, keep your hands off me!"

"I was just taking a little feel," he said.

I said, "Take another one and you're dead."

"All right, man," he said. "All right." And he backed off. He thought he was funny.

That night Killer Patulski was with me, one of my associates, a Polish fellow from Detroit. Roy Patulski was his name. We was walking from the rec hall, and Fears and a few other guys were walking in front of us. Fears was talking loud. He said, "Man, I've had every woman but one kind, and that's an Indian." He was jive-talking. "Hey, Chief," he said, you got any sister that can come up and get laid?"

I said, "Naw." I had a smile on my face. "But I'll tell you," I said, "there is one that gets it with the brothers."

While I was bullshitting, I moved close to him. I slammed him in the neck, in the cords near his Adam's apple. He grabbed his throat, staggered and fell, and then scrambled to get up. I said, "Get up, you black bastard, and I'll bust your ass. Lay off my relations, and that's all." I was in the mood to break him up.

Tree was in the bunch ahead. He was razzing. He said, "Fears, I guess you ain't going to mess with none of Ron's sisters, huh?" They all razzed him.

I said, "Come on, you got some fight in you yet?"

"You sucker-punched me," he said.

"I'm here, ain't I? I ain't going to sucker-punch you now. Come on. I'll kick your ass."

When a fight started like that, Fears got his friends, I got mine, and things got tight. I don't know if he was afraid of me or my buddies, but he sulked off.

I'm afraid of snakes, deathly scared of them. I hate them. I couldn't be more afraid of anything. Some cons found out about it. This colored guy had a big snake in the rec hall one day. I come up from the weight room, walked into the gym, and heard some hassle. "Take it after Chief," I heard.

I seen the snake then. There was a storage closet near where I was. I reached in and grabbed a shovel. I felt my heart pound with fear. I said, "Don't bring that near me or I'll cut your head off with the shovel." He kept coming at me. I swung that shovel and whapped him in the wrist. I didn't catch him with the iron part, just the handle. I near broke his wrist, but I was going to break his head. He dropped the snake, and it was crawling on the floor. I ran then and didn't come back till that snake was gone.

D. J. Williams, a colored guy in our shack, liked teasing me with snakes. I chased him all around the rec hall with a baseball bat once. I was passing out tennis shoes, and he had a garter snake. He threw it on the desk and yelled, "Hey, Ron, look at this!"

I swear I was out of there with the baseball bat before that snake hit that counter. I screamed at him, "D. J., try it again and I'll cave your head in!"

I watched for snakes constantly. I always checked my bed and everything. I was afraid somebody would stick one in there.

I found out D. J. feared spiders. Killer and I collected fifty or sixty spiders. We hunted all over that rec hall; we found them in the furnace room mostly. We put all of them in a shoe box. I told D. J. to quit messing with me, but he didn't. One Saturday afternoon, we went into the shack. I brought the spiders. I'd been keeping them at the rec hall. I was high on some codeine pills me and Killer had got from the hospital annex. We was lit up. So D. J. come in the shack that afternoon. I had my spiders ready. He stood in the doorway and said, "What's happening, man?" Then he come in.

I had it planned. He walked into the center room, a little room by the stove. I yelled to him, "Hey, D. J., want to get some pinochle going?"

He said, "Sure, man, I guess so."

"Get a partner," I said.

As I was talking, I snuck up and sucker-punched him. He fell, and I grabbed him. I strapped that bastard to his bed and waited for him to wake up.

Pretty soon I heard some groaning, so I went over to his bed. I had the shoe box under my arm. I said, "Hey, D. J."

"Man, what's going on here?" he said.

"Remember I told you to quit fucking with them snakes?"

Cassidy Lake

"What you got in that box?"

I said, "I got something for you."

He said he was going to kill me. I looked at him, smiling to myself, thinking about what was going to happen. I hadn't opened the box yet. I said, "You know what I got here, D. J.? Spiders! I got spiders!"

He went crazy. I opened that box and shook them spiders on him. You ought to heard him scream. He was sweating and screaming — not saying nothing, just screaming. Finally I let him loose, and he run out, brushing his clothes and going, *"Ahhh, ahhh!"* He was shook. I thought I was going to bust a gut laughing. Killer, that crazy son of a bitch, just rolled on the floor. He really thought that was funny.

D. J. was gone for a couple of hours. I wondered if maybe he was going to get something to light me up with. He come back to the shack. He yelled out — well, he called me Ron or Chief or Pac, three names I had — "Hey, Pac, come on out."

I looked to see if he had a weapon. He said, "It's all right, man. I want to talk to you."

"OK. I'm coming," I said.

And he said, "Look, call her even, man?"

"All right, but don't mess me up with no snakes."

And the man talked sense. "Man, I know how you felt now," he said.

I said, "All right."

He said, "I'm not bullshitting, Pac. It's over. Let's drop it."

"All right."

We got along good after that. What I did with D. J. spread the word not to fool with Ron. You have to, if a guy's got a phobia. I mean, am I scared of snakes! You got to show them guys what'll happen if they mess with you.

I did hit someone there once, and I'd do it again if I had the chance. We was in the weight room. I was lifting and was good at it for as skinny as I was, and this Lefty Bush from Detroit, a white guy, come in, and he said, "OK if I lift with you, Pac?" I said, "Sure."

We lifted for a while. He was bigger than I was, about the same height but huskier. I outlifted him, but I figured to. He'd never been in a weight room before. I told him, "I outlifted you, but give yourself some time, and you'll do a lot more than me." So that's all there was to it, at least I thought so.

I got off at nine-thirty, and I went up to the shack. The screen was off my window. I couldn't figure it out; it was summertime. I got a hammer out of the center room and nailed up the screen. I was worried. Something was wrong. You got to watch. Oh, Jesus, you got to watch all the time.

Kokard, our center-room man, was a snitch. Him and I had got into it. I kicked his ass terrible. He gave me some crap, so I beat him up. He didn't like me. Here's how it come about. When I think back on it, I realize that for a couple weeks Bush was trying to get close to me. The day I outlifted him, Kokard asked me, "Did you outlift, or did Lefty outlift?"

I said, "I outlifted him, but give him time and he will."

That same day Bush went to our shack and told Kokard he was down there lifting with Pac, and Kokard asked, "Did you get him?" Killer was listening. Bush said he didn't. Well, that was all it amounted to. But now Bush was going to get me. Can you believe that?

All this went on behind my back. Kokard hated me. Bush owed him cigarettes and a gambling debt, so he said, "Take care of Ron, Lefty, and we're even."

So Killer come up to me—I didn't know him very well yet—and he said, "You seem like a good Joe. I'm going to tell you what's going on here, Ron."

I said, "Yeah, what's that?"

And he told me all what I just told you, and he said, "You know why that window was open?"

I shook my head no. He said, "While your screen was off, he was going to smash you with a rock."

"For what?"

He told me about the weight lifting deal. I said, "I'll be goddamned."

Then Killer said Lefty was carrying a pipe. I said, "Oh, yeah? He's got a pipe?" They'd take their sleeve and cuff it up and put a pipe up and pad it on their forearm. They'd walk up and smack you. Your lights were out before you knew what was going on.

Well, he had a pipe, and I got to thinking. I figured I'd get Bush, but I didn't know what to do. I went back and forth with myself. I couldn't snitch. Snitches, tattletales, did hard times with the other cons. I couldn't run away, because they'd catch me and give me more time. So what was I going to do? I figured I better get him before he got me.

I opened the rec hall doors around noon, a half an hour before everybody went back to work. Guys would get their scrip—there was quite a lineup. I was figuring out how to get Bush, and I fell into it. I was in the scrip line. Bush walked up and said, "Hey, Pac, me and you's mellow. Can I cut in line?"

I said, "Sure."

So here he was. OK, there was me, Killer, two other cons, the little white nigger I bashed at Jacktown for being with the real niggers. Pete was his first name. And D. J. Williams was there, the one I took the spiders after.

I don't know if Bush was looking or not. He should've been if he wasn't. I said, "Say, what's happening, man? I'm your mellow man." And I stood face-to-face with him and said, "How you set for pipes lately?"

He flinched, and I punched him on the left side of his jaw, cut the inside of his mouth. When he fell, his head hit the wall. I put the boots to him then. I had that bastard down, and I was going to get him. Them guys, they didn't want me to kill him. They drug me off.

Within fifteen minutes I was in detention, ready to go to Ionia. And the guys figured Pete snitched, the white nigger. I was locked in detention ready to have the counselor talk to me. But it wasn't long before the white nigger had his ass whipped for snitching. He didn't go to the hospital, but they beat him up good. Not a noticeable beating but a good scaring, and punched in the chest and the back where nothing would show.

My counselor, Rosencranz, come to see me. He asked, "What went on, Ron?"

I said, "What did your snitches tell you?"

"Don't play games with me, Ron. You're in big trouble."

I said, "Oh, yeah?"

Then he come out and asked, "Did you hit Bush?"

I said, "No, I didn't hit him." I didn't admit anything yet.

Rosencranz said, "Bush is saying that you sucker-punched him."

"OK, I hit Bush. The bastard was after me, so he got it." And I still believe I did the right thing. The way things was, what else could I do?

Well, they didn't send me to Ionia. I thank Rosencranz for that. I don't think I would ever have straightened out if I would've went to that place. I never done time there, but them other cons told me how bad it was. But Rosencranz did write up a report, and when I come up for parole later, they turned me down. All that for hitting Bush. He had it coming, you know.

Killer and I pulled a good one on a nigger one time. He thought he was God's gift to women. They probably got the stuff out on the streets to do it, but they processed their hair in there, and they weren't supposed to. You should've seen the crap they mixed up to do that. What it amounted to was lye, soap, crackers, and salt—something like that. Before they processed their hair, they'd put this pomade on their scalp. Then they'd take this goop that they mixed up and put it on their head. When it started burning, they washed it off. They combed their hair out and put a bandanna on it. They had their hair straight now like the white guys.

I didn't like that bastard, a conceited sucker if I ever met one. He was always bragging. Nothing ever come between us, but I just flat didn't like him. So I told Killer, "Let's get some Sani-Flush."

He said, "What are you going to do?"

So I told him my idea. We had to change the element in the hot water heater up at H Group, and we got in the shack. We got the key from somebody—it wasn't his buddy exactly. We went into his locker where he had that process goop going. He had a quart of it. We took most of it out and poured the Sani-Flush in. Then we put it back. You can imagine the chemical reaction that would go on with that.

He was always over to our shack. The reason why he was over there so much was we had like a tournament going with pinochle. Killer and I played together. I'll tell you, in that pinochle game you didn't say nothing. You didn't scratch your ear. There was no talking, just straight bidding. It was an important thing, whatever you were playing for—a carton of cigarettes or coffee.

This colored guy played lots of pinochle with us. He come over that day. We didn't know he was going to be there, but we was waiting for him to process his hair, and it happened to have been that day, Sunday. So he was processing his hair—he had a visit coming. His mama, his girlfriend, was going to come see him, and he wanted to get slicked down.

He come into the shack, and he had this jar in his hand, and I didn't know he was going to do it in our shack. He put this pomade on, and I was trying not to laugh. He got this big stick out. They got a wide stick that they use to put that stuff on their head. He rubbed his pomade on and spread the goop. Wasn't long before he said, "Man, this is good shit. She's heating up already." It'd get burning, and they'd have to rinse it off.

I didn't know Killer did this, but he jammed the door. He stuck something in there. The nigger was sitting there, and he said, "Man, this is good shit. She's really burning." I'll bet you it was burning. But then he tried to get out and couldn't open the door. By now that Sani-Flush was really cooking, and he was in pain. He couldn't get out. I was laughing now; all of us was. He was yanking at that door, yelling to get out. Killer let him loose.

That Sani-Flush took the hair right off his head, and he had burn scars on his scalp. Was he a mess! I'm telling you, if he'd ever find out who did that, he'd have killed us. I never did tell nobody. It ruined his hair. That'll fix the conceited bastard. He used to say, "Man, when we's all slicked down, there just ain't no other hair match ours." Well, his hair didn't match nothing when we got through.

I liked my rec hall job. It was a challenge. In the rec hall we'd have quite a bit of activity. There was weight lifting going on. The TV room was there, and you could play basketball. I played a lot of basketball. There was a camp team that played games with teams on the outside. They had intramural leagues in basketball and softball too. There was lots of things to do, even a library.

On fifteen cents a day, you can't even buy cigarettes. And I didn't have no money when I went in, so I gambled at just about everything: pinochle, poker, Ping-Pong, basketball, you name it. They gave you paper for scrip. So what would that be a month? Not much at fifteen cents a day. And you could buy goodies from the store like Ritz crackers, peanut butter, candy bars, potato chips, and like that. I didn't get money sent from home, no package of any kind. I guess when you're locked up, everybody's busy leading their own lives. So I gambled a lot.

Sometimes I shortened the odds. We knew this guy got a good visit the day before, so I said to my buddies, "Let's get him in a game and stack them cards up."

So we stacked them up, got them all lined up. We was playing cutthroat pinochle. The hand he had was pretty good, but the one that got him was better. We watched his eyes, laughing to ourselves; he was stupid anyway. We watched his eyes, and, wow, they lit up when he seen the hand he had. He was bidding to beat hell. But we had fixed it so he couldn't win. It was for a carton of cigarettes and a jar of instant coffee. And sure as shit, he went for it and lost.

Then he wondered if we screwed him. "Cheated!" he said. "You guys cheated."

I said, "Bullshit. You got the hand, you bid, and you went set. You overbid your hand." He had aces, but that's no big thing. He didn't have double aces. And he had a roundhouse. Well, that's only twenty-four. He didn't have that much to bid on. But we knew him well. His own greed got him.

I blackmailed guys on sexual things. Well, there was this nigger named Jackson. He thought he was real cool. He punked out this white kid, a pure sissy. I caught them one night. He was busting him out right there. In fact, Jackson was screwing him in the ass is what he was doing. You know how they did this. They used pomade to do that sodomy. I think that's what you call it. The sissy run, but I knocked him down. He couldn't go far with his pants tangled around his ankles. He didn't have time to pull them up.

I said, "All right, boys, I want something on scrip day."

Jackson said, "What you mean, man?"

I said, "Run me some cigarettes. I want a carton from each of youse." I smoke a nonfilter and a filter. One gets too strong and one gets too weak.

"You ain't going to get them."

"OK," I said. "I'm going to the man, then. If you think I'm playing, don't run them scrip day. I'll wait till scrip day comes." I told them I wanted a carton of Pall Malls from Jackson and a carton of Winston from the sissy.

This sissy said, "Jackson, what are you going to do, man, about this?" as though his man was going to take over.

I said, "All right, punk bastard, I'll tell you what. I want the Winstons from you, and I want a jar of peanut butter and some Ritz crackers." And I said, "You ready to mouth off, Jackson?"

"No, man," he said. "I'll run the cigarettes."

"You better or you're going to the man."

They brought the stuff to me, and I watched the guys I was blackmailing to see if they had good visits from their parents or something, you know, and if they got goodies, good scrip day. Goddamn, I can't remember how much you could take out scrip day. I'm pretty sure it was twelve dollars and fifty cents. When they got visits, they could get whatever they wanted. So I watched. Once in a while I'd hit a good sissy, which I'll tell you about in a little while.

One day I went to the school to get a requisition. I walked in, and I was in one of them moods. I can't remember that sissy's name. Anyway, you know how a girl would look at a guy when she really likes him. If you was in school, you probably seen that—you know, staring them up. Here was that sissy sitting there, just gloating at that colored guy. That hit me wrong. I walked over, and I made sure that the teacher wasn't around. Then I slapped him. I said, "Man, straighten up. What's the matter with you? That'll be another carton of smokes too."

I caught one guy giving a blow job to the other guy. One of them was a tough bastard. He was going to give me trouble, squared off with me, everything. I caught him in the act, though. I like ice cream, so I had him run me some ice cream on scrip day and a couple cans of Bugler and some potato chips. I kept them two on the string for about three months. One wasn't queer; just the tough one was. And I had three more blackmail deals going. I had no trouble there, no sweat at all.

I've always said they should bring women in; they've did it overseas. There's so much tension. OK, a man or a woman is used to sex, and it's a release. I wouldn't care if they had to bring hookers in along with wives and girlfriends. I do believe that you wouldn't have as much trouble then.

When I was at Jackson, there was a sissy they called Venus. I guess she took care of a lot of dogs. They didn't give you much of a shower at Jackson. There was six showers, not stalls but wide-open space. You'd go in and take your shower. They'd say, "Six in," and a little later, "Six out, six in." The third or fourth time we took showers, Venus walked in. She had a washrag in front of her little dinger, just a'waddling along. Them guys whistled and yelled, "Come on over here, Venus. I'll take care of you." She was a parole violator. A lot of the cons knew her, and I swear if you looked at her from the back, she looked like a woman. She looked like a Venus. She just wiggled along. She loved it in there.

We had a sissy in our shack at Cassidy. I didn't know it till one night about a month or two before I was going home. He come over to my bunk and said, "I'm in love with you."

"Aw, come on, man," I said. "What are you trying to pull?"

He said, "I'm not kidding. I've been in love with you since we was in Jacktown."

"Oh, Jesus," I said. "Damn, I'm going home soon. I ain't going to mess with no sissy."

Killer was there, and he said, "Hey, Ron, send him over here," so I did.

He went over, and I heard them doing something, I don't know what. "Boy," I said to myself, "I wouldn't mess with something like that." Goddamn, man, that kind of turned my stomach. He was propositioning me. I got propositioned before, but not that directly—you know, right in my shack.

Now, this embarrasses me. I told you about blackmailing the sissies and the sex in them camps. But myself, I never indulged in busting anybody out or anything like that in the camps or while I was in prison. Most of the guys in the camp or in prison resort to masturbation. Hell, I masturbated lots of times. I don't know why—for release, I guess. But I damn well did it. What the hell else you going to do? But it's funny, really. You get clean laundry every week; you got to turn that in. Now, if you're going to masturbate, naturally it's going to be a mess, so—this is embarrassing—you use a stocking. Everybody's coming up short on stockings at laundry time. Well, some of them use hankies, but, hell, I used a stocking.

Every other night, lights went out and Killer would say, "I think

I'll whack my meat a little bit" or "slap my ham" or whatever. He was joking. "Got a date with Rosie Palm and her five sisters," he said. He'd be goofing just like he was really doing it, and all of a sudden he'd let out some little coos and yells like he was coming. And I got to thinking maybe he really was doing that right then and there. So we got a flashlight and waited. There was four of us on each side, plus the center-room man was D. J. We all waited. Killer said to me, "Hey, Ron, I think I'll jack off tonight."

I said, "Hell, go ahead. Knock yourself out. It's your meat."

He kept it up, and we waited for him to go through them things like he was coming to a climax. We turned on the light, and there he was doing it. Laughed—oh, we laughed! And was he embarrassed! He said, "I'll kill you, you sons of bitches." Boy, I'll tell you, that Killer had a temper.

There was drugs in there along with the sex. Neither was much good. I never shot up nothing or anything like that. I didn't like shooting, but I did try other stuff. They had what they called yellow jackets. They screwed me up. I would think when I was walking along that I got to step real high on anything to get over it. Killer and I had some of them. We also sniffed glue. I tried sniffing paint thinner, but I blacked out. That stuff is strong. But I sniffed glue. It's a funny high. I'd just forget everything, just forget.

Everybody was always looking for something to get high. You can look in a Bugler tobacco can, and you can take the hard stuff—unground tobacco or whatever it is—and crush up an aspirin and roll it in with that. All that ever gave me was a headache, but other guys said they got high. We'd try everything. Cough syrup—you have to drink a gallon to get flying. You get a bellyache before you get off.

Later on in the other camp, I got into some strong stuff, but just off and on. Like if a guy had a visit, we'd have him smuggle up a tube of airplane glue. That worked good, but you got to be careful. Guys can get killed sniffing. They put a paper bag over their head—I was never that dumb—and it just takes hold of them or something or else they lose them pigments in your nose. Guys lost the pigments out of their nose. Like they'd be white guys, and their nose would get black like a nigger's.

I got thrown off that rec hall job for having a personality problem. What they meant was I got in fights. So I got transferred to the mason crew. That was quite a deal. There was a guy named Penner, a fellow about thirty-five years old. What a dummy! I get mad when I think about him even now. He was an ass-kisser, just sucked up to the screws all he could—a suck-ass, we called guys like him. I got in trouble with Penner and in a bad fight, so I was shifted to the electric crew.

I'm scared of electricity. I guess you're scared of things you don't understand. But I had fun on the electric crew, quite a bit of fun. Peterson, the screw, was big, round-faced, fat-bellied—just a pig. And ignorant. Why, he'd sit there and fart, and he'd laugh. Bob Rose, the boxer, was on the electric crew, and Killer Patulski, me, and this other guy with a funny name. Ballard Tom was our foreman. He was a journeyman electrician on the streets before he got busted, nice old fellow. He had some fingers missing.

Now, Bob Rose was, I guess, thirty-two years old at the time. We got along good. Tree and him and Killer, they kind of looked out for me, curbed my temper when they could. Like one day we was sitting there, and Peterson farted. He lifted himself up and let a big fart and said, "There's something for you guys to smell."

I said, "Boy, if you ain't an ignorant son of a bitch!"

Bob said, "Ron, shut up. Cool it."

Peterson said, "What'd you say?"

"You're an ignorant son of a bitch," I said. "You act like a pig. This room ain't that big. You can go outside and fart."

"I can write you up on report," he said.

I said, "For what? For what you did?"

He didn't report me, but he did put extra work on me. That dirty bastard had me do every bit of shit work he could find. Well, we had to hang Christmas tree lights. Joy to the world, it's Christmastime. We hung them on the big spruce trees around the camp. That was hard work, and it was cold. I'd get left there. He'd take Killer and them away so I had to hang them bulbs myself. Rose was in D Group, and I was in H Group. I come to work one morning, and I said to Rose, "I got just the thing to take care of Peterson."

Rose said, "Jesus, Ron, don't make trouble for yourself."

"No," I said, "but I'm going to fix Peterson."

Killer poked Rose and said, "You hear what he's got planned?" I'd already told Killer what I was going to do.

Boy, one thing I'll tell you, to Warden Shay you was students, not convicts. I went to Warden Shay's office, and I said, "Mr. Shay, I'd like to talk to you," and I acted real pitiful.

"Yes, son, what can I do for you?"

"I don't like to do this," I said, "but something is the matter with Mr. Peterson. He's acting bad against us."

"What did he do?"

I said, "He keeps calling us no-good convicts, says we're the rubbish of society and we belong here."

"He said that?" The warden's face got red.

I was smiling inside. I said, "Yes, the last week he's been doing that all the time. I don't know why. You know, I'm just a convict."

"Oh, no, son, you're not a convict."

"But he keeps saying that."

"Son, you go back to your job," he said, "and I'll take care of the problem." I knew I had Peterson then.

I went back to our office, and a few minutes later Peterson got a phone call. He said, "Yes, sir. Yes, sir, I'll be right over." I had all I could do to keep from laughing. And to Warden Shay I had said, "I would appreciate it if you didn't tell Peterson that I was the one that come and spoke to you." Which apparently he didn't.

When Peterson come back from the warden's, he was so nice. You know what he said? He said, "You know, it's too cold to hang up Christmas tree lights, so we'll sort the stuff in the shop here and we'll get it organized." It was conduit and wiring and all that. We'd straighten it up. God, he was nice for a couple weeks.

We took care of Peterson in other ways too. I'll tell you how stupid he was. We was down at the fire hall. We had to rewire some lighting, and Ballard, our boss, was teaching us to work with hot wires. We had them rubber-handled pliers, and he was teaching us how to work with them. We had an old rickety ladder. They had two ladders. One was good, and the other was shaky; you had to be careful you didn't fall.

I said, "Ballard, why don't you tell Peterson to get us some better ladders?"

"I will, Ron," he said. "That one is dangerous."

Just then Peterson walked in. "What's the holdup here?" he said. I was standing by the ladder, and I said, "Peterson, this ladder is damn rickety."

"Goddamn. Give me them things. This job should've been done by now." He was just that kind of an asshole, you know. He grabbed my pliers, and he said, "I'll do it."

"No," I said. "Give me my pliers." I grabbed them back.

He said, "I'll get up there. There ain't nothing wrong with that ladder."

"Just look at it," I said. "It's falling apart.

He had to do a pigtail splice. He grabbed Killer's pliers, but not the ones with the rubber handles—we had several types. He climbed up that ladder; he was rocking back and forth. And he grabbed them hot wires. It wasn't that much, just 110, but that's a good jolt if you're not expecting it. Zap! Did he get a poke! Knocked him off that ladder and on his ass. I laughed till I hurt. Jesus, what an ignoramus!

Our warden there, Shay, was strictly AA. I went to AA for a while, but I'll be damned if I'd stand up and tell the cons what my problem was—my home life and all that—and expect to have any help. It was run strictly by the convicts. Here we were, hotheaded outcasts. How were we going to help each other?

I'll give an example. One night in the AA meeting I did get up and talk. They asked me what my problem was. I said, "Well, I like to fight, and I have got in a lot of them."

A guy jumped up and said, "You don't look so tough to me."

Damn! We were getting in a argument. I popped off. I said, "Try me sometime, boy," and I sat down.

What good was that going to do? You might get some dedicated guys who'd been around and knew more. You had older guys with years behind bars, but they was getting ready to be released or paroled. They'd go to the camps after they had went through the hard-core stuff. They might've helped, but then, you wouldn't get much consideration from them, because, hell, they didn't want to screw up by getting involved.

I worked for a while tending Warden Shay's flowers. He really liked flowers, a real fanatic. I was on the ground crew, and they had a little greenhouse made up. I worked there quite a while. This little greenhouse had a foundation and a frame of two-by-fours with plastic nailed on it. I raised them flowers from seeds. I had them in flats, and I got to know my flowers pretty good, the ones that was in there. I had a lot of flats, believe me.

I think I was a bit nuts. I'd walk in and say, "Good morning, you little green fuckers. How you doing?" I'd talk to the flowers. Actually I had no feeling for them flowers, but if Shay would come around, I'd name off the flowers. I'd say, "This is coming along good, and I think it's going to do all right."

Every once in a while Shay would make a showing in the camp. He'd go around to all the jobs. He'd come in that greenhouse—that was his pet. Jesus, he liked them flowers. "Oh, Ron, you are doing a beautiful job," he'd say. "They picked the right guy here."

I'd lay it on, you know. I said, "Well, a couple weeks here and these zinnias is going to be ready." And then the ground crew would take them. I spent two winters in there. I laid it on thick every time the warden come around.

The prison newspaper was next to the greenhouse. I'd go over and bullshit with the newspaper guys. They was the brains of the camp. One time while I was over there, some son of a bitch put a goddamn snake, a blue racer, in the greenhouse. We kept it locked. I don't know how they got that snake in there. So one morning I walked in, and I seen that snake crawl off. He didn't make his move at first. I was there awhile and was getting ready to water them flowers when he slid under the table. I screamed. I'm deathly scared of them pricks. I busted through that plastic and clean out of there. Was I scared! We had to fix the greenhouse where I busted through. I would've died of fright if I didn't get away. Never did find out who put that fucker in there.

Now, the head of the classification was Maynard. He was considered the camp's smart fellow. You didn't figure to put anything over on Maynard, but I did. I went to the inmates' store and ordered a pair of stockings and a white shirt. They had black shirts and white ones. You waited a couple weeks to get them, and lots of the cons had them. I finally got my stuff, but it was two pairs of stockings and two shirts. Goddamn, how'd that happen? Somebody goofed. Well, I wasn't going to give them back to the state.

My number, 111382, was on the tag. We had a movie coming up, and it was nice to have potato chips and go to the movies and stuff like that. So I asked Van Buren if he wanted my extra shirt. He said, "No, man, I don't. I got one." And there was this little bastard — I can't think of his name. I asked him if he wanted a shirt. He said, "Sure, man. What do you want for it?"

I said, "Give me a bag of potato chips and a carton of Pall Malls." Boy, that was a good deal. So he got the shirt, and I took the smokes.

Two days later Officer Sodi come to the gym and said, "Ron, you got to go to the detention."

"Detention!" I said. "What for?"

"Just go to detention."

When I got there, Officer Sodi said, "All right, Ron, what did you do with the shirt and the pair of stockings?"

I said, "Shirt and stockings? I got them. I ordered them from the inmates' store."

"No," he said. "The extra shirt and the extra stockings."

I said, "I don't know nothing about that."

"We got proof that you do."

"I don't know what you got," I said, "but you don't have no proof."

He left. I was thinking to myself, "That little bastard snitched."

Now here came Officer Sodi, Warden Shay, and Maynard. Maynard said, "Ron, you're in trouble."

"I don't know why," I said. "I didn't do nothing."

"We'll see," he said.

Officer Sodi questioned me first. He was more or less questioning and telling what he thought. Now and then they went through the lockers while everybody was working, and if there was contraband, they grabbed it. Somebody else must have ordered a shirt and some stockings and didn't get it, and the inventory showed that it was delivered to the laundry, where I picked it up. Officer Sodi and another screw went through the lockers and found the extra shirt with my number on it. That guy told them, "I swapped Ron a carton of cigarettes and a big bag of potato chips." Busted me right there.

Then Warden Shay asked me, "What do you have to say for yourself, Ron?"

"I've been having trouble with the niggers," I said.

Did I catch hell! "Ron, you don't call them 'niggers.' They are colored people." He lectured me. "They're people just like you and I." He went on and on. Then he asked me again what I had to say for myself.

"As you know," I said, "I was having trouble with mostly the colored people. Guys on this camp think I'm a snitch. Somebody is setting me up. I don't care what anybody says. Somebody is setting me up. If I traded this shirt and stockings to this guy, if I was pulling a shady deal, why would I leave my number on there?"

By God, they talked that over. Warden Shay said, "That does seem odd. If he did trade that, why would that number be on there? That would convict Ron." They went on and on.

I said, "That's what I'm saying. If I had done what you said, I sure wouldn't leave my number on."

The questioning got hot. Officer Sodi was saying, "He's guilty. I think he's guilty."

"But, Officer Sodi," I said, "it don't make sense."

I did some quick thinking and saved myself. This guy that I gave the shirt to, like I said, was little. I had told them before, "I'll get somebody for this. I ain't taking no bust like this. This is a setup."

Maynard said, "Ron, what would you do to the little son of a bitch if you caught him?"

I thought fast. "I don't know if he's little or big, but it don't matter," I said. "Whatever size, I'll get him if I get busted for this."

They got done questioning me and sent me out. I went into the other room and waited. In a little while I got called back. Maynard started talking. "I'll tell you, Mr. Shay," he said, "I don't think Ron's guilty. Circumstances show that it's not logical. He would not leave his number on that shirt."

Warden Shay said to me, "All right, you can leave and go back to your job. There will be no charges proffered."

I said, "Thank you. I sure would like to know who's trying to set me up."

And the warden said, "Don't worry, Ron. That stuff catches up with people."

That was in the morning, and when I went to noon chow, Officer Sodi was standing there, and he said, "Tell me, Ron. You're guilty, aren't you?"

I said, "No, I'm not. I did not do it." In the meantime, my buddies beat up that little guy. He didn't have to rat on me. He could've played dumb like I did. Or he could've seen me. I'd have got rid of the shirt I kept. But here's the good part. When he went to the parole board, he lost ninety days for stealing. That'll teach the snitch.

I like sports, and they help you pull your time, but I didn't get to play football while I was there. I had a sprained ankle when the season come out. I was playing basketball one day, and I could see this guy was going to get a good shot. He wasn't my man, but I rushed over to guard him. I jumped up, and rather than land on the guy — he wasn't moving — I tucked myself in and come down on my ankle. *Crunch!* Everybody heard it. I thought it was broke. They brought me to Jackson Hospital. I hoped it wasn't broke, because you got to stay in the prison hospital till you're healed. I would've hated that. It was a bad sprain. So they Ace-bandaged her and told me to try to walk the best I could. I went back to the prison camp and got some crutches. But I couldn't play no football. I became like the manager of the team.

We went to Hillsdale College one time and played them in football. They beat us. We wasn't very good. But after the game, they had a banquet for us, a nice layout of food. We couldn't eat much. Your stomach's goofed up after you play football. And the football players from Olivet College, they was nice to us. They asked us what we was in there for and like that, so we had a good time.

Jimmy Deen, a con from Battle Creek, was a quite a football player. I remember his wife was in the stands, and at halftime when we walked through the crowd to the dressing room, he embraced his wife and give her a kiss. She cried, and, oh, God, it was terrible. And me, I was just hawkeyeing the girls and watching them cheer girls for Hillsdale. Man, that was cool — looking and dreaming.

I didn't go out for basketball either. I played intramural. In fact, our team took the title. Jimmy Deen was on first string. Tree, he was with us. We had some good ball teams. When the play-offs came, we really beat them. The convicts had bets going on, and we got some raw deals on the refereeing, and we knew it. We had to go into another game then to determine the winners. We went to see Fay and Heinke, the screws, and we said, "We want you guys to referee."

They said, "No way!"

"Look," I said. "Them guys got bets, everything, I would imagine." So Fay and another guy refereed.

At the championship the warden was there. What a game! Well, hell, we tore them to pieces, beat them bad. And I remember the warden come to me after and said, "I didn't know you had such a good eye at shooting." Well, I could've played first string on that varsity team maybe. I don't know.

I had this dream about being a boxer, and I felt sorry for Bob Rose. He was a professional boxer, and he wanted to train me. Was he beat up! He was thirty-two years old, but he looked to be fifty. Damn, he looked rough. And he had, I guess, about fourteen years in the ring. He was from Detroit. Somebody always wanted to try him out. They'd say, "Man, how good are you now, you punch-drunk idiot?" They'd try to make him mad.

Rose seen my potential. He got in the rec hall with me. Back under the rec hall we had a big canvas bag filled with sand, and on the pipes we had a chain on there. That was our heavy bag, and we had something like a speed bag, a punching bag. It worked good. We'd rig up stuff to put on our hands for gloves, and we'd work out. Man, we worked out a long time on that heavy bag. Then Rose would show me how to throw crossovers, jab and hook, stuff like that. And we'd body-punch with each other with these big padded mits we had—just about like gloves but not quite.

I learned about boxing from Rose and other guys that was in there that boxed before. Scott, in our cabin, he had boxed. Man, was he quick! We was doing this for several months. And this colored guy knew karate. I worked with him at the same time I was boxing. In fact, he was there with us learning how to box. We all just worked out together, and he'd show me how to kick and the moves that karate men do.

Bob Rose got me in on one of his visits. His dad come and his sister, a nice-looking woman. Bob's plan was, when we both got out, I'd go into the boxing profession. I'll always regret that I couldn't try it. I would've liked to see how good I was. I was fast, and I learned quick. I had the instinct for fighting, and I was tough.

When we went on the visit, Bob told his dad, "Here's the fellow that I wrote to you about."

I shook hands with Rose's dad and his sister. I forget what we had to eat, but it was good—chicken, I think.

Bob's dad said, "I'm going to tell you something, young fellow. I'd advise you not to go into the profession. I know you probably won't listen, but I went through hell with this boy for fourteen years." He tried to talk me out of it.

Bob said, "Dad, you know I can put him where he's not going to get hurt that much and get him advanced before I get too much of a fight for him. I think the kid's got it."

And he did have a point. Lots of young fighters, they put them in with something too much right away, and they get their heads beat in. Well, I looked forward to boxing because, the way my life was then, it seemed like a good opportunity, but I never did get to do it. I had a chance, but my parole officer blew that for me.

That come later, after I got out of prison camp, but I'll tell it now so I don't forget. I was supposed to go to Detroit in Cobo Hall, wherever that is, to fight. They had Class A, B, and C—all them classes of fighters. Rose told me that he'd put me in Class B even if I was Class A; then the promoters would look at me better. They'd see my potential then, see? I was on parole, so I asked Parker, my parole officer, if I could go to Detroit and fight.

He said no. "You'll go down there and get drunk. You won't come back, or you'll smash somebody's head in."

I said, "I'll make you a deal. Let me fight. If I don't show up back here when I'm supposed to, throw me back in the big house."

"No, no," he said.

Here I was making ten dollars a day, working on a fish tug. And I said, "I'd make more money on one fight than I would three months on the tug."

Parker said, "Nope. No way."

I told him to go to hell, but that ended my boxing career.

Rose was a good friend—him and Killer and Tree. Them were the ones I associated with. The other ones was just there. You'd say hi to them and good-bye. I remember when Killer went home. He left before I did. It was a sad affair. I felt some loneliness. Between all of them that I mentioned, Killer and I was closest, because he was my age. Rose was older than I was, but we got along good.

I heard Killer went back. That's what I heard through the grapevine. I seen Officer Sodi at Camp Waterloo my second trip, and he told me Killer was in again. Too bad. Most of the guys, I'd say more than half maybe, end up going back like that. It shows you how much good them prisons did. I don't know why guys go back. Most men don't like being locked up. I don't know why they don't plant that in a guy's mind when he gets out, but when you get out, you're wild. You got catching up to do, and with me, I wasn't growed up yet, not by a damned sight. But I'm trying to figure out what good prison does. Because when I straightened up, I don't think doing time helped any. Maybe, but I don't think so. It's hard to explain.

My therapy in there was with the cons that I was locked up with. Sometimes when I was bothered, I talked with my counselor, but not often. I'm not putting Rosencranz down, because he was a decent man, but he was one guy to cover 238 cons. So most of your therapy is with the other convicts. You learned a hell of a lot in there, but most of it was bad. If you get in with the wrong guys or pull your time wrong or just make a mistake in the eyes of the cons, you're in trouble. So, to survive, you do it by being vicious. You wonder when somebody will jump you or try to bash your head in. Sometimes you get the other guy first, and you need friends to help you out.

We were cons, animals with numbers on our backs, no-good outcasts. We weren't supposed to know nothing. Well, I'll tell you, I had some hard times in the penitentiary, but I had some good ones too. I had friends in there that helped me when I needed it: Rose and Tree and Killer. I don't care if they were in there for murder or what, which they wasn't. They was my true friends. They liked me, and I liked them. They looked out for me, and I looked out for them. We helped each other, so who are you going to give the credit to here? The institutions or what?

It was the same way in the mental institution. I had friends who was outcasts like me. They was nuts to people that knew them in society, crazy people. But they helped me. We helped each other. Talk to any con or patient, and they'll tell you the same. We helped each other. If you had more of that outside on the streets—But people don't want to get involved, not at all. Well, there's a few who've helped me and done me good. Them people are ace in my books. You know they are.

The time come for me to go up for parole. At night you lay in your rack and think of the streets, what you're going to do when you get out, what the possibilities are, thinking of the label that you have. I don't care what any convict says. He worries about that label. You're a convict. And I know, when I was paroled, I wasn't ready to straighten up. But still, if people would just give somebody a chance.

Anyway, I went to find out about my parole. I got called in front of the board, and Rosencranz warned me that I would probably lose some good time. I went into this room, and there was three board members in there, if I remember right, with their suits and ties and white shirts. They was real polite.

"Hello, Ron, how are you?"

I said, "Oh, not too bad."

"You're being considered for parole," they said. "Now, your work record is very good, but we have a complaint here about you hitting a student."

I said, "Yeah?"

Then this guy in a fancy suit piped up, "Do you think you're tough, Ron?"

I said, "How exactly do you mean this?"

"Well, do you think you're tough?"

I said, "Do you mean do I know how to handle myself, or what?"

"Do you know how to handle yourself?"

I said, "Yeah, I consider myself a good fighter. What does that have to do with what we're talking about here?" I could see they were trying to rile me, which wouldn't have been hard. Damn, I was going to parole board to get good time. I had to be cool, and I knew it.

He kept at it, "You think you're tough, don't you?"

And I said, "Yeah, I'm tough. Is that a crime? Just because I can handle myself and another guy can't, so what?"

"Now, Ron, don't get mad." Then the fancy suit said, "I think we should flop him." Flop is six months, or two nineties.

"Flop me for what?"

"For hitting this student. You know, Ron, you're in here for violence, and you shouldn't be hitting people. You're here to be reformed."

I knew right then I wasn't getting out. Other things was said, but I knew that I was going to lose my good time, so I thought I'd say what was on my mind. "OK, I'm in here for violence. Do you know what goes on in here?"

"Oh, we have a pretty good idea."

I said, "You shouldn't have no *pretty* good idea. You should know for sure what's going on. You got three screws on a shift. How are they going to watch two hundred and thirty-eight convicts? We live together. We eat together. We sleep together. There's stuff that goes down that the screws don't see."

"We know that."

I said, "Then why are you flopping me? I'll tell you, I come into this place walking on my two feet, and, by God, I'm going to go out walking on my two feet." I was getting worked up. "That guy was going to cave my head in over some simple thing. So I hit him. I got him before he got me."

"We realize all this, Ron."

I said, "Sure, after you flop me, you go back to your families and your everyday life. You could give a damn about me. Do you realize what you're doing? You're giving me another six months in here to possibly have something else happen. This place is a school for violence."

"Ron, you just can't go hitting people."

I said, "OK, if I would've snitched, what would've happened to me? You tell me!"

"Well, uh—"

"Well, hell! I would've got *my* head caved in. If I'd run away, what would you have did? I'd have got caught, and you would've gave me anything from one to three. So what am I supposed to do? I figured getting him first was the smartest thing. He went to the parole board already and got his good time. Perfectly legal what he did, huh?"

"Oh, Ron, don't—"

"Bullshit. Flop me! Whatever you want."

We went on, and everything cooled down. The fancy-suited guy said, "Ron, we understand what goes on in here. You may not believe us, but we do."

I said, "Well, understanding and doing something about it is different things."

He asked me, "Would you do this again?"

I said, "I told you once already I would. Some man threatens me, I'm going to get him before he gets me. I mean it. You flop all you want. Max me out. Go ahead. But I'm not going to get my head caved in. I'm going to protect myself."

Well, anyway, that's what happened. They twisted me is what they did. They took my ninety. That was another six months I had to spend, because you went up ninety days before the board, and then if you got your ninety, you went home in ninety. So when I didn't get it, I knew that I was in another six months.

They asked me if I had plans to go home when I got out. I said, "I'll tell you, my family don't care if I come home. And it's just too small of a town. I would like to go someplace else for my parole if I could. I have no ties in St. Ignace that would do me good."

They asked me where I'd like to go, and I said, "I been thinking about Grand Rapids. There's jobs around there. Should be, anyway."

So that was considered. But damn, who's going to hire a convict unless you happened to have some pull? I wrote all over—they got addresses for me to write. Most of them didn't even write back. I was a good worker even if I was a hothead. But you got that label on you, and it would take a pretty good person to help out a kid with a record like mine. No job, nothing.

Well, I got these turndowns on jobs, and I wrote and wrote. The counselor called me and said, "Ron, we haven't got answers in here. You come and see us, but to get out, you've got to have a place to stay and a job."

I wrote my sister Gerry and my brother-in-law Sonny. I worked for them before. I stayed there and pumped gas and cleaned cabins, everything. So I wrote a letter and asked them for a job. I knew they'd be hiring in the summer. They always got somebody. They wrote me, knowing that it was going to keep me locked up if I couldn't get a job: "Sorry, Ron, we won't be hiring anybody this year." I knew better. They couldn't handle the summer business by themselves.

Well, I started crying. I was mad! I knew I was coming up for parole again. I had to be reviewed, and I would be going home on my ninety. I took the kids' pictures and their pictures, and I ripped them up. I put them in the envelope, threw them in there, and I said, "You guys go—" I wrote an awful letter: "Thanks for the help." Our letters were censored, but Rosencranz let it go through.

I went to his office, still crying. I don't often cry, but when I get depressed, I bawl. I slammed my fist down and said, "What do I do? Can't get no job in Grand Rapids. Family don't want to help. What can I do?"

He calmed me down. "Ron, we got what we call a halfway house."

"What's that?"

He said, "In Detroit on Alexander Street" or someplace. I'd go to the halfway house. I'd be locked up, but I'd have some freedom too. I could go out at night. And they would get me a job. I'd have a sort of tryout period.

I said, "Well, that makes sense. Why don't you just get me a job, and I'll go to work?" That was the whole shot, see? I'd get a job, I'd save my money, then I'd get my apartment. Well, that depressed me, because here I was, had my good time coming and everything. I was going home, but I'd still be locked up. And like I told you before, I didn't like big cities. "Son of a bitch," I said to myself. "When I get hold of that goddamn sister of mine, I'll wring her neck." I was really depressed. Halfway house, shit.

Some good news came. And I ain't never forgot this. My brother Floyd and I had a lots of disagreements, but I'll always remember how he helped me out. Rosencranz called me in. He said, "Ron, you can go back to St. Ignace. You have a job and a place to stay."

I said, "Where?"

"Your brother Floyd wrote me. You'll be working for a guy on a fish tug by the name of Joe Orvella, and you'll be staying with your brother." You can't imagine the feelings that rose up in me. And I haven't never ever forgotten.

Floyd told me later how he happened to talk to Gerry about it. She said how sorry she was. Crap! You know something else? They did hire a kid that summer. Damn them! So I left Cassidy Lake and headed back to St. Ignace on parole.

On Parole

It was the end of May 1965 when my parole come through. I was going home. I didn't have no money in my account at Cassidy Lake. Making fifteen cents a day, you couldn't save much. So I had to borrow from the state to get home. I got a bus ticket and had enough money left for something to eat. I can't remember what I borrowed, not much. I had ninety days to pay the state back.

Talk about a bus that couldn't get home quick enough! So I got to St. Ignace, and I had to report to the parole officer, call him up. And I got together with my brother Tom. He had a car. We had a couple beers, and, you might know, there was the old life waiting for me.

I wasn't in town, I don't think, an hour, and I was half drunk. We went to this hangout, Annette's; a woman run it. Fred, one of my buddies, was going to be jumped on by the Barton boys, Kirk and Albert. I seen what was going on, and I said, "I don't want no trouble, but if you jump on him, you got me to contend with."

Kirk had been in the penitentiary, and he said, "Paquin, you ain't going to fight. You just got out."

I said, "I'll tell you something, sucker, just try me. If one of youse fight him, fine, but both of youse ain't jumping on him."

Fred kept saying, "I can handle her, Ron." Well, maybe he could've. I don't know. There was a lot of talk going back and forth, but no fighting. Nothing happened, but it could have. I'd been in town a couple hours now, and I was damn near in a brawl.

I hadn't touched a woman in more than a year, and I was looking to get laid. Tommy said, "I got a hot one for you, Ron. She really likes to screw. I'll line you up."

So we had a few more beers, and he got this girl. But I embarrassed myself. I was so excited, hell, I come before I ever got inside her. Oh, was she mad! She started calling me names, yelling at me. I started yelling right back. I said, "What's the matter with you?" She walked away. And every time that bitch would see me on the street, she'd call me names. I could never catch her. Man, that was embarrassing. Christ, I'd walk down the street. "Hey, there's that son of a bitch," she'd say. I wanted to crawl under a parking meter.

I didn't have no sense when I got out on parole. I hadn't changed at all. I drank all the time. Ron St. Pierre and Tommy and I was drunk one night, walking down Main Street. There was that little broad that was always calling me names. She started yelling at me. I pretended I wasn't paying no attention to her. We got up close. She wasn't very big. I grabbed her, and I picked her up. And I said, "Listen, you keep calling me names like this, I'm going to bust your ass. Mouth off again and I'll smear you all over town. I'm sick of you insulting me. You going to cool it?" She was scared. I said, "Now, you shut your mouth. Next time you see me, you say 'Hi, Mr. Paquin' or 'Hi, Ron, how you doing?'" A week or so later she seen me. She said, "Hi, Ronny," sort of sexy-like, and I said hi.

She was sneaking out with this married man. She told him about me grabbing her, and he was going to front me off about it. "Leave her alone," he told me.

I said, "What the hell you going to do? What do you want to get in my face about that little bitch for?" He was half drunk. I was sober, and I said, "I don't want to fight you. I'll tell you what. Keep mouthing off and I'll give your wife an anonymous phone call. How do you like that? I know your wife. She's a nice person. I went to school with her. How's that for a deal?" He walked away. He wanted to play hero, but I fixed him.

I did a lot of drinking, so I didn't work long for Joe Orvella. But I got a job with Carl and Ray Halbert, two elderly fishermen, good old boys. To this day I really like them. They were good to me. I missed work sometimes, a few days; I'd get drunk, you know. But I tried to make it, even when I was loaded.

One time I scared Carl. He's real serious, the serious one of the two. They're both serious, but he's more or less the boss. And he wears glasses. He always looked over them. Needed bifocals, I think. Well, I got drunk at Danny's Bar, and I wanted to make sure I showed up for work, so I had a guy named Billy Alexander put me on the fish tug with a blanket over me. I was laying on the aft deck, sleeping, with that blanket covering me. I guess Carl near had a heart attack when he opened them boat doors and saw a body laying there.

I got sick that day, awful sick. There's nothing worse than having a hangover and getting seasick all at once. The first job I had was to oil the lifter. That's what pulls the nets into the boat. It runs in a circular motion with clamps on it. I tried to oil it, but I didn't hit many holes. I was drunk yet. And goddamn, the wind came up. Oh, man, she blew from the southwest that day. I puked up what I drank and ate the night before. Then I got the dry heaves. Was I sick! I wanted to die.

We had a box of whitefish in the boat with a thin layer of ice on them. I rubbed my face in that ice and fish. I felt terrible. I was laying on the aft deck in between lifting nets and running down the lake a ways to set the nets back. I laid down, and Carl said, "Ron, you have to get up so we can set."

I said, "OK. I'll help you." Bad as I felt, I still worked. When we got to the dock, I said, "Boy, Carl, I don't know what in the hell I ate."

He looked over his glasses at me and laughed. "I'll tell you something, son," he said, "many a day I come on the boat like that, drinking the night before. That's not no big deal, but one thing I like about you is you show up for work." I didn't fool him at all.

Puking on the lake, I swore I would never drink again. But once I got on the beach, I felt all right, and it was back to the bars.

I stayed with Floyd for a couple weeks and then moved into a little cabin I rented from Mrs. Langhoff. It was a little dinky thing, but I decked it out good. I had curtains in there. Man, I had that place looking fine. Every week I'd take my laundry and do the wash. I'd buy my groceries, and when it come rent time, I had money to pay.

I drank almost every night. Usually I ended up drunk. I'd drink and play pool till the bars closed at 2 A.M. Well, I came out all right; you play for a buck a game. Sometimes I'd go for bigger stakes. But I always had money at the end of the week—not much, a few dollars, more if I got lucky. Most of my drinks I got off that pool table.

One night after the bars closed, I started walking up the hill toward my house. I got up by the water tank, and I seen there was a car parked in the woods. I couldn't see anybody in it. Somebody was getting a little, I figured. I was drunk, and I thought I'd have some fun. I walked up and belted that hood as hard as I could. When I hit it, I slipped and fell backwards into a pile of brush. I could still look up there, though. Laugh! You never seen two people get their selves together so quick. "Who's that? Who's that?" they said.

I stood up, and I recognized this guy and this real good, nice girl. She was embarrassed. "Ronny, what are you doing out here in the woods?" she said.

I said, "Could I get a ride home?" I told them what had happened. I'd been in a fight; I was fighting all the time, seemed like.

She said, "Ronny, if you say a word about this, I'll never talk to you again." I never did till now. That was a good night.

I'm lucky to be here. The whole cabin was only about sixteen foot by twelve foot, if that. I come home drunk. Friends brought me home. I went to bed and woke up with a sore throat. Damn, my throat was sore. I got up and groped for the light switch. I was still drunk. I turned the light on, but I couldn't see a thing. The place was full of smoke.

There was just a bedroom and a couch and cookstove and refrigerator in there. I remember dropping to my knees, and then I crawled out. I busted the window. Jerry Curry lived next door, and he come out. I said, "My goddamn house is on fire." The corner of the bed was burnt, and the floorboards. It had burned a long time. I fell asleep with a cigarette is what happened. Usually the smoke gets you, and that place was thick with smoke. It wasn't my time yet.

Next day, my parole officer come down. He got a report. Didn't charge me with nothing, but he talked to me. He said, "Ron, you've got to be more careful when you're drinking, eh? And you got to stop fighting."

I told him that the other guys started the fights. And I said, "Goddamn it, why don't somebody go and investigate them?"

He said, "You're on parole, Ron."

"Yeah," I said, "and I got to take the rap for other guys. I see that."

He gave me a lecture about drinking and fighting. But I didn't listen. I got into some dandy fights. Night after night I was brawling with somebody. Piss on my parole officer.

I hadn't seen my friend Tom Gustafson since I been back. He come into town and looked me up. He said, "Let's get drunk, Ron." I said, "Sure."

We went from bar to bar and was having a good time. The two Lawson boys was in Danny's. It's the Driftwood now, but it was Danny's then. They was winning at pool, and I said to them, "You guys are monopolizing the table, huh?" I meant it as a compliment.

You can challenge the table — winners keep playing. You put two dimes on the pool table, so I put my dimes on the table, and Don Lawson said real low, "Paquin, put your dimes on that table and I'm going to knock you clean across this bar."

I yelled to Amanda, the owner, "Do I have the right to play pool here?" and she said, "Sure." I calmed down.

Then Jim, his brother—they called him Bighead—started messing with me. Tom and I was playing them then. Bighead come up to me, and he had the cue stick, hanging onto it, and he had the butt of it on the floor. He said, "Say, Paquin, just got out of the penitentiary, eh?" The bar was jammed; it was tourist season. Bighead said that real loud, and everybody turned around and looked at me.

I was half drunk. I said, "I don't know where you're coming from, Bighead. I ain't looking for no trouble."

He said, "This guy was in prison, and he was a nigger lover."

The Lawsons had a cousin with them from Detroit, a semipro boxer and judo instructor, so he started in on me too. I said, "Who the hell are you?"

He said, "Jump on Don or Jim and you're going to find out."

"I ain't going to jump on nobody," I said. "I'm just drinking and having a good time." This went on for a while. Finally I yelled out so everybody could hear me, "Amanda, I'm leaving. I don't want no trouble." But I hoped they would follow me outside, and that's exactly what they did.

I went through the door without looking behind me, and they snuck out single file. Tom told me afterward. I felt a hand on my shoulder. I didn't know which one, but I knew where he was, so I whirled and caught him in the cheek. As he slid down the door casing, I got him with my knee. Bighead come out and said, "Kick my brother, eh?" He put his fists up. I clapped my hands and kicked him in the nuts. I stepped back off the porch.

This judo guy, or whatever he was, stood on the porch with his arms in front of him yelling, "Hahhh! Hahhh!"—getting psyched up. He come off that porch, and I drop-kicked him in the chest and busted his ribs.

There was a blonde that worked in the bar there. I always wanted to get in her pants. She looked out. I stood there holding up three fingers and saying, "Hah, that wasn't nothing!"

Meantime, Don got up, and he caught me from the side, trying to kick me in the nuts. He hit my leg and skinned the hell out of it. I fell, and I hurt. I caught him with a fist as I got up. We started boxing. I lined him up, shouldered into him, and hit him with a right. I couldn't find him. "Where'd that son of a bitch go?" I said. Well, I knocked him out for a moment.

When he woke up, he said, "Paquin, you wouldn't hit a man when he's down, would you?" I walked over and kicked him in the ass, not hard, just kicked him. I kicked him again. He crawled across the parking lot. What I was doing was embarrassing him.

Somebody said, "The cops are coming." Don crawled into his car. The judo cousin snuck in too. I went in the car with them, right in the back seat. I knew the cops wouldn't look for me there, with Don and Jim in the front seat and the cousin in back. Don said, "You fight dirty, Paquin. You use your feet and everything."

Their cousin said, "For Christ's sake, three of us jumped him. What the hell do you expect him to do?" He shook my hand right there.

When the cops left, I went with Tom. Next day, them guys tried to sign a warrant on me, but they didn't get it. There was a couple prominent citizens seen the fight, and they told the cops what happened.

You can see how my life was going: drinking and fighting. My parole officer called me down for another talk.

"Ron, you got to cut this out."

I said, "You get a rat in a corner, he is going to fight. What am I—"

He said, "Leave!"

I said, "Am I supposed to leave every place in town? I got to have somewhere to go for fun."

So I got my lecture again about being a good citizen and how people are going to think the worst of you. "Back off, Ron," he said.

"I did leave," I said, telling him about that fight with the Lawsons. But like I told you, I wanted them to follow me. I was glad they come after me.

I got in one really awful fight. I hit a cop, and they threw me in jail. It come time for me to go to court. So I went in, and my parole officer come down. He asked me what happened, and I told him. Judge Beck, a civil judge, was talking about golf. He'd start talking golfing. I just up and said, "I don't give a fuck about your golfing." He was going to get me for contempt of court, and I said, "Go to hell! You haven't started the court. You been talking about golf all the time since you come in here."

I can't figure out what I pled guilty to. Assault and battery? On who? I admitted hitting a cop. A city cop had charges against me. Two of them did. There was two state cops sitting there. I don't know why, other than they thought I'd make trouble. The judge sentenced me to twenty days. They put my parole on special condition then: no drinking. I did my jail time. I was mad the whole twenty days too. I got a bad deal. There was eight guys fighting, not just me, but nobody else got busted. I never raised my fist to no one that night till they charged me or hit me. I should've signed a few warrants myself, but I didn't.

When I got out and was up to Detour fishing, I met this girl named Patty, and we got intimate. She thought she was pregnant, so I was going to marry her come April. On Christmas Eve I went to a party. I was supposed to be with her, but I bugged out with Tommy and Ron St. Pierre. Everybody at the party knew Patty was going to have a baby, and that's how things got going. Turned out later she wasn't pregnant. But anyway, we was drinking, and Curtis Jones's wife, Anne, said, "I don't think you're man enough to knock up a woman." That's what started the ruckus what sent me back.

I said, "I don't know about that. What do you think of this?" I made like I was going to drop my pants. I was teasing.

Catherine, Floyd's wife, said, "Ronny, don't." I wasn't really going to do it. Helen started screaming. Shit, she used to go down for lots of guys. She was a dandy to be talking.

Then Anne Jones started in again about my manhood, and she was calling me a jailbird. I was boiling mad. Everybody was drunk. I was drunk; they were drunk. Who knows what happened? I was yelling at this Jones bitch, and her husband jumped in. He grabbed me. I don't remember hitting him, but people said I did. I know he said he was going to get me with a club. Floyd told me that when Curtis said that, I bashed him and knocked him against the wall. I knocked him down — that's what people said. Floyd grabbed me then, trying to break things up. I was too loaded to realize he was trying to help me. He told me later that he was afraid that I was going to put the boots to the guy.

Floyd knocked me down, and I lay on the floor with my head cocked against the wall. Floyd straddled me with his knees on my arms. I pushed at him. Catherine yelled, "Hit him, Floyd! Hit him!" What a scene, eh?

I said, "Sure, go ahead and hit me. You're a goddamn robot to her anyway."

That's all I remember before Floyd punched me. He broke my nose, blackened both eyes, and shattered my upper lip on the left-hand side. He hit me so hard, he lost his balance. I threw him off. I remember standing up and saying, "OK, Flip, you ain't whipped me yet." Floyd looked worried. He had threw everything at me, but I got up.

Somebody called the cops, but no charges was made, so they didn't arrest me. The cops dropped me off at the hospital. They brought in Curtis Jones too. He was in the other room. Dr. Lasland, a good friend of mine—he's dead now—said, "Ron, we got to take care of that lip. Damn it, Ron, every time you come in here, either you're busted up or somebody else is."

He was going to stitch me up, and he was going to jab a needle in me, and I said, "No, you don't. You're not sticking no needle in my lip."

He said, "OK, you stubborn son of a bitch." He put the first stitch in. God, that hurt. The outside wasn't cut much, but the lower part of the lip, the inside, was shattered, and there was a big chunk hanging down. He took four or five stitches. It hurt so much that I told him to use that needle. He said, "Calm down, Ron. I want to play Santa Claus to my kids here tonight yet."

So he sewed me up and x-rayed my nose. He told me I had an old fracture. I remember when I got hit there. The new fracture was right over it. I was in bad shape. My lips was puffed up, and I looked like a zombie. But bad as I felt, the next day I went and shook hands with Floyd, apologized, and said, "Merry Christmas." Floyd told me I had broke Curtis Jones's collarbone.

I went back to Detour to heal my wounds and get some loving. While I was up there—this scared me—Curtis signed a warrant. He was going to teach me a lesson. That night, the night after the fight, Patty and I was cuddled in bed, waiting for people to go to sleep so we could get a little on the loving part. There was a knock on the door.

I didn't have no shoes on. I had my Levi's on but no shirt. I was bare from the waist up. I opened the door, and, Christ, there was two .38's facing me right in the face. Cops. I couldn't believe it. They had a warrant for my arrest for assault and battery.

Locked Up Again

Them cops cuffed me and hauled my ass to jail. I was wanted for assault and battery and parole violation, they said. I was in trouble again.

After I beat up that guy at Miller's Camp, I said, "Well, I'm going to the penitentiary and I know it." I didn't see no way out of it. I didn't ask for no attorney, because I never had no use for them that was appointed, and I couldn't pay for one. I thought I'd just leave it to the discretion of the judge. That's why I stood mute. And there was no way I could get out of it. I wouldn't care how good of a lawyer I got.

Now I was in jail again and headed back to prison, I figured. My Uncle Francis come down and offered to hire a lawyer. Said he had fifty bucks for the retainer fee, and I kind of gave up then too, because I'd already been jailed once for parole violation, and it didn't look good this time, with my having busted the guy's collarbone. Really, I did not start that one. So I just pled guilty. Maybe I shouldn't have. I did it, but there was circumstances to the event that maybe I would've got out of it too. I don't know. It's just that when you're on parole, you don't stand much chance.

I figured when I went back to the pen, I'd cool off. I'd do a year and have it over. Just get it done with, I figured. I didn't want to burden nobody no more, like my uncle. Fifty bucks would've just got it started. It would've cost several hundred dollars. It depends on how many hours of court you have, and two or three people of my family would've been involved. There would've been more bad feelings and lots of trouble. I was pissed off at my family then, anyhow, all but my sister Donna. The rest of them disowned me. I never got no letters in the penitentiary unless they were nasty ones. And I was

Locked Up Again

tired of hassle. Piss on those people. I was going to do my time and get it over with.

So I was in jail, and I phoned my brother-in-law and sister Gerry for some cigarettes. They told me to get out of their life. Damn! Damn my family! I was in jail several weeks. My parole officer came down, and he was writing a report. He needed to know some things like if I had a job and if I had place to stay if I got out of jail. I was trying to call Floyd. That was why I called my sister. Was I going to have a job? As simple as that. No answer. I didn't know what was going on while I was in jail, and then they told me I got to go back to Newberry for tests. I figured this was mostly bullshit. Cops from St. Ignace, state cops, drove me to Manistique and back to the funny farm.

By now, I was confused. I was remembering the first time I went to Newberry, and the authorities ignored their recommendations and locked me in prison anyway. So then it seemed like I was doing it for the formality. As far as I was concerned, the whole bunch could kiss my ass. I'd do my time, come back, and straighten up. I'd stay away from people that was ignorant or ignore them. I'd go do my time. I did the crime; I'd do the time.

So I got to the mental institution. "Hi, Ron, how've you been?" my doctor asked. "Not bad. Sorry you got to see me again, but here I am."

The mental institution was the same old stuff. You'd put funny puzzles together, look at weird faces, and talk weird talks. Same old crap. The first time in the loony house, I was sincere. I said, "Something's wrong with me"—not convulsion of the brain or anything like that—"and I'm going to listen to these people." I did listen, but it didn't do no good. Well, this time, I said, "We're going through a formality here. Step one, you get thrown in jail. Step two, you go to the nuthouse. Step three, you go to prison. Let's get it over with."

So I had a different doctor this time, Dr. Waters. He was a good man. I cooperated with him. I told him the same thing I just told you: "Doctor, there's something wrong with this system. I'm going back to the penitentiary." He said, "Well, I don't know." I told him what happened the first time. He should check the records of me talking to all these doctors and shrinks, accepting the fact that I was emotionally upset and how a little convalescent status would straighten me out—an outpatient deal, the recommendation they gave to the courts. As soon as they said that, shortly after the court got the letter, I was heading for the penitentiary.

You know, psychiatrists—the good ones like Dr. Waters—they don't fit in no place with the courts or with prison. Dr. Waters told me, just like Dr. Collier had—he probably seen Collier's records—"Ron, what do you think you need?"

I sat there, thinking, and he said again, "What do you think you need, Ron?"

I couldn't answer, so he told me, "You need love."

He was right about that. I was not first in nobody's heart. But if he'd presented this to the court and said, "Your Honor, this young man needs love," why, he'd get laughed right out of the courtroom. People would just howl. It would've been a big joke to them, a big goddamn joke. Can you imagine him walking up and saying, "Well, Judge, this boy needs love." Why, that would've been the most ridiculous thing they ever heard. They'd say, "No, he don't need love. He bashed somebody's head in. He needs prison. He can go there and get *his* head bashed in."

So the first time the authorities ignored the recommendations of the hospital. I told the psychiatrists and the doctors, "You took an EEG of me, a brain scan. There's nothing wrong with me. What are you going to do this time? It don't really matter. I'm going to do time whatever you say."

They kept telling me, "Ron, don't feel that way."

I said, "That's the way I feel. I'll behave myself in here and cooperate with you. We can sit here and talk, talk for hours if you want, but I'm going back to jail, and then I'm going to the penitentiary."

So I didn't have a good attitude. Well, Dr. Waters, I respected. I'd be serious with him. There was things I could learn from him. Up there we had several of them that was fresh out of college. It was more or less a learning period for them. I talked to this one for an hour or sometimes a couple of hours at a time. The next day, I'd stop in and tell her I lied. "I was just bullshitting you," I'd say. Then I'd tell her what she wanted to know. And after a while I was sincere with her because she was sincere with me.

You had your appointed times you talked to these people. And if you let it slide, you'd only see them a little while. If you was there a month, you might talk to them one time, maybe twice if you were lucky. So if you wanted help, the way I figured, you had to go on your own and say, "Hey, I want to talk to you."

When I got sent to prison, I told her, "I'll write to you. Will you answer back?"

"Sure," she said, "I'll answer."

I said, "Well, we'll see." So when I did get to Jacktown, I wrote her. Told her what was going on in there and that I had a year left on my original sentence, so that's what I had to do. I remember in that letter too, I told her that I was going to straighten out. I told her, "This is going to be my last time in here." I sent the letter, and sure as hell, she wrote right back, and she was very sincere. Now, I imagine I could've kept writing to her, but I didn't. But she did answer back.

What jobs did I do with the loonies? I helped with the recreational program. I helped the plasterer, did maintenance on the mason work. I delivered mail. I took reports around to what they called the cloister, where they kept patients. I delivered some kind of paper to them every morning. Christ, it was a mile around that thing.

I played basketball and roller-skated. They had dances. My attitude was that I was going to get along and do what I was told. Right now, I can't remember how long I was there, but it wasn't as long as the first time. Meanwhile, there was reports being sent by my parole officer to Lansing. I guess they had some review board that looked it over and decided if you were going back to the penitentiary.

Well, I didn't know for sure, but I thought that I was headed back to prison. I probably wouldn't have if it hadn't been for my family and I getting into it, Floyd and I. You got that story. And my other brother Tommy was humping Patty. Turned out she wasn't going to have no baby. Well, they all just averaged out my attitude and what my actions would be if I went and got drunk. They didn't want to let me on the streets. Fine, but it was wrong. So I'm trying to remember how long I stayed there. Regular diagnostic is about ninety days. I'm pretty sure I was there all of that.

When they got done fooling with me at the mental institution, they hauled me back to jail. Down came my parole officer. He said, "Well, Ron, you're going to have to go back. I'm really sorry."

I said, "What are you sorry for? I'm going to do the time." The whole thing pissed me off anyway, because during my parole I got in several fights which was reported to him. Not none of these was a conviction. If anybody could've signed warrants, it was me. But I didn't.

He told me, "Well, if you wouldn't have gotten into this scrape" or "If you wouldn't have gotten into that scrape—"

I said, "Well, sure, I'm on parole. I know that. What am I supposed to do if a man wants to jump in my face and kick it in? Am I supposed to say, 'Jeez, I'm on parole. I'm not allowed to fight. I'd appreciate it if you didn't hit me.' I'm in a spot, and you know it. You people sit around and talk. You ain't living this for me. I'm out there in the goddamn real world."

I wanted to tell him to go to hell. I said, "I'll go do time. I ain't got no choice. But you guys ain't never going to get me in your grip again." So, regardless of my attitude while I was being processed, back deep in my mind I said, "I'm going to straighten up. Goddamn, I have to. I can't live like this. This is bad." If I would've had a long term to do, like two to fifteen years or something like that, I don't know what I would've done.

So, like before, they shipped me to Jacktown for diagnostic. "What do you want to do?" they asked. "Do you want to be a machinist or something like that? We'll get you ready for the streets."

Maybe it does happen like they say, but I never seen none of it. I was an adult convict now. I just told them, "Well, I'd like a camp up north—Camp Cusino. I'd like to go there and get my time over with." So that's what they did. They let me go to Cusino.

Well, at Cusino we worked at the state parks like Indian Lake, in the resort area around Newberry and Manistique. They got a sawmill at the camp and deer pens. And some guys would work in the kitchen. So there wasn't nothing that would prepare you for hitting the streets in a fantastic job or anything like that. I got to the camp, and there was three others from St. Ignace that was there. I remember the Sarge saying, "What are you guys doing? Having a homecoming?" But it felt good to have somebody there that you knew. It helps pull time. It's nice when you can sit and rap with somebody that you know, that isn't just a prison associate.

I looked over the camp, and Bobby Gray was telling me what job to hit for and everything. He said, "See if you can get on that Indian Lake resort area job. That's the job I got. Really a boss job. We pick up the garbage, but that ain't so bad. It's all in wire baskets. We clean the beaches up and do tile work—tile fields and drain fields." I didn't mind hard work like that. It would help pass the time. That's the job I hit for, but I didn't get it right away.

I wanted to keep out of trouble, but when you're locked up with weirdos, it ain't easy. My biggest fear now was that I'd be caught in something awful and get a new sentence slapped on me. A couple times it damn near happened. You got all different personalities in there, and half of them are wacko.

One thing that happened was we made wine out of dry fruit and rye and rice, whatever we could get that would ferment, and we'd get started with yeast. Lots of them made it and sold it. You didn't charge much, because a man only made a quarter a day. If you sold two or three quarts to them a week, you was doing good.

Well, this one con was a big colored guy. He was taller than me, and I'm six feet two and a half inches tall. Anyway, he was selling hooch. We went into the barracks one day, and there he was. He had another man down and was beating him with a hammer because this man owed him seventy-five cents for brew. Well, this old fellow must have been close to sixty. The colored guy hit him on the shoulders, neck, and legs with that hammer.

I was standing there. We all was. I couldn't take it. I couldn't stand there and watch somebody get beat like that for nothing. Larson, my buddy there, said, "Ron, stay out of it." But I was in tears watching this. I said, "Piss." That guy was leaning over, hitting this old man. I kicked that son of a bitch as hard as I could. I grabbed the hammer and challenged all them guys that wanted to do something about me, because you wasn't meant to get involved. They walked away.

You know, that colored guy was in there for felonious assault, the same thing as me, and he had just three months to a complete maximum—home free, no parole, no nothing. And here he was beating on somebody with a hammer over a little juice. It don't make sense.

Another time we was riding in the back of this flat rack truck. We called them the green dogs—trucks with a green house built on the back of it with benches inside. That's where we rode when we went to work at the Indian Lake resort. You got some bread, a slice of bologna or salami, and a cookie or some cake for lunch. You had coffee, and that was your meal. Well, a colored guy and a white guy got into it over bologna and salami. The colored guy wanted bologna, and he tried to swap, but the white guy wouldn't do it. They got swinging at each other, but it broke up fast.

We were going into the chow hall that evening. The colored guy took a weight-lifting bar of solid iron, and he clubbed that guy from the side and behind. You know the sound a mushmelon makes when you slam it against the wall? This sounded like that. When he hit him, I turned quickly; he was only two guys behind me. George, a buddy from St. Ignace, caught the guy as he was falling. Stuff oozed out of his skull along the side of his head, but he didn't die.

The colored guy had eight years in and another eight to go. A guard came in, drew his gun, and pointed at him. He said, "Drop her." Guys in there that didn't like niggers was saying, "Don't drop her, man." There was a standoff. I imagine the son of a bitch was thinking, "I'm going to do some time now. I've done a lot, but I'm going to do a whole lot more." But maybe the guy wasn't thinking at all. We found that he had an IQ of seventy-eight. He'd go out when it was raining and hit at the raindrops, shadowboxing with the raindrops. He was nuts, really. You got to live around these people to understand.

You'd better figure these people out. You don't never know what they'll do. Maybe a man on that camp ain't said a word to you all the time he was there, but then you might say something to the son of a bitch—you might be joking—but he wouldn't know that and he'd come after you. I'll tell you, they should check these people out better than they do. Goddamn, if the man's insane, put him somewhere else.

That colored guy was crazy. They cuffed his ass and hauled him away. We never saw him again. I imagine the state police or the guards come with a state car and put him back in the big house. You just got to be on your guard constantly. Kill a man over a bologna sandwich? It ain't worth it. Christ, if I would've known that was going to happen, I would've give that guy my bologna. The salami wasn't half bad.

Being con-wise, I used my head to stay out of trouble. To keep right with the man, I kept in good with the snitches, treated them right. Most of them were scared, real timid people, but they were mixed up. So I was good to them. I didn't hang around with them or snitch myself, but I treated them right. So when a bust came down, they might be making a choice between a guy like me that had been treating them good and a man that wasn't shit to them. Then they were going to put the better part to you if they snitched on you. So that worked out good then. But I didn't like them. I remember when me and a few guys took them snitches' names and numbers and put them on a big towel, painted them on there, and hung it on the camp flagpole. Let them know that everybody knew who they was.

So I tried to be careful and keep out of trouble with them wackos I was locked up with. But I damn near blew it, screwing some girls I met over at the Indian Lakes. On this job at the resort area, we'd ride around on a truck and load garbage. Well, after you were there a few days, you'd see the same people. They were camping out for a week maybe. So they'd have a magazine for us or some cigarettes or maybe a couple beers. They'd put this stuff on top of the garbage, with a paper over it. You knew you was getting it. Some people was nice like that, but most was jerks, like young guys that thought they was tough. They was saying that we didn't look so tough, being convicts and all. It was hard to take.

One time two girls started talking to us and giving us the eye. We was on the job several weeks and knew our way around. They thought me and Larson was supercool. Lars was a half-breed Indian fellow I hung around with. I couldn't tell how old these chicks was. But I didn't really care. I mean we were in prison, and we were

Locked Up Again

going to maybe get laid. Well, we got talking to them, and after while we arranged a place to meet them. One of them said, "Is there any way we can get you guys alone?" and I said, "Maybe this is it, but you girls better be careful." Truth was, me and Lars better be careful, because if we got busted, we'd be doing time for a long time coming.

When we burned the trash, we'd go to the dump where it was private, and we was supposed to walk around and look for sparks in the woods. I told these girls, "There's a big pine tree on the north side of the dump. We'll meet you there."

So we were excited about these girls. We burned the trash and went over by that pine tree. We were waiting and waiting. Larson said, "Goddamn, Ron, can you believe this is happening?"

I said, "Not yet. They ain't come through them woods yet."

We didn't have much time before they'd wonder where we was—maybe three-quarters of an hour from the time we got the garbage off the truck. So we were waiting, and these girls weren't coming. I was imagining in my mind being with a woman, and I was pretty excited, but they never showed. Nothing happened that day. And we were mad as hell. I said, "Them goddamn cock-teasers." That's what I was thinking.

The next day, here they come again. They said, "Ron, where was you?" Come to find out they didn't know north from south or what a pine tree looked like. This time, we told them in detail how to get there. So we burned the garbage next day. They come to us, and we got them.

I was wondering which one I'd take, and so was Larson. Really, I didn't care which one. They was nice-looking, but to tell you the truth, they wouldn't have had to be nice-looking. We'd have taken anything. We were humping them for five days. Man, me and Larson couldn't believe it. Then I got to thinking. I said, "Goddamn, Lars, this ain't so good. Well, it's fun, but we're going to get caught. Goddamn, if we get busted—I only got a year to do now. How young do you think they are?"

"I don't know," he said. "Pretty young."

I said, "Yeah, they're pretty young. What other jobs can we get?"

"Well, not very good ones," he said. "Goddamn sawmill is about the only thing."

I said, "That's good enough." Anyhow, we heard the day before that the sawmill crew had a stash of homemade wine. We'd get in on that.

We went to the warden's office and said, "We'd like to quit our job at the resort area." I imagine he thought we was nuts, because that was a damn good job—a boss job, the cons would say.

"Sure," the warden said. "There's openings at the sawmill." He was probably still scratching his head about why we volunteered off that resort job into the sawmill.

Well, I was on one end of the planer, and Larson was on the other end, and we were wondering if we hadn't made a mistake. We told two other cons about them girls; in another week or so, they were going to be at the camp. Sure as hell, them cons got busted. So next day I was on the other end of the planer, and I said to Lars, "Now I know why we're here." We made a good move getting away from them girls, because I know if we'd stayed, the temptation would've been too great to stop doing it. It was too much fun. Found out them girls was only fourteen years old—jailbait, statutory, you know. Too young to be fooling with. That was a close one there.

I stayed at the sawmill awhile, but I didn't like it. I didn't mind working the planer or the edger and stuff like that, but when we had to go out in the yard and pile lumber, that was the most boring job there is. We had this big trailer and tractor. At that time, I had never owned no car, and I sure didn't know how to drive good or back up a trailer. The screw told me, "Get on that tractor, Ron, and back her up."

I said, "I don't know how to back up."

"Well, get on her."

Jesus, if that wasn't frustrating! I jackknifed that trailer. I pulled ahead, and I jackknifed it again. I didn't know what to do. Of course, everybody was an expert that was standing around. And they were laughing like hell. Well, here was this pile of lumber we were topping off, and it was about ten feet high. I hit the gas, and, zoom, that trailer went straight this time, but too fast. *Crash!* Right into the lumber. I knocked it down. They quit laughing. They were screaming at me now, and I was real mad. "I told you assholes," I said, "I don't know how to back up. Leave me alone." I yelled at them, but, mad as I was, I got down off that tractor and walked away. Just turned my back to them and got out of there.

We drank the hooch they had made out of raisins and apples. Bad-tasting stuff, but it done us good. I was falling-down drunk and looking for a party. They kind of carried and dragged me to the barracks. I crawled in my bunk and passed out. Drunk like that, I never made chow. When you went to eat, that was one of the counts to make sure nobody'd run off. I woke up at six-thirty and missed dinner, but they screwed up and never knew I wasn't there.

At the camp, you hardly ever got enough to eat. It wasn't very good amount of chow. I was real hungry that night, but I didn't worry, because Bobby Gray and me had a good deal going with the kitchen help, Youngblood, a colored guy. He brought me and Larson and Bobby sandwiches at night. We'd make him stuff in hobby craft that he'd send back to his people. We'd swap him like that. We wouldn't get them every night. Depended on what we had to eat that day. So I did get some food later.

I didn't hardly ever get drunk this time in or do no drugs. There was lots of stuff around—homemade wine and marijuana mostly, but pills too. One colored guy was getting dope every visit, and he'd swap for it. So it was easy to get. But thinking the way I was, I feared being drunk or high. You lose control and can't protect yourself when you're like that. You never know when it's coming or who's going to do it to you, so you got to be ready.

When I was in prison the first time, it was give-and-take, with me playing the tough guy. But my second time behind bars was different. From the start, I would lay in my cell and I'd think. Sometimes it would be hard to keep my mind straight, because maybe somebody hassled me in the yard or tried to push me around. But like I said, I'd think, especially when I got to Camp Cusino. Bobby Gray and the other guys from St. Ignace talked a lot too.

Bobby and I talked about reforming ourselves on the streets and keeping out of trouble. We knew it was only words and it wouldn't matter, but it helped to go over it in our heads, to kind of get ready. We had to do it on the streets to make any difference.

I'd tell him, "Bob, I know you was married to a woman what brought you pain. But I'm going to find me a good woman and get married. If I can find somebody decent that'll have me, I'm going to get married. I just hope it's the right one, because with my temperament, I know if I ever got hurt emotionally like my parents done to me, it would be bad." I told him, "I want to get married and have some kids. I want to buy a nice home and find a decent job." We talked like this all the time, and I began to work out a plan for myself.

I thought about the streets quite a bit. I'd fantasize what it would be like when I got out. I would just think about it all the time, especially late at night when I couldn't sleep. At night, when you lay in bed, you'd do a lot of thinking. Some nights I'd cry. I'd get to feeling sorry for myself, I guess. Some nights I'd lay there and I'd be mad about the circumstances of my life. Some nights I'd get real bitter. When I'd get like that, I'd get crazy mad. Then I'd stop and think and say, "This is what you got to stop doing—getting mad like this." I'd stop and rationalize. I'd say to myself, "Am I going to see trouble coming? How am I going to handle it?" Bobby and I would talk and say we'd walk away. I'd say, "Well, OK. I'll walk away, but with one eye watching behind, because you get it in the back sometimes."

I'd think, "I got to leave booze alone, because when you get too drunk, then your reasoning's gone, and you are just going to go back to the old violent ways." I like my beer. Right now I can take it or leave it. I can be in a bar having a good time. If I get enough beer, I'll call her quits. I've been in bars several times and drank Pepsi for the last couple hours I've been there. Maybe I'm playing pool or dancing. But at the time I'm talking about now, I couldn't leave it alone. I always got smashed. But I wanted to quit till I got myself thinking straight.

I'd talk with myself inside my head: "Now, Ron, look here. You're in good physical shape. You're strong. You went to the nuthouse and you ain't nuts. You just got to get yourself straight, get your head right. You got a good brain. You ain't had much schooling, but you're smart. Goddamn, Ron, you ain't been too smart up to now. Look where you're at, locked up with wackos and another year to do."

You know, it's a good idea to take your life like that and lay it out inside your head and look at it. I went through my whole life. I looked at my younger days in reform schools, at my mother who hated me. Well, I had a stretch of good time for a while playing high school sports. But it was too late to become an athlete. I'd think like that, and I'd talk about what I was thinking with Bobby Gray. I knew that to this point my life was worthless, and it was up to me to change it. Nobody else was going to do it.

Bobby and I told each other our plans hundreds of time. We knew that talk wasn't enough. You got to do it on the streets. Talk rehabilitation all you want. You have to get out and do it, prove your worth to yourself and not nobody else. I wanted a better life than what I'd been leading to that time. I'd look at other guys that have been institutionalized and wonder, "God, am I looking at me ten years from now?" But after all the lockup time I done, I never give in to them places. I broke free of them. Lots of fellows slid on from one institution to another, getting worse as they went, till they was better off locked up. I didn't want to be like that, not ever, so I was thinking about doing something with my life.

The scars was always going to be there, and the hurt. I knew that. But you got to get over that and not dwell on it. Put it behind you, and go on with your life. You can't be a prisoner to what happened when you was a kid if you're going to be a man. First off, I thought I'd apologize to all the ones I done wrong. I can't explain how this feeling come over me.

When you get out, you're excited. It's hard to describe the feeling. You're locked up tonight, but tomorrow morning you're going to be free, no more number on your shirttail. You're Ronald Joseph Paquin again, not 111382. They weren't going to let you out in prison clothes. They brought you from Cusino to Marquette Prison. They gave you weird duds, funny-looking old-style suits. They gave you a white shirt and a tie, a suit, and some black shoes. This was if you didn't have no clothes from the streets to wear. I can go to a bus station today and spot them suits. I seen them a few times and knew the guy was just out.

Settling Down

The second time I got out of prison was different from when I was on parole. I was wild then. This time I knew I wasn't never going to get locked up again, and I had a plan for myself: finding a nice woman, getting married and raising a family, getting a decent job, maybe buying a home—being the model citizen. But first I had to get my temper under control, and my drinking.

It took me a while to find them people so I could apologize. At the firemen's ball, I seen one guy that I brawled with at a wedding reception two years before I got thrown in the penitentiary the first time. He was eyeing me, wondering, "Ron's getting drunk. Is he crazy like he was?"

I knew how he felt, so I walked over to him, stuck my hand out, and said, "Bill, how about letting bygones be bygones?"

He said, "Sure, Ron. No hard feelings." Most cases was like that.

I looked hard for my brother Tommy, but for a couple weeks I could never find him. I had left prison on December 13, and now it was Christmas Eve. I heard there was a party at my sister's. You'd think, after I just got out of the pen, they'd invite me to a Christmas party, a family gathering, but they never did. I went anyhow, walked right in. Everybody pretended they was happy to see me, but I could tell they wasn't. My aunt was, but the rest of them was feeling squirmy.

I shook Tommy's hand and told him, "I'm sorry for everything bad that I've ever said or done to you."

He said, "That's OK, Ron. You made it. You learned your lesson."

I wanted to slug him. I could feel the old heat rising, but I kept my cool. "Learned your lesson," my ass. I didn't stick around for long. Everyone was feeling so uncomfortable, they was telling me to leave without exactly saying the words. I talked to everybody, said hello, and then I left before I got in trouble. So much for my screwed-up family.

Over the next several months I apologized to lots of people – ones I had beat up or abused in some way. I'd tell them I was sorry, and they'd usually say, "Well, OK. Let's forget the past." That's how the apologies went. All of them was pretty much the same, except Curtis Jones. I'd broken his collarbone at that party and got sent up again. That was a close call when I apologized to him. I mean if these people would've just accepted my apology, that would've been all right. But I could've broke his head when he said, "Ron, I'm glad you learned your lesson."

When I came out, I'd meet guys on the streets and in the bars. I got in some hot arguments, but it wasn't like before. One guy I apologized to, and then a bit later we were arguing, really going at it. I can't remember why. I shoved him, and he plowed through some chairs, but I didn't go after him. I apologized to him again. So that wasn't nothing serious. In the old days, I'd have gone after that guy, wanting to smash him, but I didn't do that no more. I tried to choke back my anger.

I didn't get no satisfaction out of them apologies, but I learned some stuff about being mad. I want to tell you about my temper for a while. We'll get back to the story soon. I never learned, as a kid, what to do about being mad. When I was real young, I lost my temper when my feelings was hurt. I'd start crying, and I was dangerous because I was riled enough to fly out of control. And when I tore into somebody and I felt that way, I didn't recall much of what I done. I'd do just about anything. I didn't care. What do you call that? Rage?

Other times, when I was older, if I got in a fight and lost my temper arguing with somebody, my temper was bad, but I was under control – cool. I had learned to use my temper for fighting. When I made a move on somebody, I knew what I was doing with that move, to get him off guard or whatever and beat him up.

But when I lost my temper in the mental institution, that was my feelings getting hurt and frustration, but I didn't go after people there. I took it out on things, like I'd hit the door with my fist or the wall. I never did hit nobody in there. I don't know why.

A temper is a bad thing. You lose it. You're mad, but what are you going to do about it? If I'd had somebody to talk to as a boy, to relate my problems to, it would've helped. But there wasn't nobody there for me. I was all alone, so I brought my temper out by fighting mostly, not knowing what else to do.

Now, the person what just sits there and lets it build up inside him—you probably know people like that. I do. Well, that guy is in trouble too. They sit there and decay inside something terrible. They don't tell their troubles to nobody, but they don't fight either. They don't do nothing, but it's working on them, eating at their insides, building hatred. To somebody that didn't know what was going on with them, why, they're just sitting there, sulking maybe. But watch out for them people, especially when they's drinking. They can just run amok. Them are dangerous.

As a kid, I never bottled my anger up. I did some awful things with my temper, like try to kill my father that time. To this day, I feel lucky that I didn't kill somebody or that they didn't kill me. God, I'm thankful for that. I could've killed that guy I stabbed with the pool cue or that big Swede in Ludington. I think about that, and I shudder.

Now, there's just no way not to get angry. You've got frustrations all your life, what with family problems and selfish people in the world that don't give a rat's ass about anything but their self. I'm wondering how you ever do get by without developing a temper. It puzzles me why I had to wait till I was twenty-five—I still had one when I was twenty-five—to learn some self-control. I still got a temper now, but I got a little more rationality to me too. Well, you generally sense that trouble is coming, and I try to stay out of it. That way, by avoiding it, I don't get into it.

Don't get me wrong. I ain't some wimp what's going to let himself be pushed around. I'd get to fighting again if someone assaulted my wife or son or threatened me or either of them. I'd retaliate. I ain't going to talk to the son of a bitch, that's for sure. I'm not going to plead with him or beg. I'm just going to beat him to a pulp. Throw some fear into him. Kill him if that's what I got to do. An eye for an eye. I'm going to protect my family, no matter what I got to do.

Now, I ain't been in no fights in a long time and not no real-out-of-control brawls since I left prison that second time. I try to let my temper out in other ways—by talking or playing sports. Like I'm golfing now. It's good for me because it calms me down. But getting mad still problems me, especially when it's with good friends or with my wife or son. Usually, then, I walk away and let things cool down. I don't want no emotional scenes, so it's easier to avoid that stuff. But I don't worry no more about being crazy mad and doing stuff

Settling Down

like I done before. There'll never be a day again when I'll flare up and won't have control of myself, because I'm not the only one I got to think of now if I'd do this. I got a wife and son and responsibilities—stuff like that. And self-respect. So I think that's going to stop me from doing it. I hope so.

But I worried plenty when I went around and apologized to all them people. I'd probably have smashed some of them if I hadn't been sober. Drunk, I would never have held back my anger like I had to. To this day, if I'm in a real dark mood, I don't drink. Drinking caused lots of my problems back then. All them times I hurt people, I was drunk. I was pretty rational when I was sober. I blew my temper a few times, but it'd be all verbal—no physical stuff. So if I'd left the booze alone, I probably would've been OK.

Booze does strange things to people. I bartended a few times—real underpaid work, if you ask me. When you bartend, you watch people go through changes. They come in with one personality. They have a few beers. It might take two beers or maybe ten before their personality changes, but now you're not dealing with the person what come in the door. Different people go different ways. Watch out for the quiet ones; they explode. With me, well, at first I'd be laughing and dancing and cracking jokes—the life of the party, don't you know? But then something would snap inside me, and I'd want to hurt people. I had to get over that if I was going to survive.

Back when I'm talking about now, I knew booze was a big part of my troubles, and I figured that I should totally quit drinking, but I couldn't do it. I wasn't making no money. I was depressed about being poor, having lousy jobs, and fishing was bad. We couldn't fish all over like now, and I never owned no gear. I just worked for other guys, white men. They made the money, not me. There'd be times Floyd and me would only make forty dollars each in a week. But it was easy to get drunk—to hide from myself in a bottle, blur the pain. I did want to quit drinking, but then, in a way, I didn't.

Drinking was a cheap escape. All my buddies drank. Going to the bars was fun because I'd always find friends there—not real friends maybe but people I hung out with anyway. There was action, excitement, and my lousy life faded for a while. What I really needed was a friend who'd stop me from running away and make me look at myself. My wife's been a friend like that, but we wasn't married yet and wasn't nobody else helping me then.

I wanted to get my drinking under control so I could have a few beers and behave myself and be comfortable. If you can drink and get a little high and enjoy socializing with people, you're all right. And that's where I wanted to get, because I'll never quit drinking

completely. I enjoy it. I like to go out and dance and have a good time. What are you going to do? Sit inside and look at these walls all the time? Around this town there ain't much to do for fun.

My wife's name is Carole. She helped me get my boozing and fighting under control. I'm getting ahead of myself here, but I think I should tell you the rest of this while I got it started. I met Carole not long after I got out of prison. Her and I started going together. One night we was out, and somebody said something raunchy about her. I wasn't sure who had mouthed off, so I said, "I'm going to whip all five of you bastards," and I started swinging. Them guys run, and I started after them.

Carole grabbed my shoulder and said, "Let them go, Ron." She was pregnant. She said, "I love you, but I don't want a man who's in trouble all the time. What's going to happen if every time you get riled up, you start fighting? You're going back to the pen, that's what. I don't want to marry a man like that."

I loved her too, and I wanted to get married, so what she said made sense. How could I be a husband to her and a dad to our child if I was locked up behind bars? So she curbed me on that.

I decided I had to stop fighting, but I kept right on going to the bars and drinking with my rum-dum buddies. I drank a lot when we first got married. I wasn't over the bar life yet. I never raised much hell, just drank. Well, Carole put up with this a long time. I was working on the pipeline then, making good money. Them pipeliners was big drinkers. Most every day after work I went to the bars with them and drank a few beers. I wasn't chasing women. I'd never go out on Carole. I just had a good time drinking with the fellows.

I met Carole not long after I got out of prison. . . . And I was lucky to find a woman like Carole. She's really helped me over the years. I'm a better man having married her, that's for sure. That was the happiest moment of my life when I married her.

Often I stayed out late and come home rolling drunk. I did this quite regular.

Carole never said nothing about my drinking and going out. Me being so ignorant, I never thought about what I was doing. I never figured out that with her personality being the way it was, she wanted to say something but never did. Looking back now, I can't see why a woman would put up with her man running around the way I was.

I played pool a lot and drank. Being in the bars and bullshitting with the guys is fun. Pretty selfish of me, eh? But I goofed around in bars all the time, so I didn't think about Carole. I done this for a few months, I guess. One time I come home, and Carole was gone. She had left that afternoon before I come in. I figured she went downtown or to visit her sister. Nine o'clock, no Carole. I started to worry. It got late. No Carole. Usually if she was going to be gone a long time, she'd leave me a note, but not this time. Finally a little after 1 A.M. she tumbled in with a friend of hers. They'd been drinking, and Carole was loaded.

I'd been real worried till she showed up, so I got mad and started yelling at her: "Where you been? Why didn't you tell me?" Stuff like that.

She'd had enough to drink, so she stood right up to me, giving it back to me. "You do it all the time," she said. "You never ask me. You don't tell me where you're going or when you'll be home. If you do it, why can't I?"

I realized that she was right, and I stopped going to the bars with my buddies. I seen that with many couples. The guy goes out. Then she goes out. They keep trying to get even with each other: Well, if you do it, I'm going to. Carole and I could've went on like that, but we never did. We go out together now, except when we're playing in a pool league, so it worked out OK with us. But I seen marriages break up on account of guys going to the bars like I was doing there for a while. I learned a good lesson from Carole.

When Carole and I first got married, we kept vodka in the house. We'd mix up a drink. I noticed this. We'd mix up one. Then after while it'd be two, and then several. So I got to thinking, and I figured this wasn't going to work. I could see what was going to happen. Pretty soon we'd be drinking a bottle a night and some beer too. Drinking becomes a habit. That's like the guys going to the bars every night and can't stop, whether they need company or conversation or what. Mainly you got to figure they want the booze. Leastways it ain't long before they can't do without it. So Carole and me just cut it out. I think that was a good idea, because people become alcoholics real easy without knowing what's happened to them. I could see where it might happen to us, and I didn't want that. So we stopped keeping liquor in the house for a while.

But to say that I got to where booze ain't no problem, I think it was after five years. We've been married over twenty years. Even when we come back from Iowa, when we'd been married five years, we partied to beat hell. So I guess we decided at times that we would quit drinking. We would stop and not have nothing to drink for two, three months. But we always went out together and kind of looked out for each other. I can take it or leave it now, like last night I think I left two beers there. I seen the time when I wouldn't leave that beer. I'd have to drink them all. I don't need it. I'm not going to quit completely. I probably never will. I can drink and be comfortable now. I got booze whipped, I think. We can have a six-pack in this house, and it'll sit there for months and nobody will touch it. Well, that six-pack in the refrigerator, that's been there since Easter—a long time. I can take it or leave it.

And I look at another deal here with these people I know. All the people we know, we can have fun with. We tease each other, and nobody's feelings get hurt. That's the kind of people I want to associate with.

I worried about going back to the pen. I promised myself I wasn't never going back, but sometimes I'd get to drinking, and there would be a fight brewing. That's when I'd get upset. I'd hit somebody, and I'd be afraid he'd sign a warrant on me. But I never seen a day in jail since I got out that last time. I'll admit that sometimes when I'm drinking and driving, I deserve a couple days in jail like you generally get. I get scared when I see the jail, like when I went for my driver's license. I saw them bars, and it gave me bad feelings.

When I came back to St. Ignace, people feared me. The people that are afraid of me aren't usually going to bother me, but they will when they drink. I mean, what protection do I have against their slanderous remarks? They always say, "Goddamn it. You committed a crime against society. You got to pay." Well, society has committed crimes on me too. Who pays for what was heaped on me? Who paid in reform school when I got slugged by a grown man? Who pays for the nightmares? For the abuse? Where do I get protection? I don't know. It tees me off.

When I got out of prison, I wanted to get married, part of the plan I told you about. And I was lucky to find a woman like Carole.

She's really helped me over the years. I'm a better man having married her, that's for sure. That was the happiest moment of my life when I married her.

I first met Carole a few days after I got back to town. My cousin and some other girls was riding around, and they picked me up. Carole was with them. I'd been drinking and worried I might make a fool of myself, because I liked her right away. We rode around awhile and talked, but next day all I could remember was I met this cute girl who said her name was Carlos. She was teasing me—her dad called her that. She was very attractive to me, but I didn't know who she was—not the usual thing in a small town like this. I hoped I'd see her again.

Next day, I was delivering coal for my uncle, and she lived over on Rolling Hill, I think. She lived in an apartment up there with her mother. We delivered coal, and there she was on the balcony, saying hi to me, and we started dating right after that.

I'm surprised that she went out with me at all, because she was afraid of me. She'd see me in a dance hall and get away. She told me later that she'd been scared of me. And I remember one time Ron St. Pierre and I was walking down the street, and Carole was with another girl I took out, Tisa. Tisa come up to talk with us, but Carole stood back. So I was lucky she went out with me.

Carole was shy back then—quiet, never said much. I brought her over to Floyd's place one night. We was there three or four hours. She said hello when we got there and good-bye when we left. That's the extent of it. She more or less kept her feelings to herself, so I never knew quite what was going on inside her. What a pair we was back then, eh?

I could feel that I was falling in love with her. I was pretty mixed up at this time, but I knew I was having feelings I hadn't felt before. I remember the first time I said I loved her. "Oh, go on," she said. Right after that she said she wouldn't go out with me no more. I figured I'd get high on nutmeg. If she won't go out with me, hell with her. I did the nutmeg, and damn, here came Carole to see me. She really looked good. Here she was wanting to talk to me, and here I was higher than a son of a bitch.

We went to the movie show. Her and I took in every show that year. I didn't have no car, so we couldn't do much. We'd go to a movie and walk up to the apartment where I stayed. I never made enough money to buy a car. I didn't even have a driver's license. Got it right after we was married. Anyway, we went to the movie that night. You get hallucinations on nutmeg. I was watching the movie, and suddenly a squirrel run by me. That wasn't so bad, but he had boxing trunks on. I asked him, "What's the trunks for?" I shook my head, trying to get things straight, drinking pop, one after another. Anything cold reduces it some.

We watched the first feature. I got through that. The squirrel never come back. The introduction music to the second feature scared me. I asked Carole, "Would you like to go?" She didn't care about the movie, so we left and went to the Homestead Cafe. I was drinking milk, not my usual in that place. I felt stupid. I liked her and thought I was playing the fool. I was looking at her, thinking that she knew I was high. It was my imagination, because she had no idea. Finally I told her what I had did.

But after Carole told me about curbing my fighting, that was the first time she said that she loved me. It made me feel good. I loved her, and what she said about my fighting made sense. I mean, there was reality staring me in the face. She wouldn't marry me, even though she loved me, unless I changed. I could see that her feelings toward me was mixed up, and she didn't know quite what to do. I mean, my personality was so strange that it would drive a person nuts.

Here was Carole living more or less a sheltered life, and she was going with an unstable person like me, an ex-con. Wouldn't that confuse you? Even being friends with a guy like me could be difficult in them days. I'd get moody and decide, "Well, piss on being polite to these people. Piss on reforming myself." Who wants to be friends with a person like that? Being married to me like I was—I wouldn't wish that on no one.

When Carole become pregnant, there was part of my dream coming true, but she wouldn't marry me. I got her under Dr. Lasland's care, which was a very good friend of mine. He used to talk to me, counsel me. One time Carole and I went to him. This was November 1967, a couple weeks before we got married. We went for Carole's checkup, and the doctor said, "Well, Carole, are you ready to marry this crazy son of a bitch?" That was his exact words.

She looked down and smiled. "Yes," she said. "Yes, I am."

He laughed and said, "You better hurry up, or you'll be adopting your own kid."

We got married December 23, and Chris was born four days later. Carole gets mad sometimes when I talk about it. The ink wasn't hardly dry on the marriage papers, and I was getting a birth certificate for Chris.

I knew Dr. Lasland before that. He's the one patched me up after Floyd pounded me that time trying to keep me from busting up Curtis Jones. Before we was married, Carole would get upset sometimes about being pregnant and having a baby, being with a guy like me—everything. One time she got so depressed and confused, she told me she was going to kill herself. She didn't mean it, but I didn't know that. She worried about what was happening and wondered what to do. She would've talked herself out of what she was thinking after a bit. But stupid me, I said, "Want to commit suicide? It's easy. I'll show you how to do it."

I got crazy drunk on Thunderbird wine and went to the drugstore. I bought some Contac pills. Why I picked them, I don't know. I walked home snaked to the gills, and I said again, "Want to commit suicide, eh?" Now she was sorry she said that. Don't get me wrong. I wasn't trying to commit suicide. But yet I was taking all them pills. I swallowed them, downed them with Thunderbird. I said to her, "I'll show you how it's done."

I was crazy. I was awful drunk, and I didn't know quite what I was doing. Carole called the cops. My friend Jimmy Riersey was a cop then. He called Dr. Lasland. The doctor told Jimmy not to worry. I'd get an awful headache and would be severely dehydrated, and I'd get the flurries.

Next morning when I got up, I didn't know what the flurries was, but I soon found out. I went to work on the fish tug with Floyd. I only slept a couple hours. I got up and was in the truck, and I got a raging headache. Floyd felt something was wrong, so he brought me home. Well, what the flurries is, you're not comfortable no place. You get up and got to move here and there, restless. I couldn't get no saliva in my mouth.

Why did I do that? I don't know. I never did figure it out. I mean if Carole felt that way, I should've just talked to her, calmed her down. Talk about a screwed-up young man!

My nerves was bad. I remember one time Carole and I was laying alongside the stove. We had a mattress there where we'd watch TV. The place didn't have no furniture. She didn't want me to fish for a living. She was pregnant. I was probably going to marry her, and I wasn't making but forty bucks a week when I was lucky. Fishing wasn't doing it. I was asleep, dreaming. I woke up, and I said, "Don't want me fishing, eh?" She didn't know what's going on, and I said, "I'll fix that. I'll just fix myself so I can't fish." I smashed my hand into the door—cut my hand. I got a scar there and scar there, all over. That was after I took the pills, a couple days, maybe a week.

I was bandaged next morning, and Floyd said, "What's wrong with you?" I started talking, and then I cried. I said, "I got to get help."

Settling Down

I went to see Dr. Lasland. He said, "I wondered crazy ass would be here. You know you should be wine you drank plus the pills. You're nuts."

When Riersey had called him that night, Dr. Lasland "Don't force him to come down here. Let him do it on his own." And that's how I got started golfing.

The doctor said, "Ron, you're nervous. Your nerves are shot. You're a high-strung person, you're mixed up, and you need help. I'll do all I can to help you, and if that doesn't work, I'll tell you what I'll do. Now, this isn't charity." He knew how I didn't like that. "I will get the best psychiatrist," he said. "You won't have to go into an institution like Newberry. I'll get you the best help I can. But for now it's strictly up to you and me. You can confide in me, but you got to straighten up."

And that's when he said, "You like sports. I know that. Have you ever played golf?" I shook my head.

He said, "Have you ever played tennis?"

I said, "Yeah, but I hit myself in the nose with the racket one time, and I quit."

So I took up golf. I love it. He told me, "Ron, you're like a cat. You have nine lives, and you've used up eight of them. Now do something with the last one. You've got one chance left to make something of yourself."

He was killed in a car accident. He helped me a lot. A good man he was. Them are hard to find.

A few times I'd get real troubled, and I'd talk to him. I'd meet him on the street, and he'd start talking with me. Now, you're in trouble if you do that. I'm going to talk your leg off. But he would listen even when I went on and on. I can tell if somebody's genuine or if he's conning me. Dr. Lasland was just a real good man. He knew a lot about me, and I didn't know where he was finding this out. I considered him as a friend for the time that I knew him. He helped me when I was in trouble. It broke me up when I heard he'd got killed.

After the doctor told Carole and me about we'd adopt our own kid, we decided to get married. We was going to get married before, but there wasn't no actual plans. I told Carole, "Don't feel bad if people don't show up at the wedding reception." We invited people, and then our friends told other friends about it. Turned out quite a few people did come to wish us well. We got married by the justice of the peace. Beck was his name. I wasn't nervous. It didn't bother me a bit. I wanted to get married.

My buddies gave the reception. The people that come was

more or less my age, friends that didn't care about my reputation and wasn't afraid there was going to be a fight. My ma and dad didn't show up. We had it in Allenville, near Moran, in the town hall. They decorated it the night before. My best man, Mike Clark, got loaded at the wedding reception. All he wanted to do was fight.

But what pissed me off about the wedding reception was what my brother Tommy, and my brother Leonard did while they was there. Leonard drank and couldn't handle it. I stayed sober, just sipping on a beer. Carole was pregnant and wasn't feeling good, but we did go. They had too much whiskey. Them guys, within about two hours, went through over a case of whiskey. Speed Sales, a very good friend, was there, and his brother-in-law was just out of boot camp. He wore his uniform. We never got along with none of the armed forces; there was quite a rivalry between the townspeople and them. But this kid wasn't bothering nobody, and he was in the Army.

Tommy started bugging him, razzing him. He took the guy's hat, put it on the floor, and stomped it. Well, Speed Sales was going to take the part of his brother-in-law. I walked over to quiet things. "Come on, guys," I said. "My wife's not feeling good. I'd appreciate it if you'd just have a good time."

Tommy kept picking. He was the one what started the fight. Pretty soon Leonard grabbed Speed. I waded in. I slapped Leonard. I said, "Damn it. Calm down, Leonard." That's what you got to do with him.

Well, I shoved Speed, and now he wanted to fight me. I calmed him down, and there was another fight breaking out. Shorty Pimmerton, an old high school buddy, swung at Tommy. I broke that up. I put my foot behind Tommy and knocked him on his butt and told him to stay there.

Shorty squared off, and I threw a foot up by his face, and I said, "Shorty, the next one's coming in. I don't want no fighting here." I was playing the peacemaker, if you can believe that.

Shorty said, "I'll fight your brother, but I won't fight you."

"Come on," I said. "I'll buy you a drink." So I got him a whiskey. Speed decided to leave, and he was trying to get in his car, but Tommy was swinging away at him. So Tommy screwed the reception up good.

Bobby Gray and some friends drove in while the fight was going on. They seen what was happening and left. What a way to start a new life, eh? We didn't stay the whole time, because Carole was feeling tired. We come home. I was renting a little place on Lake Street then. Carole was happy, and she said she loved me a lot.

Settling Down

She told me how much she was looking forward to having the baby.

Getting married changed my life. It's what got me straight. It give me responsibility and something to work for. I can't find the right words to tell you what it meant to me. All them years nobody had loved me, but now someone had took me into their heart.

Carole didn't show much when she was pregnant. She didn't get big like most women do. I was anxious for the day to come and was wondering what it would be, a boy or a girl. Well, anyway, my sister-in-law Catherine was over. Carole and her was playing cards. They was sitting there talking. Carole was fidgeting, and Cathy said, "What's the matter with you? You in labor?"

Carole said, "I think so."

I hurried up and got Floyd because I didn't have no car. And jeez, Carole was in pain now. Her water busted in the car. And we didn't know where the hospital was in Cheboygan. There was just two stoplights there, so we took the second one, and there it was. Lucky for us. The doctor said, "If you guys had missed the light, you would have had an experience you would have never forgotten."

When we brought her to the hospital, the nurse asked us what was the matter with her. We brought her through emergency. I said, "She's going to have a baby."

So they wheeled her in right away, and I had to go sign some papers. I was nervous. I don't like papers, and I didn't know what was going on. Where was Carole? Was she OK? I was wandering around the hall, didn't know where I was going, being excited and everything. I saw a guy and asked him where the delivery room was. He said, "That's down the hall. Is that your wife in there?"

I said, "Yeah."

He said, "You better hurry up."

I went in there, and I didn't even have a chance to smoke a cigarette or nothing and pace the floor like everybody does. She had the baby just a few minutes after they wheeled her in.

I heard some crying. I got scared when I first seen Chris, my new son. He was purple. I wondered if there was something wrong with him. Well, I know now that dark-skinned babies look like that. I watched him being weighed and measured. He just screamed away.

I talked with Carole for a while. I told her the baby was OK and how happy I was. I headed home then. Everything was all right. I paid the bridge fare. It was $3.75, and I had just $1.25 left to my name. But I didn't care, because I was a father.

Next morning, me and Little Ron, Carole's brother, painted totem poles to beat hell so we could go back to see Carole. I'll tell you

more about totem pole painting a little later. We got paid ten cents each. Over the years I've painted lots of them goddamn poles. Anyhow, we did up about two hundred of them, I think. We had enough money to get to Cheboygan and back now with some left over.

We didn't have no health insurance and no money. I paid them when I got a little ahead, bit by bit. Carole was only there two days. The doctor asked me, "Can you take good care of her when you bring her home?"

I said, "Sure!"

I bought a little blanket with totem pole money so we could bring Christopher home. I went to the hospital. There he was, still crying. We wrapped him up and brought him home. I was excited, and I worried about taking care of him. But I was happy to be building a family like I never had when I was young.

Carole has high blood pressure, and the doctor told her not to have any more kids. We was careful, but she become pregnant again. It's painful for me to talk about this, even after all these years. Carole and I wanted more kids, at least two, but Carole was not supposed to have got pregnant that second time. But it happened, and she carried the baby good for a while.

Well, I was excited about having another child, and Carole was too. We talked about it. Carole got to seven and a half months with no trouble, not long to go. But then she was not feeling good at all. I brought her to the hospital in Petoskey. They got good doctors there: Dr. Kenny and a baby specialist.

She was bleeding. They said that it was critical, and she could hemorrhage. That scared me. I could lose her.

My son Chris. When Chris was born, I had just $1.25 left to my name. But I didn't care, because I was a father. . . . I was excited, and I worried about taking care of him. But I was happy to be building a family like I never had when I was young.

Everything went good for a while. They hooked her up to a machine where they could monitor the baby's heartbeat and hers too. I waited for several hours, and everything was all right because Dr. Kenny said the baby was fine and Carole was doing very well.

Well, jeez, I felt better, but anxious, don't you know? I was hungry then, so I went to the cafeteria and got something to eat and met a guy there. I ate dinner with him. I don't even know who he was. But he was sitting there, and I got to talking with him. He told me his problems, I told him mine, and at the time it was no problem. I told him everything was all right. Well, we ate and sat there and bullshitted for a while and smoked a couple cigarettes.

I was heading back upstairs, and my sister-in-law Catherine was crying. She wasn't there when I left. I said, "Oh, my God, what's wrong?"

Dark things went through my mind. Maybe Carole was in trouble. I didn't know what to think. I rushed in there, and Dr. Kenny didn't want to talk to me. He felt bad too. It's not often you meet a doctor with compassion like that man has. He said he was real sorry. He told me what happened. The afterbirth pulled away and smothered the baby. It happened real fast.

Poor Carole, she went through hell. She was in labor when this was going on. I hoped the machines was wrong, but they wasn't. The baby seemed alive when you first looked at her, like she was sleeping: a little girl. She looked like Chris, only with more hair. I stared at her, and, oh, God, I couldn't accept it. I wondered, "Why? What kind of justice is this?"

Carole stayed in the hospital, and I had to arrange for the baby's burial. I went to the funeral home in St. Ignace, and I buried her at the Indian cemetery. My brother-in-law, Howard Owens, dug the grave for me. I couldn't do that. We had a service for her. When you have a healthy baby, you think of a name. We didn't have a name picked out. We called her Marie.

Carole came home from the hospital, and she seemed OK, not depressed or anything. I didn't get over that for a long time. I still ain't over it. I'd cry. I cried sometimes when Carole wasn't around. Damn! A little girl too.

I never had no home when I was young, a safe place where people loved me. I got shifted around to aunts and uncles, the Catholic school, mom and dad. As a kid, I had no sense of who I was or where I belonged after being tossed from place to place like that. So I hoped to have a home of my own someday where I could raise a family.

Carole and I lived lots of places after we was married, most of

Settling Down

them pretty small because we was poor. I call them matchboxes, they was so tiny. The first one was that dinky house over on Lake Street. The kitchen and dining room was all together, and there was just one bedroom. When we had the boys, Carole's two brothers, staying with us, they slept on the couch. It was real small and too crowded. When I worked construction on the high rise in Escanaba, we lived in a house with some friends of ours. We shared the rent and everything. But I didn't like that, because it cuts down on your privacy.

Now, in Iowa we found a great little house where senior citizens usually lived. It was small but comfortable, and we enjoyed being by ourselves. There wasn't no furniture. The only thing in the place was an electric stove, so we went to a thrift shop. We paid twenty-five dollars for a pullout-bed couch, some chairs, a table, and a refrigerator. What a deal! I gave everything back when we left. I donated it back to them people at the library when we left, because that's what they used the thrift shop for was to finance the library.

That town was something else. It was as dull as Iowa, if you get my drift. I don't think it had five hundred population. But the people was nice. Like when Carole walked out of the store with groceries, some young fellows opened the doors for her. I was talking to the city cop, and he told me the last vandalism there—what they called major vandalism—was about eight years back. It was just a little farm town but a good place to live while I was working construction.

When we come back to St. Ignace, we lived in a big place, two bedrooms, great big dining room, and we had lots of room. Somebody moved in there when we went to Escanaba. I didn't give the landlords notice, because I didn't know when I was going to be going to the job. Well, I left in the middle of the month, but they charged me the whole month's rent. And at that time it was kind of hard to give it up. But I believe that old saying, What goes around comes around. And it did. When they tore that house down, I helped move the antiques out and helped the landlady sell them. I bought the leftovers for $20 and sold them for $540 within a few days. So here she could've made all that money. Good enough for her, right?

We left there for a big house on South Street. It couldn't be heated. Goddamn, it was cold. We had the upstairs bedroom, and the stovepipe run through there. When we went to bed, we'd bring Chris with us and put an electric heater on. The wood stove was roaring downstairs, and the pipe was hot, but that room was cold as hell. The house wasn't insulated, so that's how we slept. We had to shut off one room to make another room comfortable. We'd even light the oven. What a mess! So we moved out of there and to one other place after that before we built our own house. In fact, the year I worked on the Ramada Inn in Sault Ste. Marie, we stayed in a trailer park. That was the worst yet. The trailers are awful. This was a small one, real tiny, a sardine can. I didn't like being packed in like that.

Me and Carole talked about buying a house. We heard that we could go through the Federal Housing Administration. We called the Soo [Sault Ste. Marie]; that's where the office was. We couldn't get no mortgage from the bank, but these people was nice to us and said we could buy a home. I was making good money then, working steady for Tom Shaw, a contractor around here. The FHA talked to me and Carole several times about how much money we was making, what kind of house we could get, how much we could borrow.

Before we talked to FHA, we bought land over on Fourth Street to build a house on. Me and Carole paid for the land. We saved and saved. What a mess that turned out to be! There was people already on the land, on the west end of it. I got the land surveyed; FHA said you had to do that. Here was this vacant land sitting there. Nobody was paying no attention to it. We bought it from my Aunt Agnes. People had just snuck on her land, and they was getting away with it for years, I guess. There was a trailer on the property. I looked at that land. I knew about surveying from my pipeline work, and I knew something was wrong. Well, this Don Goodreau was giving me a rough time. His mother was the one got the trailer there.

"What are you doing?" he said.

"I'm going to build here."

"Where's your land?"

"Where's yours?" I said. "Show me the surveyor's stake. You're on my land." So that's when I decided I should hire a survey company.

When the surveyors showed up, Don Goodreau was right in their face, making trouble. I was mad then. I took a chain saw in there and started cutting. He heard me and come down. I told him, "I'm cutting this tree and them birch trees over there and them ones over there too. Sue me if you want." I knew I was on my property. He said nothing. Just stood there. The survey company didn't stay long. I asked my aunt what the trouble was, and she said the plat maps was screwed up. I figured something was up.

"What's you and Goodreau planning? What's going on?" I said.

"What are you saying?" she wanted to know.

Me and a friend surveyed it—nothing official, but we knew what we was doing. Half of Goodreau's trailer was on my land. I

Settling Down

went and got him and showed him that it was thirty feet inside the line. His mother called me and offered to swap for some land down on South Street, but, hell, that land's too steep to build on, and not much land either. So with all this hassle, I figured I'd better look for another place to build.

Finally Carole talked me into facing them papers at the FHA. I'd wanted to do it, but I feared them papers because I can't read very good. I'd always tell Carole, "Hon, we better wait till I got a better job." But I was just putting things off so I wouldn't have to sign stuff I didn't understand.

We started making out papers at FHA. They got to know this, know that. We looked at several homes. We really liked one in the First Ward there, but the foundation was bad. FHA's real particular about that, but I wish I'd known enough about their rulings to say, "Well, I'm going to buy the house, jack it up, and put a new foundation under it." We give up on older houses after that and decided to build a Wassau home, the Rockford, a two-bedroom ranch. The salesman offered us a honey of a deal, he told us, but we soon found out things wasn't so sweet like he said.

I was working on the Ramada Inn in the Soo, and the woman from FHA come up. She said, "Ron, I got good news for you. Everything went through. You got your loan. Can you be in my office at eight-thirty tomorrow morning?"

I said, "Yeah. I'll ask the boss for the time off."

I told Carole. We was delighted about it. It was springtime then, and after we signed the papers, if we was renting someplace, we had to pay rent plus our payments, which would be rough. We had a ten-by-ten-foot tent with a nine-by-five-foot porch on it. Carole's mother told us we could put it in the front yard, and we'd camp with her for the summer. I got sick of camping pretty fast. We did save money, though. If we wanted to wash up or anything, we'd just go in the house and we generally ate in the house. Well, it took quite a while to get things straightened around, and it got too chilly for the tent, so we rented a cabin at one of the motels here.

Carole and I come to the lot, and I was cutting the brush and was getting it cleared. We subcontracted a lot of work. We should've cleared more for a backyard and a lot of stuff. I didn't know about all this. And you can look at the front yard now and see it's screwed up. That was their fault. They didn't fill enough. I put more dirt in there, but it still ain't level. So there was things I didn't know, but then it come to the point where they said, "If you do the foundation, I'll just pay you, Ron."

So I did the foundation, and nobody from my family come to

help. Not one of my brothers said, "Here, want a helping hand, Ron? You're getting a new house. I think it's nice for you." It was Carole's family what helped. That bothers me because if one of my brothers was building a house, even though they didn't come over to help with mine, I'd say, "Well, hell, get the footings in and you tend for me. I'll lay the foundation up for you." That's something I can honestly say I'd do. But not a single Paquin offered to help me.

Some friends come up and worked. Never charged me or nothing. That's nice of people to do that. Eddie, my nephew, tended for me, worked real hard. So we was all doing it and drinking beer. We had to quit because everybody got too drunk. We finished next day. So I went to collect my foundation money, and he wouldn't pay. He tried to con me on the deal. He looked at this brochure for Wassau Homes, and he said, "Well, now, if you would've got that in the wintertime, you would've got your appliances free, but I can't pay you for your labor."

"Bullshit!" I said. "I know how to get your ass."

He said, "Oh, no, you're getting that refrigerator for your work. That's the deal we made."

"No, it ain't," I said. "I'll get my money one way or the other."

I asked around and found out I could go to small claims court. I figured for my block work I had $184 coming. But when I brought it to small claims court, I pushed it up to $300. I charged him for the raking, the clearing that Carole and I did, and the other work too. Really we didn't have to do that. That package deal was $23,500 to move in. So I got everything ready, and I decided I was going to defend this case myself. I wasn't going to hire no lawyer.

We went to court. The circuit court judge handled small claims. The Wassau guy talked about refrigerator this, refrigerator that. He said I was getting the refrigerator for my work. He presented his case first. I got Carole on the witness stand, and she started to freeze because she's not used to talking in public. The judge shouldn't have said this to her, but he said, "Tell us what you know, not what Ron told you to say." I don't think he should've said that. She almost didn't get out what I did tell her to say.

She was really nervous now. So finally I got up, and I said, "Look, a deal's a deal. Judge, here's the brochure right here. Read it. Article nineteen says, 'All appliances.' 'All' means the refrigerator too. I want my block-laying money, and for the clearing my wife and I done. We worked hard for lots of hours. I want paid for that. I'm putting the total at three hundred dollars." I figured I had it won. The judge was smart. He could see I was being cheated.

When the hearing was over, we was standing there, and I said,

"Why do you try to cheat poor people like us?" I made sure the judge heard me. I said, "We never done nothing to you."

Weiss, the Wassau guy, was going bankrupt, darn near. He didn't know how to do business. He bought this, bought that, and got too far ahead of himself. So $300 would have been good money for him. When we got to the courthouse lobby, he said, "Tell you what, Ron. I owe it to you. Would you settle for just the block work?"

"OK," I said. "That's all ever wanted."

"I'll write you a check right now for one hundred eighty-four dollars."

I said, "All right."

About a week later, I got a paper from the court saying that Harold Weiss owed me $300. I won the case. Carole had told me to hang on, that we'd get all the money, but I just took the $184.

We picked out our carpet. We got the carpet contractor, and our kitchen linoleum, which is hard to buy now, the stuff that's there now. It's really nice. Carole chose all that. We picked out the carpet together. We got a real good deal on the carpet in the front room. He gave us a price on a carpet, but when we got there, they didn't have it, so he gave us higher-grade stuff. A deal was a deal, so he just did it for us. We got the whole house carpeted for eight hundred dollars. That's a good price, and it lasted with no sign of wear.

Now on the outside of the house, it wasn't stained or painted. It was up to us to do that afterwards. He give us some stain. Wrong damn stuff! It didn't match. He had to pull two panels and put them back in because we bought the stain from him. So he constantly screwed us around.

It got cold, so we moved in the house before it was done. We didn't have no furniture yet, just a bed. We slept in this room right here, the living room, Chris and I and Carole. We had a big candle, and we kept the stove on. This was fall, quite chilly. We slept real good that first night. Here we were—we had our home. It was nice getting up in the morning, bare feet on the carpet. It was really nice. And I said, "Boy, this is comfort. This is where it's at."

My dreams was coming true.

Work

I've did lots of jobs in my life, mostly not no good ones. When I was real young and living with the Hartwicks, I never went out and worked then. But after I left their place and went to my parents', when I was eight years old, I worked for Dr. Holly, an elderly fellow from Florida. I took care of his garden, and he gave me twenty-five cents an hour, which was at least spending money. And then Mrs. Taylor, a colored woman, give me jobs, like in the fall to gather bittersweet berries. She made a cough syrup out of it; it worked good, too. And Donny, my twin brother, took care of her geese and goats and stuff like that.

Next year, when I was nine years old, I worked at Colby's fishery, taking care of smelt and herring mostly. And I learned to dress fish. I worked at Gessenger's fishery and at Fritz Halbert's fishery when I was twelve. I'll tell you about that later. I split wood for people too in the fall. They'd get the wood and hire me to split it. So even at a young age I was always looking for work.

In reform school and home school you had duties to do. I learned how to run a lathe and how to sew sheets and pillowcases and stuff like that. I got damn fast on that Singer sewing machine. And I learned how to mop floors good and wax them and buff and stuff like that. Then I worked in the gym there when I was office boy. I didn't have to do much but run messages between there and the administration building. At that time I was turning fourteen years old, and you got your working permit, a Social Security card.

I did things that were not too constructive, but at least it was work. I worked in restaurants, pearl diving—what they call washing dishes. Later, when I stayed at the Hartwicks' again in my first year of high school, we cut pulpwood and fireplace wood. That's damn

Work

hard work. Later on I went in the woods several times during life, but I've talked about that in some earlier stories, like about Big Boy Curry.

When I come out of the woods, I went over to Mackinac Island and got my first construction job, mason tending. I always wanted to become a mason, and I figured someday I might if I got the right deal. I asked lots of questions on that first job because I wanted to learn. Once in a while they let me use a trowel, but it was a union job, so I wasn't allowed to do much other than carry. That's when I worked with John MacCumber. I cement-finished for him too, and I worked on his farm near Ludington. I fed cattle, and I pruned cherry trees and apple trees. I even picked cherries. Never did pick apples. A farmer's got to be able to do lots of things.

When I went to prison, I was on a ground crew and an electric crew. I learned some about how electricity worked. And I was foreman of the rec hall there, but that didn't amount to much. Mostly, I didn't learn nothing worth knowing about work in prison. You remember that, I guess.

When I got out of prison, I worked on the fish tugs, and I probably would've appreciated it a lot more if I'd made any money doing it. They paid terrible. Then I went back on construction, so when I first got married, I was drawing unemployment. Another job I had around then was I went over to the island and painted boats, ferryboats to bring tourists to Mackinac Island. I got $1.75 an hour, bad pay for tough work, scrubbing boats and painting them.

The first job I got after we was married was surveying on the pipeline for Williams Brothers. Now, I learned quite a bit there. I would've liked to have learned how to run that instrument for the surveying part, but I was only head chainman, just a laborer. But I liked it. Well, the depression fell on the pipeline, so I didn't get no jobs after that. I made good pay pipelining, but my wife and I didn't know how to handle money then, so we didn't save a dime. If I could do it over, I would save quite a bit of money, but I didn't.

I even drove a Head Start bus once. And I'm still picturing myself with all them little kids. That was quite the job. It didn't pay good, but it was a job, and I needed one real bad at the time because we was broke. Sometimes I'd grab work in town that came through, like when these guys built swimming pools. And I was foreman when the waterworks went through town.

Mostly, you can see, I did different jobs in construction during them years, but I couldn't get nowhere doing that sort of work. I wasn't union, and I had no education. The brickies—the masons' union—said I was too old to join. Over the hill was what they said.

At thirty-one years, I was too old? Bullshit! I didn't have no pull, I think, no good connections.

The guy from the brickies told me I was too old, but then he turned to me and said, "Ron, don't you have Indian in you?"

I told him, "Yeah, I do."

So he said, "Well, go in on a minority deal."

I thought about it. It really pissed me off to have to do that, but I needed a good job, so I said OK. He was going to take care of the papers and let me know. Well, it come time to put apprentices on, but I never heard from him. He didn't do nothing, I think. I suppose I could've fought it, but I let it go. See, I don't want a job because I'm a minority. I want it because I'm a good worker. That's how I held all my jobs all my life is being a good worker.

I like to work. I think it's good for people to work and sweat. I can't stand people who just live off other people's labor, and I cannot tolerate anybody that's lazy. You get lots of them that are friends with the boss or the foreman or something like that, and they just don't do nothing, yet they get the same pay you're getting for doing less work. And I honestly believe when you work for a man and he pays good, you should give him a decent day's work. If they see that you're working hard and there's a raise available, you should get it. Like when I worked for Brumm Construction Company. Nobody liked him, because he was nonunion, but I worked my ass off for that man, and the next week he appreciated this and give me a raise. And that gave me some incentive. Not that I wasn't doing a good

You got to do lots of jobs if you're going to make it in a place like this where there ain't much steady work. But through the years, I've fished for a living more than anything else. Fishing is in my blood. I love doing it. I hope I don't never have to quit. When I first started commercial fishing in the mid-1970s, for five years, maybe, we made excellent money.

enough job for him before. It was a fifty-cent raise. Well, fifty cents is fifty cents.

I was always trying to advance myself. See, I have nothing against labor work. Laborers is important. Where would our economy be if you didn't have laborers? I didn't want to be a laborer all my life. But while I was laboring, I thought I'd be one of the best, and I think I was, but I wasn't satisfied to be the best laborer. I wanted to advance myself. And of course when you advance yourself, too, there's a difference in money. I mean, you can't live without money, so what you're really striving for is to get a trade and make something of yourself, but in the other sense, if you want to stay a laborer all your life, I don't condemn that man. The only man I condemn is the lazy SOB that won't work. I got friends that are strictly laborers, and they'll be that way all their life, but they're satisfied and they support their families good. Hey, he's a man in my book. You don't make a better man because you're an executive and that other man is just a laborer. That ain't what I'm saying. But I was not satisfied to be a laborer.

We'd be a lot better off if more people worked for a living. As long as we got all them white-collar guys running things, we're going to have trouble. They don't know nothing but what's in books, and they don't give a damn about a working man like me. It's all politics, them guys looking out for their own. You got congressmen making more than forty thousand dollars a year voting on a lousy 10 percent raise on the minimum wage without stopping to think that that's all these people are going to make. So they can't be truly thinking of us. I remember seeing this goddamn congressman on the TV a while back. He said, "I can't live off twenty-nine thousand dollars a year," but at the same time they're only upping the minimum wage to $3.35. Here they voted themselves a thirteen-thousand-dollar raise. So there's forty thousand dollars a year this man is making. Plus he gets expenses.

Well, goddamn! Nobody can tell me that this country's ever going to get straightened out under these circumstances. When it costs you millions of dollars to get into office, you know damn well some poor bastard like me ain't going to make it. That's for sure. So here we got our fate held by rich people. They got a fifteen-room home with a heated swimming pool, and they spend more on heating that pool than most people spend on heating their home. Oh, the life of luxury! Here they are, they got maids and chauffeurs, and then they go make rules and regulations on us. So I don't know where we're ever going to get any fairness out of this.

I'll tell you, we ought to make them elite people go out and dig a ditch for twelve hours a day and see if they like it. Let them live on hard work and minimum wage for a while. Don't be blaming the working people for screwing this country up. Don't blame them. Them elites figure, "We can't make mistakes, because, boy, we got doctorate degree of this, a degree of that, and a degree of everything. Oh, are we ever smart! Goddamn, are we clever people! We don't got to listen to dumb laymens. We don't make mistakes—we was educated." Educated idiots, if you ask me. There ain't no better education than hard work and common sense. That's where we get our idiots, the ones that don't have common sense. And they got to have compassion, some feeling for the people. But everything just goes on in their heads, always thinking and scheming. They ought to pay more attention to their hearts.

But on that affirmative action, white people been putting the boots to Indians around here for as long as I can remember and before that too. I know that. So what are you going to do? I can't get jobs sometimes because I'm an Indian. That's a fact! So maybe there's nothing wrong with protecting minorities and helping them get ahead. I don't know.

What really done me in was no education. I can't do numbers, I can't spell, and I can't read much. If you told me your name, I couldn't find it in the phone book. I can't hardly read this book I'm writing here. My wife helps me do that. Don't get me wrong. I'm not dumb. I just never had no education. I can fool most people into thinking I graduated high school. When you're like I am, you got to con a lot.

But with jobs it's different, like on the pipeline. I worked my way up as high as head chainman. I would've liked to got at the instrument and had somebody teach me on that. I know I could've learned that, how to run degrees and stuff like that. I'm damn sure I could've learned that. Thad Ray, one of the head engineers, told my wife when we visited them one time, "As long as I'm ever on the pipeline, your husband's got a job. He would probably make inspector in a couple of years." Which is no big deal. After a year of being on the pipeline, as far as being inspector, all you got to do is be able to read the specs and understand what it's saying, like the depth for a road crossing. I think an inspector's job is kind of a boost up after you been with the company awhile. It pays more.

I really lost out by not having an education. There was an opening for a right-of-way man on the pipeline. To be a right-of-way man, you got to have some degree. I think you could get along without the engineering degree, but you got to be a half lawyer, and you got to be able to type. They called me up and everything. Tom

Thaxton at the division office in Petoskey called and asked me, "Ron, how much education you got?"

I said, "None."

"Damn," he said. "There was a right-a-way job."

At that time, it was fifteen hundred dollars a month and all expenses. If you didn't have a car, they bought you a used one. I wanted to go in a corner and cry. But there wasn't nothing I could do.

What went on there has happened other times: no education, no job. Just last year I probably could've worked running the Father Marquette Museum here in town, but they hired somebody else because I can't spell. I didn't even apply. Looking back on it now, I'm pissed off about the education part. I didn't get enough schooling, and that formed a depression on my life, like when I was nineteen or so, even before I went to prison. You can see that I could never land no real good jobs. It was always a fish tug for eight or ten dollars a day, or washing dishes, something like that.

But some guys graduated high school. They went into the service and got that over with and come back out and had their education where they could become an electrician or a plumber or, at that time, a mason, which you had to go through a four-year apprenticeship for. But for those jobs you had to have that high school education. So that was frustration for me. It would come out in a bar sometimes or whatever. Like guys would say to me, "Ron, why don't you do this? Why don't you do that?" I'd say, "Jesus Christ, how am I going to do it without no education?"

I had determination to get ahead, always had that. One day I said, "I'm going to learn to lay block," and I did it. I said, "Well, I'm going to learn to weld," and I did that. I said, "One day I'm going to own my own fishing rig," and I did that. I did lots of things I said I was going to do. At least they was constructive things. Sometimes I said, "I'm going to beat so-and-so's ass," and I did that too. But I'm not proud of that.

I had determination in constructive things, and I did this without no education. It might take me longer to figure out my bond when I'm laying block, but I will get it. I'll make it up in physical work. I'll put ten more blocks on a wall by the time that man will, so I'll make it up in that. It frustrated me when I couldn't figure that bond right out. But I'd get her. Towards the end there I had a handy-dandy calculator that helped a hell of a lot.

There's been times I just couldn't find no work at all. When the tourists go home, there ain't no jobs. Half the people around here is unemployed in the winter. You may not believe that, but it's true, and that's only counting the ones looking for work. One time I looked and looked for a job. We got so desperate—no money at all—that I had to go on welfare. I hated doing it. I felt so ashamed when I went down to see about it. It's like telling them I couldn't take care of my family. So we got an assistance check—you know, to help pay the rent and heat and stuff like that. We got checks a couple times, I think. I did it just that one time, and it wasn't long before I found work.

Usually, when Carole and I were out of work, we did handicrafts and sold them, mostly totem poles and jewelry, but other stuff too. Calvin Tamlyn had the totem pole factory over by Evergreen Shores, a sort of suburb of St. Ignace. He made several sizes and shipped them out. He had a franchise for them. Well, we painted them, and I was really glad they was around, because they put money in our pockets when we needed it. So we'd get busy painting totem poles. We did five-inch, seven-inch, and ten-inch poles. These would have colors on them: red, black, and white, mostly. We painted neck stripes, eyes, a beak, and on the sides and breast we'd make some Chippewa designs like rain clouds, arrows, little tepees, lightning, stuff like that, whatever struck your fancy. We made them all ways. A couple or three hundred, we'd put crossed arrows on them. Several hundred we'd do with rain clouds. We'd change our design to take the monotony out of it. Genuine Indian-made, eh?

For painting the five-inch poles, we got five cents; seven-inch, we got seven cents; and for the ten-inch, we got ten cents. Our house, when we was doing this steady, was pretty small, a two-room job: Carole and I's bedroom, and then the front room was the kitchen, living room, and dining room combined. The whole house was only ten feet wide. We'd line them totem poles up on strips of cardboard, stack them, and we'd get an assembly line going. I did one color and one part of the totem pole, Carole would do another, and Little Ron, Carole's brother, did another one. Carole did the detail painting. She's got a good eye and a steady hand. She'd outline stuff in black, around the eyes, lips. She had more patience than me.

We used water-based paint so them poles would dry fast. I enjoyed doing them at first, but it soon got old. But we did it because we had to, not because it was fun. I seen times since then when I didn't have no good work and I wished them totem poles was back.

We'd figure we needed fifty dollars for groceries, so we'd go get five hundred big totem poles. We'd do them all in one night. The women working at the factory couldn't believe we could do so many.

We painted thousands of them sometimes. One month we made nearly a thousand dollars painting totem poles. We run them right out of unpainted ones. I paid for the first car I ever owned by painting totem poles. Carole and her family painted totem poles for years. Her dad had designed the damn things. I got started because of her family.

Another time we was broke and there wasn't no totem poles to paint, and I got thinking what we could do with pinecones. In the winter, we'd make wreaths with nuts and cones and evergreens — quite nice pieces, really. But this was summer, and tourist season was on. Damn, there wasn't no work no place. So we thought we'd make little birds out of cones. We collected different kinds of cones, every sort we could find. We made goony birds, with beady eyes. We bought packages of eyes and bought glue and some paint. We went to rummage sales and bought these old-time hats with feathers on them, and we used wild bird feathers from road kills too. Them goony birds was real cute when we got through. I made birch-bark stands for some of them. We'd glue the cone birds on there and then paint feet on them.

God, did we sell them birds! I sold them for $5.50 a dozen, and we sold the hell out of them. Doesn't seem like much money now, but back then it kept us going. Me and Carole done other handicrafts for selling: porcupine-quill chokers, black-ash baskets. We made chokers, triple strands and single ones too. I make pipes out of horn. I like working with my hands, and there's been times we really needed the money. We wouldn't have had nothing otherwise. It's keeping up the heritage too, especially with the baskets and quillwork. And there's special feelings in doing good work with your hands. But I'll tell you, handicrafts has put lots of meals on our table. It beats being on welfare, that's for sure.

Carole and I would keep stuff we'd made in the car — chokers, quill boxes, different things. We'd be in a bar or visiting somewhere and get to talking. I'd mention stuff we'd made. And heck, I don't know how many times they'd say, "You got any of that stuff with you?" I'd say, "Well, yeah, I do. Just a minute. I'll be right back." I'd go to the car and get several chokers and a box or two, and we'd end up selling them.

Sometimes you get pissed at the cheap sons of bitches that want to buy it like they did fifty years ago from the Indians. Everything for nothing. They don't realize the time involved or the skill. And if it isn't the tourist trying to cheat you, it's the one selling to the tourist. They want stuff for nothing, and then they double or triple the price.

Work

Years back, from the stories my Aunt Agnes told me, the Indians didn't have no room to bargain. They made black-ash baskets and did quillwork. By God, they needed the money. They wasn't in no position to hold out. They had to sell stuff to eat. People knew that. I talked to my Aunt Agnes. She knew she was getting screwed, but she was hungry. She told me she'd make a big market basket. I don't know if you ever made baskets, but let me tell you, that's hard work. She told me the best she could get out of it was two dollars. For the little baskets, she'd get maybe a quarter or fifty cents. That's the way it was when an Indian was hard up.

Indians was exploited back then. Like at the Indian Village tourist shop down there along the harbor, they got dirt-cheap wages making baskets and little tepees, tourist stuff like that. They never got decent pay. Old man Eby kind of took care of the Indians here. He owned the Indian Village. He let them live down there in shacks covered with birch bark. That's where most of Carole's family was. I hung around with an Indian fellow, Frank Moses, then, and we'd go in them shacks. This was in the 1950s, but it went way back through the years. Indians would sit in them shacks and make baskets. I'd look in there and see them when I was a kid, just like the tourists did. Eby didn't pay no good, but he was nicer to Indians than most of the people around here were.

White people controlled things back then. Mostly they still do. They always run things, I guess. I don't know of any Indians my age that have businesses or stores and like that. Whites own them. Whites run the fishing tugs, and Indians was hired hands. Whites made the money. Indians did the work. I can see that now.

Indians mostly lived near other Indians, scattered around, but near too, like Vee Pash, the Third Ward, down where Paquin Street is. "Empty pockets," it means. That was an Indian area. In the old days, all the Paquins fished out of the old dock there, just down from Miles Cabins. The old Third Ward school was there. The story was that my great-grandfather and great-grandmother donated that land to the city for the school. Somehow white people ended up owning it. But that's the way it goes around here.

Groscap was another Indian area. Old Indian families lived there: the LaVakes and Antoine Paquin. But in the town area it was mostly Third Ward where Indians lived. Now that I'm thinking on it, some of this seems odd to me. How could Indians have owned land to give to the city? My grandmother owned property down there where the Dairy Queen is now. My Uncle Eddie had land on the harbor near where the tanks is now. He lived in a little shack there. White people own all of it now.

Sometimes in the winter when there wasn't no work, I'd run a trapline. I did quite a little of that, but not on a big scale, because I couldn't afford much gear, like stretchers and traps. Them are expensive. But I did it when I could to make a few extra bucks, and I did it because I like being in the woods that way too. I haven't trapped for years, though. I trapped muskrat, mink, beaver, coyotes, and rabbits too. I enjoyed trying to outsmart rabbits. I enjoyed trying to outsmart all them animals. The last animal I caught that was worth anything was a fox. God, that's been a long time, maybe ten years. I had two foxes stolen on me that year. I got thirty-four bucks for the one I got.

I remember when I was young, I set traps for beaver. The water wasn't deep where I was. Generally you set two or three traps on a spring pole. I found a nice sapling, and I bent it. Usually I'd knock a spike in a tree and hook the sapling under it so when the beaver got caught, he'd pull it out from under the spike and—*whoom!*—up goes the spring pole.

One time I had trouble getting this pole set right. I slipped it under the tree limb. "A pretty slick job," I was thinking. I was squatted there, admiring my work, and wham! That spring pole popped and cracked me across the nose. I fell backward, out cold. When I woke up, I couldn't remember what happened. It's weird when you're knocked out like that. Well, I got it set OK after that. By now a big bruise was rising across my nose. I went back the next day, and, damn, I'd caught a little black dog, cute little fellow. I had a hell of a time getting him out. I took him home and fixed his paw up. We kept him for a long time, but then he run off.

I never made much money trapping. And people stole animals out of my traps when I worked the day shift for Tom Shaw that time. I'd walk my trapline in the evening. When I was done, I'd sit there listening to the sounds in the woods, lots of sounds. I like being in the woods like that.

Other times I did the flea markets. Carole and I went to rummage sales and auctions all the time. Then I got more interested in antiques. Carole did too. We did our house in antiques, but then we sold them all. I still fool around with them when I can find a good deal, one I can turn over quick and make a few bucks. I sold to dealers a lot. You don't make as much that way, but you can move stuff fast.

I'd set up at the flea markets. I usually did good. I like wheeling and dealing with the public. Everybody's hustling, trying to put something over or trying to grab something for cheap. So you get some scheming going on. I was good at it. I could tell the lookers from the buyers. When I first started with antiques, I wish I had known more, because ten years ago you could pick up stuff pretty reasonable. Now it's rough to find antiques without paying a lot for them. Then it's hard to turn a profit.

I been stung a few times, but I made more money than I lost. There was times I didn't have work and kept us going with antiques. I'd go to a rummage sale, look around, and not see nothing, and I'd ask them, "Any more stuff around?" Well, sometimes they'll let you look in their attic or garage or barn, and you find real good stuff. Lots of times you don't too. Or I'd hear that maybe some people had old things in their house, and I'd go knock on their door. I'd say, "So-and-so told me you had some antiques for sale," just trying to get my foot in the door. I found good stuff that way sometimes.

So I'm always looking to grab a few dollars buying and selling. It's fun.

Fishing

You got to do lots of jobs if you're going to make it in a place like this where there ain't much steady work. But through the years, I've fished for a living more than anything else. Fishing is in my blood. I love doing it. I hope I don't never have to quit.

I never made much money fishing as a kid, but I learned things what come in handy when I went into the business myself. Floyd got me my first real job at Colby's fishery, where he was working. What Colby did was he'd ship herring and he'd box these smelts after they was cleaned by us. He hired a bunch of women that boxed them in little pound boxes, and they had a little machine that put cellophane on them. They shipped them into Canada, I think.

For cleaning fish we had a great big long bench—the gut board, we called it. You could stand up to it, and it had holes in it where you scraped the fish innards into a bucket below. I was short then—I was only nine years old—so I stood on a box. We got four cents a pound for smelt and a cent for herring. We got them pan-ready—cut the heads off and cleaned the innards out. For scaling the herring, they had a big circular-like drum with diamond-shaped mesh all around it and a belt on it with a motor. They'd stick eight or nine hundred pounds of herring in there, turn it on, and round and round it would go, taking the scales off them. Then we'd get them.

We had a galvanized bucket with handles on each end. It held probably fifty pounds of cleaned smelt, and the same amount of herring. When we'd fill that up, another bunch would be over there. They'd weigh them. Then the women would wash them up good. That was their job.

When Colby got these smelt in, Jerry Paquin—my distant cousin—was steady making boxes. Couple other guys did too. All

Fishing

the guts of the herring and of the smelt were saved and packed in trays about four inches tall and three feet long by two feet wide. Then they froze them. They'd ship them frozen guts to mink farms all over the place. So nothing went to waste. Nobody does that around here anymore. They just throw them in the dump. Seems like a waste, if you could feed something with them.

Colby's wife hated me. I didn't like her either. She'd say to Colby, "You ain't going to pay that little son of a bitch. He's not worth nothing." She was on me ever since I come in there. Donny and I locked her in the freezer one time. Goddamn, we never told nobody she was in there. Somebody happened in there to get something and found her. She wasn't half froze or anything, but her ass was damn cold. We cut her hose when she was cleaning the windows one time. I always gave her the finger when she wasn't looking. I can't remember how it started with me and her. But we never got along.

Then we'd go over to this eating place. They had a little coach, part of a boxcar. There was two of them in town. We'd sit there. I'd always order a hamburger, a Pepsi, and peanuts. Used to put the peanuts inside the Pepsi after you take a few swallows and eat them like that and drink it. I felt proud about having my own money to spend.

I worked for a guy named Fritz Halbert and his wife, Bonnie. We're very good friends to them to this day. I really like them. Of all the fishermen, Fritz and his two brothers treated me the best. Never that much pay, but they wouldn't work me over eight hours a day. Not like them other fishermen. They work you sixteen, eighteen, hours for eight bucks or ten bucks a day and never an extra dollar. With Fritz and them we worked hard, but if we was over eight hours, they paid me overtime.

When I was twelve years old, I went down there and asked them for a job. Oh, boy, did he do a business! We had the Mackinac ferryboats then, and the people had to wait for the ferry to go across, and they'd sit sometimes for hours. Fritz had several people selling smoked fish for him. They got 25 percent of what they sold, and they was making over a hundred dollars a day each, just the sellers.

Halbert's was called Lazy Bob's, and the restaurant was right next to it — the Bellaire restaurant. Talk about a business! We'd open that smokehouse, and people would rush down there, sometimes thirty or forty of them, sometimes more, just waiting for that fish to get done. They'd follow you right up to the fishery.

I scaled and cleaned fish for tourists that stopped in to get fresh fish. Bonnie was steady weighing and packaging the fish. She put a weight and price on it so we'd know what to charge. It was a pretty good business. You'd go through with the smoked fish, and other ones go through selling pop. They made good money. I think Fritz to this day is living off of that. I know he is. He just tinkers around now. He don't fish much. He fishes out of a rowboat too and hates the state game officials just like we do. They had a pet raccoon come down there. He'd steal my fish knife all the time and my broom. I always knew where to find stuff: right down that hole in the floorboard.

In the winter we'd go out and cut ice on the big lakes. Quite interesting work, the old-time way of doing it. At that time it was all done by hand with regular old ice saws and cedar saws. Now they got ice machines. They're bigger businesses now, so they really need them. I don't know of anyone around here now who puts up ice. That's quite a chore. Some got a little modern towards the end there; they cut it with a chain saw.

Back then you'd cut the ice in blocks that would weigh about a hundred pounds each. You'd buckle them around and get them on the truck. Then you'd have to unload them at the ice house. Fritz had a big ice house, a big old ugly-looking building. They'd put a layer of sawdust, then a layer of ice, and then sawdust over that. Sawdust would be covering all the ice when you was done.

In the summer, you'd go get a truckload from the ice house and bring maybe five or six chunks down to the fishery and hose the sawdust off it. When people would want a small chunk of ice, you'd buckle that ice around with a set of tongs and cut it and knock off a piece. I got so I could get nice square chunks off there. I think Fritz sold it for two or three cents a pound, maybe more. I know he got a few cents for it anyway.

Then, of course, I'd shave a lot of ice too. You'd shave some for packaging and for when people bring their coolers in. You can get a pretty good price for them old-time ice shavers right now. They had seven or eight points on them, a tapered edge. I got pretty handy with it. I could really shave it down.

It was time for me to get my paycheck the first week I worked. Fritz called me in. Bonnie was there and asked me what my Social Security number was. Well, jeez, I didn't even know what they was talking about. Finally Fritz said, "Well, how old are you, son?" and I said, "I'm twelve."

I was a damn good worker, so they talked it over and asked me to stay on. And I imagine if I would've got hurt or anything, Fritz would've taken care of me. I said sure. They paid me twenty-five bucks a week, big money to me. Every week Fritz or Bonnie called me aside and gave me an extra five or ten dollars. Bonnie would say, "Don't tell Fritz," and Fritz would say, "Don't tell Bonnie." Either one or both of them would sneak it to me at the end of the week. Why, hell, that was a good deal. Of course, they must have appreciated my help too. We worked hard. We really did. I earned that bonus.

Hagan had a fishery down there too. I worked for him off and on. I made boxes for him. One thing I did a lot for him is clean perch. Goddamn, I hate to clean perch. I got five cents a pound for cleaning them. He put us in a separate room, not even part of the fishery. We closed the doors to keep the flies out. You'd have to scale them perch by hand because that cheap son of a bitch wouldn't buy an electric scaler. Sometimes I'd make twenty-five bucks a day. Well, if I made twenty-five bucks, that meant I scaled and cleaned five hundred pounds of perch. Usually he'd have two hundred pounds or so for me to do. Perch have sharp fins what cut your hands. Goddamn, they're hard on the hands.

That's more or less what the fisheries was like. The boats was a different story. I first started on the fish tugs with Hagan, dressing fish. They was fishing chubs then, a delicious fish but they're real oily. You can't fry them to eat them. They use them strictly for smoking. I guess it was in 1964 when they got that botulism scare. Really, I don't think there was any botulism at all caused by the preparation of these fish. Some dumb son of a bitch bought one and left it in a sunny window for a couple days and then decided to eat it. They got awful sick or died; I can't remember which. So the scare was on. For years people wouldn't buy chubs. Before that, they was a good seller, but people was afraid of them after that. Floyd and I run a fishery in 1972 for Butch Slayover down here. We had chubs, and people would come in. They'd have you eat it and then come back later to see if you was sick before they'd buy one. You got to be careful when you smoke fish, that's for sure, but there's too many rules now. Them politicians always screw stuff up, and probably none of them know nothing about smoking fish.

I worked on fish tugs lots of times. Damn, I'd get seasick. And I was usually drunk the night before. Ain't nothing worse than seasickness and drunkenness or hangover. A few times I wanted to die. I don't get sick on an outdoor boat, but on them tugs the greasy smell and the old fish smell down in the bilge, where it's hot and everything is close, hangs heavy on you. It makes you puke when you don't feel good.

You set your nets using a spreader with a wheel on it. You put your corkline, which is the top line on a net, onto that wheel, and it

You set your nets using a spreader with a wheel on it. You put your corkline, which is the top line on a net, onto that wheel, and it spins around as your boat moves. Another guy stands there and lets the net out through his right hand if he's right-handed, and he watches for snarls. That's called spinning the net. That spreader takes the place of another man, because otherwise a man woud have to stand there and spread the top and bottom lines. You tie your nets together as they're going out.

For cleaning fish we had a great big long bench—the gut board, we called it. ABOVE *You could stand up to it, and it had holes in it where you scraped the fish innards into a bucket below.*

spins around as your boat moves. Another guy stands there and lets the net out through his right hand if he's right-handed, and he watches for snarls. That's called spinning the net. That spreader takes the place of another man, because otherwise a man would have to stand there and spread the top and bottom lines. You tie your nets together as they're going out.

When you lift them on a tug, they got what they call a lifter. It's a big circular wheel with cogs on it. Once you get your net in there, that wheel keeps rotating and pulls the net in. There's a tray on the boat side of the wheel and then a big board, like a dressing board in a fishery. These nets come in and across the tray onto the board, and you steady pick fish out of the nets. Now, when you're fishing chubs, you got what they call an awl. You put it in your hand, and you punch the fish just below the lower fins or in the belly to puncture a sort of air bag inside the fish.

Another guy stands there and boxes the nets up after the fish is picked. He gets out snarls and packs the nets in boxes, and you got a man at the wheel who's steering the boat, keeping it up to the net so that the net stays close to the boat. You want the nets straight up and down when you're pulling them. The guy at the lifter picks fish too. Then the other guy will box, or else the guy off the lifter will box. Everybody does a lot of helping. Usually three men can run a tug. I've done it with two, but that's awful rough.

When a box is full of nets, you bring it to the stern, where they're going to be set out. They had me on the tug when I first started for just dressing the fish, and oh, boy, I'd get a few hundred pounds dressed and I'd start feeling sick. Damn! I'd puke every day – dry heaves sometimes. We usually dumped the guts for the sea gulls next morning, at break of day, because when we went in these tugs, we'd have about a three- or four-hour ride just to the nets. The guts in that barrel would be a foot deep, and them chub guts is a stinky mess. Oh, they're rank. One time I began feeling terrible sick. They tied a rope in the bow. I'd hang onto that rope and barf. I had my head over the gut barrel. That damn *Falcon* – that was the boat's name – she'd roll before a storm would even start the sea going. An awful son of a bitch to work on, she was. But it blew wild that day. She took a flip, a roll, and I lost hold of that rope. I fell headfirst into them rotten guts. Did I puke then! My friend Bob Henry laughed. He just roared.

Talk about a bad day! We had an old potbellied wood stove, and we had a good fire going. God, the wind really howled that day. I was bent over when she took a roll. I lost my balance and slid

Fishing

backwards. That stove was red hot, and I went ass-first into that stove and burned myself. I fell and bashed my elbow. Bob was out of control, laughing. He really thought that was funny. I didn't think it was very goddamn funny. I hurt.

I worked on this other tug with Elvin Gustafson. It had a little Kahlenberg diesel engine in it. Hagan's had a marine gasoline engine in it. We called this Kahlenberg a one-lunger; it was a one-cylinder engine. We was fishing up to Cedarville then. Damn, it'd take us four hours to get to the nets sometimes. On a rough day we'd go up one wave and slide back two. I don't think it went eight miles an hour. I worked on that one for a while, not long.

This other boat I fished on was called *Hans*. It had a big ninety Kahlenberg in her, a three-banger; it had three cylinders. When I first looked at that motor, I said to Floyd—he was working there too, "How do you ever start the thing?" Well, you should see what you got to do to get it going. I'll try to remember. Before you shut the engine off, you had to build your air up in the tanks because it took air to start them. Well, them tanks were full of air. There was a jet on the top of each cylinder. You had to turn them on and torch them—get them jets hot and the head hot on top there. But first you had to turn your flywheel to a certain position, so you took a big rod there—the flywheel had holes in it. You turned it. You had to fill two oil resevoirs and oil several places on the engine.

When these heads got hot, you torqued it down. That flywheel started up, you added the air, and that was supposed to start the engine going. Usually it did. Boy, talk about a job! You had to oil them all the time too, because it used a hell of a lot even when it worked right. On a day's run, we might go through several gallons. It was spitting oil into the bilge there. It shouldn't have been doing that. Something was wrong. Usually they have a return on there where this oil accumulates. Then you can put it back into the oil boxes—Kahlenbergs is really quite the deal. They'd just chug along. I swear them things would run underwater.

I worked on the *Seaberg* too, an old wooden ship. It was a diver—ready to sink, I mean. But the nicest tug I worked on was the *C and R* for Carl and Ray Halbert. They still own that boat. They'll probably sell it soon. Carl's fished since 1919. They're getting old. They're both in their eighties. Every year you ask them if they're going to quit, and they says, "No. Well, we might." But they won't. They'd die if they quit.

The *C and R* is a thirty-eight-footer, all steel, with a Caterpillar engine. I enjoyed working on that boat; it was really nice. And Carl and Ray was always good to me. Every spring before we'd head out, I'd help fix the boat. I'd clean that bilge out and put Rust-Oleum in her and paint her up every year. She looked brand-new.

Boy, that one time, though, I was lucky. I was below, down by the bottom part of the engine, in the bilge. It was greasy, so I asked Carl to give me some gas. I don't know why I said that or why Carl even gave it to me. He had a little yellow bucket there, and he put a couple inches of gas in it and handed it to me. I got this rag, and I was dipping it in there and wiping out that oil and grease. All of a sudden I began singing—I was getting high. I remember saying to myself, "I got to get out of here." I climbed up through the hole in the bilge and fell to my knees right on the deck. I was dizzy and felt weird. Boy, I'll tell you, if I was ever sentenced to death, the gas chamber would probably be the way to go, because other than the mental thing of knowing you was going to die, you'd go out smiling. But that boat there I really liked.

Well, that's about the gist of it on the fishing, on how it's done. But there's other things too, like the elements against you—the winds, the waves, the fog, and the snow—and that's just on top of the water. Here's what you'll get in your nets. You get red bug, they call it—little red bugs that get in the web of the nets, in the knots. What a mess! Then in August and September you get hair snakes. They ball up like snakes, but they're real skinny like a hair. You get balls and balls of them. I've seen them a foot deep on the aft deck after we got done setting nets back. You don't want them to dry in your nets or you'll never get them out. The only way you can get them out of your nets is to soak them down with a soap solution, and they straighten out. The movement of setting the net back knocks them loose. So that's really a mess with them hair snakes.

You got green moss and black moss. Now, when you get green moss in your nets, you got to bring them in to dry. You put them on a big drying reel. You reel them on there and let the sun hit them. That moss turns like powder when it dries. So you usually put on a pair of gloves, and you reel these down and rub them and the moss comes out. Black moss is the worst. It's like steel wool, and it sticks to your nets. You got to put the nets in shallow water and the surf will take it out, or you set them where some suckers or a lot of trout will get in and shake it out. But usually when we set them nets back with the black moss in them, we soak them good with soap, and it makes them slippery. Some fishermen, if they got lots of nets, they just soap them down and leave them, and that black moss rots. It comes out a lot easier then, too.

Then there's the brown slime. If you're lifting on the ice, brown

Fishing

slime in your nets looks like about forty guys stood there and spit tobacco on the ice. Oh, it's a mess. We usually take soap with us and get that out of there.

So you got the red bug, the hair snakes, the black moss, the green moss, the brown slime. Now, that's just nature's elements. You also got human stuff. There's lumber; there used to be a sawmill here. We've got cables, lamp chimneys, women's underwear, tampons, paper, clinkers from the freighters. You name it, I've caught it in my nets.

One time during an east blow Floyd and me was fishing out front in the St. Ignace harbor—that's what we call it right off St. Ignace here. Them nets was going right down the lake. They was moving. I had to stand on the splash rail of the boat to catch the buoy. We got it in, and the nets was full of lumber. I was boxing nets, and I seen something purple. Floyd didn't catch them, and they come around the tray. Human bones! There was a skull and some other pieces in the nets. They must have been down a long time, because they was purple.

I get bad feelings from dead things. Floyd shut the lifter off, and we talked about it. We thought about bringing them in to shore. Bodies been lost out there, and they never find them, because there's so much current. I've always been afraid I'd get a body in my nets. I'm not a religious man, but I have prayed in my life. I bunched the nets up and hung them over the lake. I took my knife, said a prayer, and cut them loose. Down they went. That's their proper burial ground. Why, you know what some idiots would've did if we'd took them in. First thing they would've thought was that they're Indian bones. They'd have taken them and chipped them and x-rayed them and took pictures and put them in a museum. To me that's not right.

For years here, just right down from the place where I used to live—the last place on the right when you're going over the hill—there was an Indian burial ground. There must have been either a war or big sickness or something, because there was more than fifty Indian skeletons there and their belongings. So what'd they do? They left a big open grave and let people charge admission to see the graves. These tourists just got to see some Indian bones. Damn, that makes me mad. Well, it took that organization we had, the North American Indian Association, a while, but we closed the place down.

I'm getting off the subject, but let me tell you how ignorant people are. Just north of town there's the Kabaret Bar—used to be the Harbor Light. Well, the story was that there was a paupers' graveyard there. I knew it was true. So we was putting in water lines, and there was maybe a dozen skulls and all sorts of bones. I got out of the ditch. Well, some tourists at Shore's Restaurant comes over. This girl about ten years old stood there. She said, "Oh, Mommy! Oh, Mommy, Daddy! Will you get me some Indian bones?"

Did that make me mad! And he was going in the ditch to get some. I took a skull. Normally I wouldn't touch anything like that. I dropped the skull, and I seen this other piece of this bone. I grabbed it, and I said, "You ignorant bastards." I threw that bone at them. I said, "Take them. They ain't Indian bones. They're white man's bones. Still want them, you ignorant bastards?"

My boss rushed over. "Ron," he said, "cool it."

I said, "Yeah, I'll cool it. I'll cave his head in." I said, "You ignorant sons of bitches. You want them now—white people's bones? You want them now? Want to bring them home and put them in your showcase? Or bring them to school?"

"You better quit mouthing off," that guy said, "or I'll come down in that ditch."

I said, "You don't have to come down here. I'll come up there." I quick climbed out of that ditch, and you want to see somebody run? He took off.

People are such fools. I wonder how he'd feel if I dug up where his ancestors is buried and put them on display? I wonder what'd happen if I went over to the Catholic cemetery with a shovel and started digging? Well, I better get back to the fishing stuff I was telling about.

Fishing is a dangerous way to earn a living. If I was to list all the fishermen I know who's drowned, it would fill a couple of these pages you're reading. I know that's hard to believe, but it's true. These lakes have claimed my friends. I've almost drowned a few times. My nephew Eddie died when he went through the ice with me while we was winter fishing. God, that was such a terrible day, I hate to think about it. I'll tell you that story some other time. I haven't got the stomach for it now.

Like I told you a while ago, I did mostly construction work after me and Carole got married. But a few years later—around 1970, I think—Indian fishing got going, and I saw a chance to get into the business for myself and make some good money. I been fishing ever since—other things too, but mostly fishing. Let me tell you about Indian fishing. It's quite the deal.

I better explain some things first. My ancestors, the Chippewa people, signed treaties with the United States in 1820, 1836, and 1855. They signed other ones too, but them are the important ones

Fishing

for fishing. The Chippewas sold most of their land to the States, but they held on to some property and kept their 1 hunt, fish, and gather the natural products of the land—the "usual rights of occupancy," the 1836 treaty says. That's what the treaties read, and that's what the courts have said is true after a lot of legal hassles the last few years. White people forgot about them treaties right after signing them and just tromped all over the Indians. They took their land and rights and never paid the money they owed. White people made Indians into paupers, drove them right down and never gave them a chance to make something of themselves. They discriminated against them. All them years, the state of Michigan claimed to own the animals and fish and flat ignored our treaty rights till we started fighting back.

At first, things was real uncertain as far as the Indian fishing went. Nobody knew what was going on. We was sneaking nets in the lake. We had heard the Indians had the right to fish, but we didn't know just what the deal was. The name *Jondreau* was mentioned. We always said an Indian someplace got the right by going to court.

My brother, Floyd, and me was working in Slayover's fishery then. We heard about a meeting at the St. Ignace Legion Hall, and that this Jondreau fellow who had the right to fish would be there. So we went. Maybe two hundred people showed up. This was probably in 1972. Old man Hatch was there—Fred Hatch, Sr., who sort of fathered the Sault tribe of the Chippewas, got it started. He brought something to the meeting what looked like the original Durant roll, a 1907 list of Indians put together by the government. He gave a talk about how we had an Indian right to fish. "Show me your grandparents on that roll, and I'll give you a card so you can fish," he said. Hatch was the only one there from the tribe, but Jondreau was in the audience and he gave us a speech saying, "Don't let them take your rights away, whatever you do. I won my court case."

Now, I had never thought much about my genealogy or about being an Indian. I didn't know nothing, not even who my grandparents was. But I got the drift that Indian rights was real. When people was through talking, everybody got in line to look at that roll. "Find your grandparents, and I'll write you a card," Hatch kept saying. Well, I got in line like everybody was doing. Floyd and I was standing there with no idea at all who our dad's parents was, and my dad was dead by then. My Aunt Agnes come up. "Do you boys know who your grandparents was?" she said.

"No," we told her.

She said, "Come here. I'll show you." She went right to that book and showed us our family descent. So we got our fishing cards from Fred Hatch.

I got interested in my Indian heritage. Chief Lambert, another founder of the Sault tribe, worked for the Indians then. He's in Washington, D.C., someplace now. I talked to him and older Indian people. I wanted to see the Treaty of 1836, to read it. I can't remember who got a copy for me. I wanted to know stuff for myself so as not to play the fool. I wanted to go to meetings and speak out, so I figured I ought to know what I was saying, not talking through my ass and just blowing hot air.

I got excited reading this stuff. It was hard because I don't read good. Carole helped me, and I struggled through it. But I got to know quite a bit. I saw in the treaty where the white people got lots of money, and the Indians didn't get nothing. Rix Robinson, a fur trader, got land and money, and them others like Henry Schoolcraft, the Indian agent, made out too. Some old Chippewa chief would get maybe a hundred dollars, and the white men got rich.

Waunetta Dominic, head of the Northern Michigan Ottawa Association, gave me some histories of Indians. I got to know her through Indians from down below in the lower Penninsula of Michigan. She was one of a few people who spoke out for the Indians around here at that time. She tried to organize the fishermen so they could protect their rights by drawing up some regulations. She set up a meeting in Petoskey. About forty of us showed up. She said

Fishing has been good for Indians around here. . . . It give them some pride and made them see things they ain't never seen before. I never knew nothing about my heritage till this got going. . . . I also began to see how white people discriminated against me and other Indians. They won't never do that to me again, not to me and not to no other Indians, if I can help it.

that us fishermen should pick a chairman to run the meeting, and they chose me. So we talked out what we should do, and I had a chance to meet Mrs. Dominic. I asked her lots of questions after the meeting, and she gave me stuff to read.

When Indian fishing seemed like it really would happen, I wanted to know more about the treaties and being Indian and all. After I read the stuff Mrs. Dominic give me, I talked with people, mostly older white commercial fishermen about their troubles with the DNR, Michigan's Department of Natural Resources. And I talked to my Aunt Agnes. She'd tell stories about Indians and fishing. Everybody fished, she said, white and Indian, to get food for their families.

For the first time, you could get something for being Indian, something worth having. People started claiming Indian who you'd never figure for it or who had even denied it a few years back. They wasn't necessarily so much proud of being Indian as trying to see what they could get out of it. The proudness come later, I guess.

Fishing has been good for Indians around here. It riled them up, made them mad. It give them some pride and made them see things they ain't never seen before. I never knew nothing about my heritage till this got going—never learned no history, no treaties. Well, maybe that don't mean much. It's no big deal, I guess. But I also began to see how white people discriminated against me and other Indians. They won't never do that to me again, not to me and not to no other Indians, if I can help it.

I had seen what a fisherman could make for money, so I knew that I could do good if I had my own rig instead of working for someone else. I began treaty fishing in the summer of 1972. Man, it was all hassles for a long time, several years there. Jondreau's people signed different treaties from mine, so his case didn't apply to fishermen like me. The state of Michigan decided to fight the Indians. My tribe went to court too, but till it was decided, the state threw the works at us.

The night after that meeting with Fred Hatch and Jondreau, I set nets in the St. Ignace harbor—out front, we call it. The state game wardens knew what was going on, but they only watched for a while and didn't do nothing. Then one Sunday they started pulling our nets. Me and an Ottawa friend, Johnny Alexander, seen what they was doing, so we hopped in our boat and started chasing them. They dropped the nets, didn't get them all. The wardens went down the lake, and we come right behind them. I held up an oar. We heard later that they thought it was a gun. My cousin was working at the jail then and heard on the two-way radios that we was chasing them, going to shoot them maybe. They pulled in by one of the docks in St. Ignace there.

I seen that the nets were Johnny's and Floyd's, so I asked Johnny what he wanted to do. I leaned over to look at the nets, and one of the game wardens grabbed my arm. I said, "You better cut loose of me, because you have no right to touch me."

There was a rookie cop there, a new one probably fresh out of the academy. Johnny told him, "You guys don't have no right here."

That new cop got real mad then and told us that he'd soon show us. He was going to strip off his badge, everything.

I said, "The smartest thing for you to do is just put that hat and coat back on." And he did do that.

The game wardens took Floyd and Johnny to civil court in St. Ignace. Floyd got a sharp lawyer, Bill James, from the legal services in the Soo. He had the case dismissed on some technicality.

Next thing they tried was on a day when it was real foggy, so Floyd and I didn't lift our nets. We had set some old nets we bought from a friend, and they had wooden corks on them, so they was easy to identify. Genie Thomas, my cousin, come up to me and said, "You better check that DNR boat there. They got nets with wooden corks. Are them yours?"

I said, "Yeah, probably." I went down there, and sure as hell they was mine.

I got on the phone to Jack Douglas, our game warden for this area, and I said, "Jack, what's going on? You got no right to pull my nets."

"They weren't marked," he said.

"Yes they was," I said. "You guys ran around in the fog and found some jugs. They was marked. You better set them back in the lake tomorrow."

I think that was the first time in history that the DNR set back so-called illegal nets they had seized. They was reset wrong, but they were set back. The DNR even picked clean a big snarl. I asked them where the fish was. "Oh, you only had eight fish," they said.

I was mad about what they done, so I wrote to Governor Milliken. It took several months to get an answer. He told me that a very qualified man on that boat, Mr. Olson, used to be a commercial fisherman. He said that if I thought any damage was done, we could take it to small claims court. But the nets did go back in the lake.

The DNR tried to grab my nets another time. They was steady on us, and they kept it up for years. I had eight boxes of nets out here in Lake Huron when we heard that we had to pull all our nets. I called Jack Douglas and asked him what the story was. I said, "Did you get a letter or a phone call, or what did you get?"

He said, "A phone call. You guys got to pull all your nets." He told me we had to have them out by noon.

I said, "I got eight boxes out there," so he said he would give me more time.

Next morning, it blew wild, really storming. We did lift the small mesh. We had about five hundred pounds of menominees, which isn't much. You only get thirty-five cents a pound for them dressed. So I told Paul Simkins, my partner, to bring them fish to the fishery and sell them. I told him I'd pull the whitefish nets, but I was going to leave half of them in. We had four boxes set. Paul's a trembler sometimes. He didn't know quite what to say, so he kept quiet.

I pulled the two boxes. Just as I got done and started the engine up, here comes a DNR boat. Olson was running it, I think, a fatso. He pulled up beside me and said, "You got your nets pulled, Ron?"

I pointed at the ones in the boat, and I headed for my other gang about three-fourths of a mile away. Olson followed me for a while and then moved on ahead. He found my buoy and lifted it aboard his boat. I headed toward them, but they pitched the buoy back in the water and turned toward shore. I drove to the dock. My wife was waiting there. She told me the DNR had come into the marina and had took their gear off.

Everything looked OK. Paul come over to see what happened, and we stood on the dock, shooting the bull. Good thing we did, because, jeez, I looked up and there was them DNR, heading for my nets again. Well, we jumped in my boat, but we only had a seven-horse engine on it, and it was foggy. By the time I got to the nets, they was starting to lift my nets into their boat. I yelled at them, "Hey, you sons of bitches, them are my nets."

The game warden looked at me and raised his fist. So I zipped to the other end of the nets and got a hold of the buoy. I never pulled nets so fast in my life. We was headed toward each other now from opposite ends of the gang. And I was wondering with Paul what we was going to do when we met up with the DNR. I told Paul, "I'm going to board them. They ain't getting my nets. Them are the best ones we got."

Paul never said nothing for a while. Then he said, "Well, I don't know, Ron. We got to be careful."

I said, "No we don't! They have no right to pull them." I had about five nets in when we heard a motor far off. Real dense fog had

Fishing

set in. Here came Floyd and Johnny. Carole told them what was going on, so they come out on the lake to help. We could hear them cursing them game wardens. We was getting close now. I yelled at them, "I'm boarding you. There's four of us now and five of you. We're kicking ass."

They untied the nets and zoomed off. They ended up with four on their boat, and I had six. Johnny and Floyd yelled, "We'll meet them at the dock."

I wanted to go with them because they had twenty horsepower on their aluminum boat, and it moved good. But I didn't, and I come in; seemed like it took forever. Carole met me at the dock, and we went looking for the DNR. They hadn't come in yet. We went to the Shell station, where their car was. They went to pull in, but when they seen us, they whipped the boat around and headed for the marina. We beat them to the marina and waited. Police cars was there too. They turned completely around and headed for the Coast Guard station. I was happy about that because that's right on our turf—federal property.

So we drove up there. The state police had blocked the driveway, so I couldn't get in. The state cop said, "Ron, cool down."

I jumped over the hood of his car and ran to the dock. The DNR come in, and I grabbed the line and tied their boat up. The argument started. I said, "Give me those nets. They're mine, and that's it. You guys don't own them. You had no right to pull them."

That one game warden was taking pictures; he took them on the lake too. He kept smiling, like it was funny. I was standing above him, and I said, "I'll tell you one thing, mister. You smile one more time, and I'll kick your teeth in." I was wild mad but under control too. I said, "You think it's funny, but this is my living we're messing with. If you think it's so goddamn funny, smile again, you son of a bitch, and I'll show you."

The state police lieutenant grabbed my arm. He said, "Ron, cool it."

"You know he's wrong," I said.

He said, "Well, he shouldn't be teasing you like that."

They started to unhook their boat and head out, so I jerked away from the state cop, jumped over the rail, and got on their boat. That fat Olson yelled, "Get off my boat."

I said, "I ain't getting off. I don't care where you're going, back to Beaver Island or wherever, but I'm going with you. You got my nets, so I'll go where you go."

They idled the engine down so we was just floating. Johnny said, "Well, Ron, take them f-f-f-fuck-fucking nets and throw them right in the lake. We'll d-d-d-dive for them later." Mad as I was, I laughed because he stutters when he gets excited and when he gets mad. John is a handful when he's mad.

They had three nets in one big bucket and one net in another bucket, a gray plastic fish bucket we use. When I grabbed Olson, the game wardens jumped me. They held me around the neck, the legs, the waist. And that pig of an Olson stepped in the box so I couldn't lift it. But I got it partway up, and Douglas put his foot in there too. I broke loose and shoved Olson to the deck.

Douglas stood there, and he said, "Ron, I don't want this."

"Why don't you stop it then?" I said. He was the boss in this area.

I stopped for a minute and then rushed for the nets. They jumped me again. The lieutenant of the state police was yelling, but he couldn't do nothing. Things were turning wild now. Then the Coast Guard commander, who we knew quite well, yelled, "Stop it! I'm in charge here. I don't know about this fishing deal. I don't know what your rights are. But I'll tell you one thing. You state people don't have power here. Tie that boat up till it's settled. Now, get in here and dock it." So they did.

We got in the car with the game warden for our area with Jack Douglas, and the state police lieutenant, and we were arguing. The state police said, "Ron, I don't know what to do."

"We do have the right to fish," I said. "It's been court-proven time and time again that we have the right." So I said, "What order did you get, Jack? Did you get something official? Where did you get the right to pull our nets?"

He said he got a phone call.

"There you go," I said. "What's going on here?"

"Ron, I got to do what I'm told," he said. "If I said what I believed and they heard me, I'd get fired."

I feel sorry for the game wardens sometimes. They're the laymens in the Department of Natural Resources, the blue collar. The white collar sit on their asses and give orders, but the poor game wardens are taking the rap for the whole works.

Jack told me, "From one week to the next they're writing up laws which aren't laws. They're rulings. And they're doing it all the time. I can't keep track of them." He's a dedicated man. We've had our differences, but I respect him. He tells the truth.

We went into the Coast Guard station then, and we were talking. Well, before that, the DNR signed an agreement with the reservation Indians that they would not bother them until the court cases went through.

"Who gave you the right to sign with them and not us?" I said. "That treaty don't mention about no reservations. It says, 'Indians, Chippewa and Ottawa.' That's what we are in this town. You have no right to make an agreement with them without making one with us. I better get my goddamn nets back, because the next time I go down there, I'm going to kick some ass." Goddamn, I was mad.

"I'll tell you what I'll do," I said. "I'll give you one fish and one net for evidence if you want to bring me to court."

"Aw, I can't do that."

"OK," I said. "I'm going down there, and I'm going to tear up some green uniforms." I headed out the door.

"Hold it, hold it," he said. "It's against my principles, but, Ron, OK. That'll be the deal."

So we went down to the boats. He said, "Give Ron them three nets. We'll keep that one." Well, within the three nets, they said there was a couple brown trout in them. Then he said, "Ron, can I have one of them when you pick it out?"

I smiled. He said, "Ron, goddamn it, I mean it."

I said, "OK."

It's funny. They was going to trick me. They think we're all dumb because we're Indians. We don't have no degree or a college education or whatever, so they think we're stupid. Well, what it amounted to was they're going to give me the nets and not take me to court. I wanted to go to court. I demanded a ticket. The state cop said, "That's the first time I ever heard of anybody who wanted a ticket."

I said, "Use your head. If you arrest me, you got to have a reason. You can't take my equipment and not give me a ticket. If you take my equipment, you got to accuse me of some crime. You've got to give me a citation. You got to appear in court. So that's it. I want a ticket."

Nobody from the DNR would sign it. And that book passed around to different game wardens. Finally it come back to Jack, and he signed it. It read, "Ronald Paquin was illegally fishing in closed waters with gill nets without a commercial license."

So within ten days I was supposed to appear. Floyd and Johnny had to go to court on the following Monday, so I went with them to see what I could find out. I was standing there, waiting for them to get started, and I seen Jack Douglas come in. So I thought I'd see what he was going to do.

I hurried up the stairs and waited by the bathrooms; they're in the same hallway as the 92nd District Court. Jack stood in the courtroom doorway there, and he was talking to the magistrate. He said,

"Don't you go bringing Ron to court. We're not ready for him yet." So I took the ticket in, and I asked the judge what he was going to do about it. I laid the ticket down. I haven't heard nothing about it since.

I went to meetings after that. One time at Escanaba, Fred Dakota, the chairman of the Keweenaw Tribe, was there, and Art LeBlanc from Bay Mills Indian community. Chief Lambert of St. Ignace and another leading local Indian, Edwin Moses. Neither knew much about fishing, so they asked me to go with them. We went on our own, with no invitation. We sat there, and everybody stared at us, wondering who we was.

Well, reporters from TV channels 9 and 10 was there, and when they come into the meeting, Fred Dakota told them to get out. He said, "We never get fair coverage from the news media."

Well, this reporter got mad and called us "no-good fucking Indians," his very words. Later on, when they let him back in the meeting, he apologized for what he said and promised that we would get fair coverage.

I was sitting there when they asked us who we was. We introduced ourselves, and I said, "We're here representing the St. Ignace Indians." That was all we said, "St. Ignace Indians."

The meeting consisted of the reservation Indians trying to cut us nonreservation Indians out. Talk about underhanded. But there's a clause in the treaty that says if you live on or near a reservation, you are considered a reservation Indian. So I asked, "Does anybody in this meeting know how far 'near' is?" Nobody answered. Well, far is really near nowadays, what with the transportation we got.

The meeting went on and on. Nothing got done. Some lawman for the DNR, used all them million-dollar words trying to confuse us. I told him, "Break it down into layman's language, and we can talk all day." The only reason they use them big words is to be evasive anyway. They don't want to answer you, because they might find out that you have some kind of challenge to their facts.

During intermission, Fred Dakota came to me and introduced himself, and he said, "Ron, Indians got to stick together here."

I said, "Yeah, let's stick together."

The bigwigs from the DNR was there too. Prior to this I never even knew who these men was, let alone meet them. At intermission time I was standing on the porch, and I got a hand on one shoulder and a hand on the other, and there they are standing one side of me and on the other. "How you doing, Ron?" they said.

I said, "Oh, I'm doing fine."

They was up to something, but I didn't know what. So we went back into the meeting, and I was pretty worked up by now. I stood up and told Fred Dakota, "You reservation Indians, you blanket Indians, you sit on your ass, cross-legged, and let the government feed you, clothe you, house you, and you're going to condemn us and try to steal our rights to commercial fish. You going to condemn us for hustling for a living? Who do you think you are?"

Till now, I hadn't grasped what they were scheming. Then I did. They had a brochure on commercial fishing, and they had a little card written up for the nonreservation Indian. It said, "No commercial fishing."

I asked, "Can I see that?" I pretended to read it, skim through it. The whole thing was clear now. I said, "You can't do this." And I ripped them papers up in front of all their eyes. "This isn't worth wiping my ass on," I said. "You have no right to do this, and you know it. We have the right to fish. It don't say nothing in that treaty about reservation Indians having priorities to the rights. It says, 'Indians, Ottawa and Chippewa Indians,' but there's nothing about reservations. So we're going to keep fishing."

After that, the reservation Indians tried it again. They were on some TV program, and the news media asked the chairman at Bay Mills, "Does it hurt you reservation Indians to have the nonreservation ones fishing?" He said, "Oh, yes, it sure does." So they really tried to get away with it there, to make us look bad.

I don't know what happened then, but we got along good after that. Indians stopped scrapping with each other. But white people just never quit, not for years and years. They steady went at us, just steady.

The attorney general for Michigan is Frank Kelley. What a jackass! He's elected by the people. He takes the sportsmen's part and tells the newspapers all sorts of things about Indians and treaties. He's going to win it in the courts, he says. Governor Milliken was just as bad. He was real good at using treaty fishing to win votes. He never even tried to present our side, let alone tell the truth.

Probably the worst of them politicians is Bob Davis, our congressman from up here. He presented a bill in Congress to the effect of abrogating the treaties and giving us some money. He runs all over talking against Indians. I seen Davis on TV, telling all this crap about Indian fishing. A couple days later I went to the high school basketball game in St. Ignace here. Who comes in but Davis! My wife got shook up because she knew what I'd do. I went over to

Davis, and I grabbed his hand. I shook it and held tight. I wouldn't let loose. I said, "Davis, what are you trying to pull, putting all that stuff on TV to rile the public up?"

"I believe you Indians are depleting the lakes," he said.

I said, "Listen. I'll tell you something. If you would've talked to both sides and then come to your opinion, I could converse with you. But you didn't give us a fair shake."

"Oh," he said, "I'll be glad to talk to you."

Yeah, I'll bet he would. I said, "We don't want to talk to you now. You already made up your mind. I can see as a politician you're bound to kiss ass with the majority, but get your goddamn facts straight!" I told him about Indians taking only about 25 percent of the total catch. I said, "Get that on TV and see if people still think we're raping the lakes. Goddamn, man, where are you coming from? You don't care about the truth. You're just looking for votes."

Well, my wife thought I was going to hit Davis, I guess, so she grabbed me by the arm and said, "Ron, what are you doing?"

"I'm trying to talk sense to this ass-kisser," I said. "That's all he is: a vote-hunting ass-kisser."

I know Davis's dad. I respect his dad, golfed with him. But how can we have good politicians? And it's going to go on forever. When they depend on the people to vote them in if the majority of the people is against something, whether it's right or wrong, they're going to go with them. So how can you have a decent government what gives minorities a fair shake? If they go with us, the people are going to vote them out. Goddamn that Davis! Why don't he quit his Congress job? Why in the hell don't he quit it and come fishing for a while, see what it's like? Don't condemn me because I, out of my Indian heritage, decided to go fishing. So he's got to explain himself before he can say I'm getting rich. He's fat-mouthing on TV about my goddamn living, and he's probably making forty-five thousand dollars a year. Well, why don't he put himself in the minority? We all can't become congressmen. Talk about money! They're the ones making the bucks.

There's nothing worse than a politician that hangs with the crowd. Them guys just go with the majority. Oh, yeah, Davis sat up there in a public hearing and said, "Well, I'll be glad to help with all the other programs for the Indian people. No doubt that they were mistreated." Crap! He didn't really feel bad about the Indian people. But seeing that everybody's against us on commercial fishing, well, he's going that way too. And he don't have much to do with our other programs. They've already been put through Congress. Who's he kidding? Are we going to get a fair shake out of these politicians? No way.

Sometimes I think there's more going on here than them political bastards hunting the people's votes. Just around St. Ignace, Indian fishing feeds and clothes and houses about two hundred people. That's two hundred people that aren't on welfare, and I don't see nothing wrong with that. But people don't want us to better ourselves. They'd rather keep us as laborers. And this commercial fishing's been going on for over a hundred years, not by the Indians but by everybody else, by white people. So now the Indians are exercising their rights, and that's wrong? I mean the government kept it secret a long time. Here this treaty was signed in 1836, and we just found out about it in 1972. I'd say that's sneaky, and it's no accident. The government has no right to make this a goddamn sportsman's paradise. Talk about greed. The sportsmen has got ten thousand lakes in Michigan. They got thirty-six thousand miles of creeks, rivers, and streams to fish, plus thirty-six thousand square miles in the Great Lakes, and they want them all. They're so greedy that they don't want to share nothing with us.

Them politicians mouthing off like that sort of gives the OK for the people to attack us Indians. I ain't through telling you about them politicians yet. They made a poor man out of me when I was doing good. Them are bad people. You got to watch them. I'll tell you more about them in a while. Right now I want to talk about the cops and vigilantes.

Everywhere we went in them early years, the cops was after us—some state police, but mostly the local ones, sheriffs and city cops. They wasn't upholding the law in no evenhanded way. They was flat out to get us however they could. We'd drive through Charlevoix, and you can spot an Indian fisherman a mile off, trailering a boat full of fish boxes, a spreader in the back, stuff like that. Well, you could probably smell some of them guys too. So we was driving, being real careful, and here'd come that goddamn sheriff. "You're going too fast," he'd say, or "Your taillights ain't working." And you know you're in for a lot of hassle: "Where you headed, fellows? Let me see your driver's license. You got your registration for the truck? How about the trailer? The boat? Well, you're going to have to come down to the station. Your trailer license run out two months ago. And I got to write you a ticket on that broken taillight." So there'd go a couple hours and fifty bucks. And they'd do it all the time: Wait for us by that sharp bend before you hit the drawbridge. Them bastards!

But when there was trouble on the beaches, them cops wasn't nowhere to be found. We been threatened and attacked. People wreck our nets and boats and trucks. They try to swamp us on the lakes. They shot at us a few times, trying to scare us off. Cops wouldn't help us then. They never come down to keep the peace. When we called them to complain, they was real evasive. I found out later that the cops was right in the middle of them troublemakers. A deputy sheriff was in that bunch what shot up our boats and blasted them sweet old people's house where we parked them. Piss on the cops. They got one law for white men and another one for Indians.

The state boys was in on this stuff too, in that group what got started in Charlevoix and Traverse City—Stop Gill Netters. SGN they called them. Now, them guys was talking violence against us. The Traverse City newspaper said they ought to put on sheets and join the Klan. People in the DNR helped them SGN guys. They gave them stuff and talked at their meetings. SGN was handing out Wanted posters with an Indian's picture on it. That picture was took by Myrl Keller. He works for the DNR. Them guys passed out bumper stickers: "Spear an Indian and Save a Fish." The FBI and the federal marshals sent here from Judge Fox's court in Grand Rapids stopped that stuff.

You people probably don't believe things like this goes on anymore. Well, it does. This is 1987 when I'm saying this, and there's guys on the TV talking all the time about the U.S. Constitution, how wonderful it is, and how we got all these rights because we're Americans. Bullshit! A man like me, a poor man, an Indian, ain't got no rights but the ones I fight for. And you people fought real hard to take them away too.

Them guys wasn't through when SGN busted up. The ones from Traverse City got another group going, the Grand Traverse Area Sportfishing Association (GTASFA). They wasn't no better than them first ones. This one guy, a public relations man from Lansing, flat denied there was any Indian rights, and he was talking violence. Hit the beaches, he said. John Scott, who run the Great Lakes Fishery for the DNR, gave a couple speeches to GTASFA. And Judge Richard L. Benedict, that judge from Leelanau County what convicted an Ottawa Indian, Art Duhamel, went to a few of them meetings too. Art went to jail for treaty fishing. All them guys was in it together. In cahoots they was. Put the boots to the Indians—that's their message.

I didn't worry about them guys so much. They was mostly mouth, yapping to their buddies at the Holiday Inn. On the beaches, they was mostly talkers too, but you wasn't never sure. Some of them had guns.

All them people, no matter what they did, wasn't going to keep me off the lakes. No way could they do that. I was making good money, and I wasn't going to let it go. I seen an opportunity to bring my dream together. Commercial fishermen around here what had a big rig or even a not so big one did OK. Their kids went to college. They had nice homes and drove new cars. You look at that and figure you could have it too. I could just picture myself being better off like that.

We got big lifts at first. To make $250 in one day was more than I had ever dreamed of. You didn't make it every day. It was feast or famine. But you made it often enough back then. I lived good that first summer, fishing out front of St. Ignace here. I paid my bills and put some money in the bank. Then they slapped that restraining order on us, and I couldn't fish no more. I figured, "My God, this is all going to stop." I worried about it and didn't know what to do. Even when they took it off, which wasn't long that first time, you never knew when they'd throw it back on.

I fished through that winter and the next spring, getting mostly beautiful lifts. It was sometime in the early 1970s, probably 1973. You didn't need many nets to earn a good living then. For a man like me, who'd been poor most of his life, the money seemed too good to true.

We began fishing to the south, then at Petoskey, Charlevoix, Torch Lake, and Rex Beach. Them areas hadn't been touched for years, and the lifts was hard to believe. We caught thousands of pounds of whitefish and trout—mostly trout, as I remember. We made excellent money, more than I had ever had before. This went on for several years, five maybe.

The big lifts stopped after a while, and we wasn't tonning up—catching a ton of fish—all the time, so I went into the fish business myself to see if I could make more money. Wholesale fish prices go up and down all the time, and it's hard for fishermen to make money. Mostly the fishermen get poor while middlemen make the bucks. The price of fish today is pretty much like it was twenty years ago, but the price of other stuff is way higher after all that inflation. For me, a small fisherman, it was hard to make enough money to live off when the big lifts stopped, so I figured to be a middleman myself.

I had did everything around the fishery when I was young, so I learned a lot. I helped brine the fish before we smoked them. Fritz Halbert would tell me to put so much salt on them. He put an egg in there or a potato. You had enough salt when the potato would float. I washed the fish after they was brined and put them on the racks in the smoker. I didn't know just when they was smoked enough, but he showed me how they was a deep brown when they was done. I knew how to run a fishery, in other words.

I got a smokehouse. My brother-in-law, Francis Moses, built it for me. I got a recorder for temperature. It's like an oven thermometer. You got to have one. There's lots of laws about smoked fish since somebody got botulism a few years back. I made a cooler from an old freezer to keep the fish in. Some fish I sold fresh; I filleted them and took them to restaurants. I had several that bought from me.

Whatever I couldn't sell fresh, I chunked up and smoked. I did pretty good that way. Now, I pocketed maybe $1.50 a pound for my fish instead of 30 or 40 cents if I took them to the fishery. After doing this for a while, I realized there was good money in it. I enjoyed it too.

Next couple seasons, I quit the business because I began catching so many fish down below. I didn't have time to travel so far, fillet, and smoke fish too. But it wasn't long before the big lifts was gone again and the price went to hell, so I got back into the business in a big way. I started packaging the smoked fish in shrink wrap and Styrofoam trays like they do meat in the grocery stores. Right away I got customers that wasn't interested before I packaged. I could sell all the fish I could smoke. I even bought fish from other Indian fishermen, but you don't make out so good that way.

I kept my business going right through the tourist season, till after Labor Day. And I'd try to smoke up a batch of menominees for the deer hunters in November, when we couldn't fish whitefish. The business was hard work. You put in long days, twelve to fifteen hours on the days you lift nets, but the money was worth it. I sold to about a dozen places during the summer—gas stations, grocery stores, fruit stands, and like that. Things went good for three years. I wasn't making the money I did at first, but I was doing OK. I was paying my bills and taking care of my family.

Then the closures started. You couldn't fish here. You couldn't fish there. They shut the waters, and I couldn't earn a living no more. For a while I had figured that I would be a fisherman. Fishing would be my job. The closures ruined that. I couldn't plan. I didn't know what to do. Get in? Get out? Buy more stuff? Sell everything?

Bureaucrats closed parts of the lakes because they thought so many fish was being caught in them places that the fish was being depleted till they couldn't reproduce. This is mostly bullshit. The lake trout is all planted. Don't none of them reproduce. If you want

Fishing

more fish, you just plant more of them, but you don't close the lake.

Everybody's talking conservation. The state claims the Indians got no rules. They say we're unregulated, that Indians are raping the lakes and ruining Michigan's multimillion-dollar sportfishing industry. Mostly it's the DNR saying this, but governor Milliken and Frank Kelley are saying it too.

Don't none of what they say make sense to me. How can you have conservation of planted fish? You can't. The state just wanted rich white people to catch them fish, not poor Indians, and that's the truth. Conservation had nothing to do with it.

Now, the DNR messed up people's minds in this town. They're always saying there's no rules, no limits. *Unregulated* is the word they used. These Indians is unregulated, just lawless, they say. Local people believed them lies after a while, and it made things bad for us. The newspapers printed this stuff too. Indians is raping the lakes, they said. The *Weekly Wave* in Cedarville, Michigan, was probably the worst, but other papers said things like I'm telling you now, and for a long time none of them told the truth or give us a fair shake. Their lies was hot copy.

At first, people in town wasn't worked up over Indian fishing. We had tiny beat-up boats, old motors, and just a few nets. Most of us had fished all our lives. Everybody knew we was fishermen. But outsiders stirred things up—MUCC [Michigan United Conservation Clubs] and Tom Opre in the *Detroit Free Press*. Things got hot around here. People was mad, but we just felt all the stronger about being Indian and keeping on.

In the old days I'd go in the bar to have a couple beers, and they'd say, "How's it going, Ron? How's fishing?" But when I'm fishing under treaty rights, they call me a no-good Indian behind my back and don't talk to my face at all. The bar turns hush when I walk in. Nobody's got nothing to say. Maybe it was outsiders caused it, but as I think of it, the more I believe it was envyness and old hatreds coming out. Even the Catholic priest here in St. Ignace give a talk right in church about it. He said, "You people should be ashamed of yourselves, abusing Indians because of fish."

The lawyer for the tribe, Dan Green, started talking like the DNR, said he was all worried about the fish. I agree that you got to practice conservation, but he didn't know what he was saying. Our tribe is run strictly by a few people, a tribal board of eight and a chairman, but really the chairman and the lawyer control most things. Out of all them people, there's two fishermen. I don't know what the other ones do, but they don't know nothing about fishing.

The board is the one what closed the lakes. They took away my living. Indians did that to me. They wanted to make money off the fishery like the DNR. They jacked up the license fees to pay our lawyer's salary, and then he shut the lakes off. It's hard to understand.

I was on the tribe's conservation committee for a while. I went to different meetings, and I listened to what people had to say. I negotiated with people from the state, the DNR, and the governor's office. I went to federal court in Grand Rapids and Charlottesville, Virginia. I met all them big wigs and watched them operate: judges, lawyers, college professors, politicians. I think all them people in white collars is all the same. It don't matter whether they's white or Indian, lawyer or politician. Watch them sometime. Listen to them. They all dress alike. They talk alike. They even walk alike. They must go to white-collar school somewhere to learn that stuff. But when they get together and start signing papers, a poor man like me is going to get the shaft. That's for sure.

Through them years, politicians and lawyers was sending all them papers back and forth, talking about this, negotiating about that, and discussing something else. They were drawing salaries while all this was going on, and collecting fees, getting fat off treaty-right fishing. But I was trying to pay my bills and feed my family by catching fish and selling them. Them lawyers and politicians never worried about whether my family was hungry or if the bank was going to grab my truck or the FHA take my house. They just pushed paper around and drew their pay.

I suffered when they started closing waters. I had took the risk and invested in a new truck, a good boat, motors, and nets. Part-time fishermen wasn't hurt like I was. They could go back to their jobs and wait it out. Maybe they was the smart ones. But guys like me what was trying to earn a living strictly by fishing got hurt bad, especially the small fishermen. It just went all to hell. I'm struggling for words, and I'm fighting back the tears. I don't know how to say it. I can't express the terribleness of them times for me. They were dark days. I lost most everything I had worked for over the years, and I haven't caught up yet.

When the bureaucrats closed the lakes to fishing . . . I couldn't pay my bills. By 1984 I was terrible poor, and I couldn't see no way out. . . . Chris took it real hard, us losing our home. It was the only place he could remember living in. . . . I felt sad too. I had lived in that house longer than anyplace in my life and raised my son there. I felt that I had lost something I'd fought hard to get. I liked living there. It give me security. It was my home.

Broken Dreams

When the white collars closed the lakes, I just could not catch very many fish. A fisherman like me has got to hit the spring and fall runs hard if he's going to make it. That's when you get big lifts. You got to make money then, or you're going to go under.

Well, every time they negotiated, they closed more waters. Pretty soon we couldn't hardly fish no place. Before this, in the fall I'd make enough to get my twine up and save some money to get through the winter. They closed us out of the fall runs for three years. I'd get so broke by December that I had to borrow money to survive.

They talked about conservation, protecting the fish, but I think it was all politics. And I don't believe them people ever considered the Indian families what was being fed and clothed from fishing money. They looked at maps and numbers and pushed papers around while we got poor. There was never no feelings for the human element—Indians trying to earn a living. Them white-collar bastards busted my dreams by shuffling papers like that.

This went on for several years, closing here, closing there, and each time I sunk lower. I couldn't pay my bills. By 1984 I was terrible poor, and I couldn't see no way out. When you're helpless like that, some people have compassion for you, give you a hand, cut you a break, but a lot of them see a chance to put the boots to you and rip off what's left, like vultures sitting in the trees, hoping you'll die.

The utility companies put it to us. That one terrible winter when my nephew Ed had drowned, we was awful poor, with no money at all, broke. I wasn't catching no fish, and I got busted because my helper forgot to buy his new license. The electric company called every few days and threatened to shut off my power. This was January, and it was below-zero cold. I talked to the head guy down there. He said, kind of snottylike, "Just what is the problem, Mr. Paquin?"

I said, "We're not catching no fish."

We only owed them forty dollars, more or less. He said, "You better pay your bill when you catch some fish." But hell, when I caught twenty pounds of fish, I bought groceries. We had to eat.

The bill got up to eighty-five dollars by March. They were still calling and threatening, but no one gave me no certain date for shutoff. They never called for two weeks. I was watching TV one afternoon, and this guy knocked on the door. "Mr. Paquin," he said, "I have an order here to shut off your electricity." The guy had no choice. He was doing what the boss told him. He walked around the corner to the meter, and zap—no power.

I was really mad. They shut me off in March, right in winter, for eighty-five dollars. I know businesses in town here what owed hundreds of dollars, and the electric company never shut them off. Goddamn! Put it to the poor man, eh? My family could've froze in that house for all the company knew, with no heat at all. Of course, we had the wood stove, but they didn't know that.

I was lucky, though. Otto Hyslip, a friend, come by, and when I told him we had no power, he loaned me ninety-five dollars to get it turned back on. It cost me ten extra bucks because I was already cut off.

They never shut the gas off on us. We didn't use much—just for hot water. They'd threaten us, put a yellow tag on the door when they read the meter. They'd call sometimes too. We had quite a few of them yellow notices. Carole would go pay them a few dollars, and they'd leave us alone for a while. If I'd get a big lift of fish, we'd stock up on groceries and divide the rest, try to pay all them utilities a few dollars to keep them off our backs for a while. If you dribble a little money out to them, they leave you alone.

One time I called up this lady at the electric office, after we got a notice. I said, "I'm having problems right now. I'm out of work, and I ain't catching no fish."

She said, "Well, I don't know. I've never been in that shape."

Piss on her. I told Carole, "I'm not even going down to the office." I knew I'd get into it with that woman. Why would they have a heartless person like that collecting bills anyhow? She's never been in that shape. Who cares about that? I didn't call to find out what kind of shape she's been in.

Now, at the phone company they don't fool around. They shut you off real fast. Reach out and touch someone, hah! They turned it off, but it was in my name, so Carole had the phone put back in with her name. She waited a couple weeks and done that. They called me on Carole's phone. It was ridiculous. This phone woman said, "I've been trying to call you about this bill, Mr. Paquin, but your phone was shut off." They were trying to call me on the phone *they* shut off. It's funny now, but it wasn't funny then. Everything was going wrong, and there didn't seem no end to it.

The tax collectors, IRS, got after me. They tried to make me pay on fishing money. They started in 1980, I think, when I was catching lots of fish and making good money, but they kept it up even when I got poor. We had heard that there was a federal court case in Washington State, and we did not have to pay, but IRS kept the heat on us.

I thought I would challenge them. They called me and sent me letters. "Please come down and meet with us," they'd say. But I never went. I figured that they wasn't sure of what they was doing, because they was being nice and not trying to push me around.

They kept calling and writing. I decided to meet with them. I don't know why. This was when everything was going wrong. Probably it just wore me down, and I wasn't feeling so cocky as before. Anyhow, I went to Petoskey to talk with them. The man was real nice and polite. He showed me some papers about the Osage Indians and that they had to pay on timber and corn.

I asked him, "Where does it say they got to pay on fish? Did the Osage Indians fish commercially like my people did in the old days?"

"No," he said, and he give me some more papers to look at. "There," he said. "Look at that." And he pointed to the paper.

I don't read good, so I went real slow. At first it looked like Indians had to pay on fishing. That's what it said. Then I saw that he was tricking me. I asked him, "What are these papers? A court decision? A federal law? Or what?"

He looked at me puzzled-like. The other fishermen had told me, "Yeah, Ron, we got to pay it. The Osage Indians. . . ." But they never seen what I saw.

He said, "Those are IRS rulings." He was conning me, in other words. He asked me, "Ron, what does the treaty say?"

I laughed at him. "Man, you got to be kidding me. There wasn't no income tax in 1836. You think I'm a stupid Indian, but I ain't. I know what's going on."

They sent a guy to my house to figure my taxes. He itemized it

Broken Dreams

all up for three years, 1979 through 1981, and I didn't owe no taxes, just two thousand dollars for Social Security. "Are you going to pay that?" he asked.

"No," I said. "Federal employees do not have to pay it, so I ain't going to either." Christ, I was broke. I couldn't pay it.

They start sending me bills, and they were charging 15 percent interest. Then they wanted to audit me. That was silly. Their man did the work in the first place. Didn't they trust him? I never went to their audits. I got a bill from IRS that I owed them thirty-two thousand dollars. What a joke! I couldn't pay a light bill for eighty-five dollars. Where was I going to get thirty-two thousand dollars? I don't owe them that anyhow.

IRS sent a collection agency after me. We was living on State Street then and poor as hell. Them collection guys come asking questions. They decided that we was broke and had no money to pay IRS. We was spending everything we made for stuff we needed.

IRS was just crazy. They'd try to scare us. We'd get bills for ten thousand dollars or twenty-five thousand dollars. They made them up, I think. The bills was all different—no relationship from one to the next. The last call I got from IRS was maybe a month after the collection agency figured out we could not pay. "Mr. Paquin," they said, "you called and said you were going to pay this all off."

"What the hell are you talking about?" I said. "What are you trying to pull? Your people was just here, and they found out we can't afford to pay you nothing at all. What the hell do you mean, pay it off?"

Now we were arguing. I told them to leave me alone. I didn't owe them nothing anyhow. I ain't heard from IRS since then, but they grab our tax refunds real quick. Damn, that was awful, though. Something else to worry about.

With my truck, the bank refinanced me three times. They was in a bind too, but they treated me fair. I got mad at them a few times, but mostly they tried to help me make the payments and keep the truck. Otherwise I wouldn't have the damn thing now. I'm working on my fourth loan officer since I bought that truck in 1980. I won't pay for it till 1991, just in time to leave it at the dump probably.

I didn't have no money for house payments, and my real estate taxes was three years overdue. Carole and I thought we'd get rousted out of the house, thrown into the streets, evicted. We thought FHA would just up and say you got to get out by next Tuesday or whenever. Our friend Jane Josephson, a sweet old lady who lives up the street, told us, "I talked with my son. You kids can live in that old house on the beach by Graham's Point. You'll have to fix it up, but you can stay there rent-free."

We went down there and tried to do something, but we didn't have no money to fix it up. The place had been empty quite a while and needed things done. Me and Carole and Chris worked there for more than a week. We fixed the water system, cleaned out the trash, and got it ready for sheetrocking. But then we saw it needed more than we could afford. We was too poor even for that.

FHA showed some feeling for me. They wasn't like the utility companies. They was good with us. They hung on a long time, helped us out. We wouldn't have payments for a while. They put us on like a moratorium. Right after we built the house, we had trouble with the payments and got behind a thousand dollars. They talked with us, and we paid five hundred dollars of it back in one crack, and then they added the rest to what we owed. They brought our payments right down to poverty level. We stayed with that a long time, a couple years, making payments every month when fishing was good, before the closures started. The payments was just for the money we borrowed and not no taxes. You pay the taxes separate, plus pay the insurance. When things turned bad, me and Carole talked with FHA—told them we was completely broke. They explained what we could do. We could go on a moratorium with no payments for six months. They helped us when things was rough.

The taxes just kept coming, like city taxes. We was so far behind, we wasn't ever going to catch up. They were putting interest on and interest on the interest. There was new taxes on the way. We was back three years and thought that the city would take our home.

I found out that these companies are bloodsuckers. They see where people are having a rough time. They check the records, and they know when places are put up for tax sale. They pay the taxes and grab the house. That's what they do. They hide back in the bushes and steal people's homes.

The city was steady adding interest, but they just sent a notice. "You're delinquent," they told us, but no phone calls or harassment. Everything else was getting behind too. We owed and owed.

Me and Carole talked about our money troubles. We hoped things would straighten out, but they steady got worse, not better. Carole called FHA, and they was nice to her. They told her we would definitely not be thrown out, even though we owed three years' taxes.

Finally we decided to get out from under it. We called FHA again and thanked them for helping us like they did but told them we was going to move out and let the house go back to them. We went to the Soo and signed it off. All through them times, FHA treated us decent. They let us stay a long time after they could've pushed us out. They gave us a chance to save our home. I was glad that we kept the house in such good shape that they sold it fast and didn't lose no money, not a dime.

Chris took it real hard, us losing our home. It was the only place he could remember living in. It was home to him, in other words. Carole and me didn't feel so bad about it as him, because we was gaining too. A big load come off our minds when we left there. A relief is what it was. But I felt sad too. I had lived in that house longer than anyplace in my life and raised my son there. I felt that I had lost something I'd fought hard to get. I liked living there. It give me some security. It was my home. I hope me and Carole can buy another house someday.

People loaned me money, trying to help me through them bad days. I want to thank them. There was times when I wouldn't have made it without them pitching in, like when Otto give me the money to get my lights turned back on or when my mother give me fifty dollars for groceries.

My ice machine broke down. I needed it to run the fishery, but I didn't have no money to fix it. The repairman, Bob Wheaton, worked for a day and a half and got it going. He never sent me no bill. It would've been for several hundred dollars—he did a lot of work. I asked him about it a few weeks later, and he said "Aw, Ron, don't worry about it. I know you're having a rough time. Bring me some fresh fish when you can." Wheaton knew the bind I was in. You can't be in the fish business without ice. I didn't have no money to fix the ice machine. Without the machine, I couldn't process fish. If I didn't process fish, I didn't make any money. I was trapped, in other words, without Wheaton's help.

There's a long list of people that helped like Wheaton did. I want to thank them: Jane Josephson, Dave Bosset, Stu Carlson, Clarence Maggo, Warren Highstone, Mickey Melwing, Bob Doherty. I could go on and on. I've forgot some people, I imagine. I apologize for that. It ain't that I don't appreciate what they done for me and my family.

Fishing is dangerous work. Even a careful fisherman has got to take risks that no normal man would. Tremblers ain't going to make money fishing. But when we got real poor and I needed money so bad, I took some chances I shouldn't have took. Out there on the ice that day, my nephew Ed died because we was poor. He could've died the December before when we was fishing at Big Rock.

We was fishing off the atomic plant at Big Rock, near Charlevoix. It was December and cold. Back then, I was cocky on the lake, figured I could always find my way. I never carried no compass. Our nets were not far offshore, a couple miles maybe. Generally, we could lift them in two or three hours and be back in. I seen before we left that we didn't have much gas, but it didn't matter because we were just a little way out.

We had two gangs set, and things went good. There wasn't no sea. We just about got the second gang lifted when it began to snow, heavy wet stuff, and it was coming down till you couldn't see but only a few feet. I hadn't heard no forecast that day, and the weather looked good when me and Ed left Big Rock—sunny with an easy southwest breeze coming onshore. But it sure was snowing now, and no wind at all.

We lifted our nets and headed in. I figured I was going the right way, but we weren't hitting the beach. "Damn, Ed," I said, "we ought to be there by now. We should've hit the beach."

"I don't know," he said, "but I'm getting cold."

We didn't have much gas left. We'd run quite a while, I guess. I shut the motor off, hoping that the storm would pass or we'd hear something, but it was snowing harder than before, and the wind was blowing now. We were drifting in the swells, and the sea was rising. Ed and me took empty net boxes to protect us from the wind and snow. It had turned bitter cold. My hands and face burned. I had no idea where we was, so I didn't know which way to go, not having a compass.

I talked with Ed. "We got to do something here," I said. "You're in this too. I think that the wind has went northwest on us. We got to quarter that son of a bitch and go. What do you think? It's up to you too."

He had my rain jacket on, and I had one of them big old army coats. It was soaked, and we was both shivering. Ed said OK, so I started the motor and headed away from the wind. It was quartering on my left shoulder. If I was wrong, we were headed for Wisconsin, going to run out of gas and spend a frozen night on the lake, drifting on a big sea.

We'd ride awhile and then drift. We found out later that Keith Grogan, who was guarding our truck, was worried, so he called the Coast Guard. "Are they in immediate danger?" the guy asked. Keith

Photo courtesy of Robert G. Doherty

Fishing is dangerous work. Even a careful fisherman has got to take risks that no normal man would. Tremblers ain't going to make money fishing. But when we got real poor and I needed money so bad, I took some chances I shouldn't have took. Out there on the ice that day, my nephew Ed died because we was poor. . . . The two of us was riding the snow machine and pulling the sled. . . . We hit some slush spots on the way, but nothing bad. . . . We started to circle, and—it happened so fast—a hole opened in the ice.

told them, "How the hell would I know?" They come down and talked to him, but they never looked for us.

Man, was I happy I had a lot of cigarettes with me! Ed had a pack too. We were joking around, nervous about the fix we were in, so we were smoking to beat hell. I told him, "Ed, we got to stay awake. Don't fall asleep." I worried about hypothermia. It was getting grayish dark, late afternoon, and still we ain't seen land. We'd been on the lake since early morning.

All of a sudden, the storm broke. It looked like a boat at first, but it was land. I cranked up the motor and headed for shore. I told Ed, "I don't know where we're at, but if we're on an island, we'll find a cabin. We'll break into it and get warm. We can pay them for it later."

There was just a little beach and real steep cliffs ahead. I never seen nothing like that near where we was fishing. Man, did I ever feel good when we hit shore! I didn't care where we landed. We was safe.

Ed and me looked at that cliff. We wondered how we was going to climb it. We just went straight up. It took us about a half hour to get to the top, but we was warm now. We got up there, and roads was going here and there. I started seeing No Trespassing signs, and I said to Ed, "We're not on no island. We're on the mainland someplace."

Well, we must have been a sight. We had on our oilers and hip boots. Here came this truck. There was a man in it and a girl. I waved my arms, and the guy stopped. I said, "Sir, could you tell me something?"

"Sure," he said.

"Where are we?"

"Where did you guys come from?" he asked.

"We been lost on the lake all day. From Charlevoix."

"Man," he said, "you're a long way from there. Get in the truck. You guys come on home with me. Change your wet clothes and get warm. Come on. Get in."

It was nice and warm in that truck, and it sure felt good. He brought us to his house and took real good care of Ed and me. And you know where we was? Near Cross Village. Clear across Little Traverse Bay from Charlevoix and up the coast a way.

So after Ed and me got warm, I called my brother Tommy. He lived near there. He come and got us. We left that guy what helped us fifty pounds of fish and some money for the phone. Most white men around there wouldn't help an Indian fisherman in no way at all. So we was lucky there. He was a real nice fellow.

Broken Dreams

Not long after that, Ed drowned. I saw that the ice was bad that morning. But we was broke, and we needed to lift our nets. We always took chances. Me and Ed had some close calls. That's part of being a fisherman. But if we'd had any money, we wouldn't have went out under them conditions. Ed would still be alive.

The ice didn't make good that winter. It was too warm and windy. We'd get a little ice and then heavy snow would insulate it. We had set our nets the day before. This was early February. Chris and I and Ed went out to set the nets. We went out in the snow machines, dragging a sled. We lifted some nets, and there wasn't nothing but brown slime, no fish.

We set three nets, and I began having bad feelings about the ice. "Let's head in," I said. "That's enough nets. We ain't catching nothing anyhow." God, I think of that. Chris was with us that day, the day before Ed drowned. It could've been him gone through the ice.

Next day, me and Ed went out on the ice. The two of us was riding the snow machine and pulling the sled. I saw Floyd and his crew out there, so we went over and shot the bull with them for a while. We hit some slush spots on the way, but nothing bad. They was having trouble with one of their machines. I told them we was going to run south and check our stakes to make sure they hadn't melted out of their holes. We'd lift our nets and go in.

We fixed two stakes and headed for the outside end of our furthest south gang. We started to circle, and—it happened so fast—a hole opened in the ice. We didn't have no warning, didn't hear the ice crack. Probably there was just real thin ice with snow on top, so we couldn't see trouble coming. We broke through. I revved the machine to see if I couldn't get it back on the ice. I don't know why I did that, because it's impossible. We were in the water but still on the machine. It was starting to sink.

"Ed," I said, "we got to get off before she goes down. Make sure it don't catch your clothes." I couldn't see Ed. He was behind me. I knew he must be scared, because he couldn't swim. "We'll be OK," I told him.

We slid off the machine into the water. There was a big hole open now. I got up on the ice in a few seconds. Ed yelled, "Ron! Ron!"

I said, "I got you." I kneeled down on the ice, and I grabbed Ed's right arm. We were face-to-face for a minute. He didn't look scared. "Easy, Ed. I got you." I had him half out of the hole, and the ice gave way. We were back in the water.

I swum over to Ed and grabbed him. "Take hold of the ice," I said. "Break it till it gets strong. Pull yourself out."

I couldn't get out of the water now. The ice around us was too thin. I'd get halfway out, and the ice would break. I lost track of Ed and began to worry about myself. I wondered if I wasn't going to die. I saw Ed then, by the edge of the hole near the ice. He wasn't trying to get out.

I was tired now. I thought I should rest for a minute and then give it all I got. I knew I wasn't going to last much longer. I grabbed hold of the edge of the ice, figuring to rest, but the current pulled me under the ice.

"I'm drowning," I thought. But I wasn't going to give up. I took my fist and blasted straight up through that ice. I was losing it now, having thoughts about death. I remember saying to myself, "I'm going to die." I almost quit. I was at ease, but the ice was solid where my fist broke through. I grabbed hold. I heard Ed making noises, but I couldn't see him. I scrambled onto the ice and turned around. Ed was gone. His jacket was floating in the hole.

When I was in the water, I seen Floyd leave, and I knew no help was coming. But after I got out, I crawled away from the hole and stood up. I saw Floyd and started waving my arms. When he come over, I was wandering back toward the hole yelling, "Ed! Ed!"

Floyd grabbed me and asked what happened. "Ed drowned" was all I could say. I started crying and to shiver out of control. They loaded me on their sled and took me to shore.

I've thought about that day a lot. Ed and me was real close. We fished together for five years. We worked hard, made good money for a while, took risks together, got drunk, shot pool, and had fun. We was good friends, almost like brothers. I miss Ed very much. I still think about him when I'm on the lake. I'll never get over what happened.

I made mistakes that day. I should've lay down on the ice when I tried to help Ed, and I should've used my jacket to pull him out so I could keep away from the edge. We should've been wearing life jackets. I do now when I go on the ice. But mostly we should never have went on that ice at all. I had nine dollars to my name at that time, no more. I went on the ice because I had to have money, because I was poor. That's why Ed died.

Carole and I felt quite a turmoil wondering what to do. I love fishing, but at that time it was more a hindrance than a trade and I had trouble going on the lake after Ed died. There wasn't much I could do but wait, so I hung on. Meantime, my bills weren't getting paid—my house, my truck, everything.

Carole and I talked about our money troubles. Then she went

and looked for a job. She told me, "Ron, I got a job interview today." The next week she began working. When Carole done that, it forced me to do something too. She was saying to me that the time for talking was over. She's been doing motel work in Mackinaw City three years now. The people treat her good. They pay her a decent wage and give her a bonus in the fall. They make sure she gets enough weeks for her unemployment. She likes the boss too, so she's happy.

I knew I had to get a job like Carole done, but I didn't know what kind of job I'd hunt for. Then one come hunting for me. Back around 1980 I built a longhouse in the visitor center at the Father Marquette State Park there by the boulevard just north of the Mackinac Bridge. The state of Michigan contracted me for that. I like working with my hands, so I enjoyed building that house, and I done a nice job for them. People complimented me on it. I got a reputation around town as an Indian craftsman that done nice work.

The town fathers in St. Ignace, the Downtown Development Authority (DDA), decided that they was going to fix up the little museum and park in the center of the city into a nice tourist attraction. They wanted to put the place in the vintage of the seventeenth century, with Indian stuff like people always want to see.

Well, just about the time I began looking for work, Paul Garlitz, the head of DDA, asked me if I'd take a job with the city making stuff for the museum. I needed work bad, so I said, "Sure! What do you want me to do?" Paul said, "You'll do craftwork, Ron, and oversee the CETA employees in the museum." I went to work the next day.

Just inside the museum's front door there was a living scene with a bark-covered wigwam, one of the utilizations of nature the Indians lived in. It consisted of cattails, birch bark, and a sapling framework that was tossed together. The guy that built it had no idea how to do it right.

I tore the wigwam apart. It had white-man stuff in it like safety pins and nails. I'm not knocking anyone, but it wasn't built good. So I got some books, and I studied up on old-style Indian housing, Chippewa dwellings. When Indians used nature, they used whatever they could find. It wasn't like you had some official way. Anyhow, I read these books—Carole helped me—and went to work. I began building what them books said was a Chippewa-style hut. I didn't have much time, because the season was opening soon and you couldn't work in there then. In two weeks I finished the hut and fixed up the living scene. I was proud of the job I done. It looked good.

The guys at DDA wanted a project at the museum to draw tourists. I was fixing the hut when Bob Specito walked into the museum. He was on the DDA. Of all of them, he was more interested in history and Indians. We got to talking, and he mentioned about me building a birchbark canoe. I said, "I've never built one, Bob. I'll attempt it, if that's what you want. But I need to know soon because I got to strip the bark now while the sap's running fresh. I believe I can do it. I'd sure like to try."

Bob was gone for about an hour, and he come back. If they had a meeting, I don't know. Probably they had a meeting on the phone. He said, "The canoe is go, Ron."

I said, "All right!" I was excited, and I was worried too. I wondered what this was going to consist of and could I do it right.

I got a real good book by a guy named Adney and also a book where some Chippewa Indians from Lac du Flambeau, Wisconsin, made a birchbark canoe in the early 1950s. I studied them books. The more I looked at them, I could see that it was quite an undertaking I got myself into.

I worked on that canoe all summer. I gathered stuff from the woods: birch bark, black spruce roots, and white cedar. I learned as I went along. I made some mistakes, but most everything worked out good, and the canoe come out just excellent. I felt really happy. I liked my job, and it give me some security after all them years of

The town fathers in St. Ignace . . . decided that they was going to fix up the little museum and park in the center of the city into a nice tourist attraction. They wanted to put the place in the vintage of the seventeenth century, with Indian stuff like people always want to see. . . . Just about the time I began looking for work, I was asked if I'd take a job with the city making stuff for the museum. . . . I worked on the birchbark canoe all summer.

Photo courtesy of Sue Branister

worrying. I'm getting toward fifty years old, and I can do any kind of physical work now, but you never can tell what might happen. Besides, in a place like St, Ignace that closes up tight in the winter, there ain't hardly no work lasting year-round.

When I first took this job, I thought, "Well, get away from the fishing for a while. I'll adjust to this job and see financially how it will suit us. I didn't get paid much—$5.25 an hour—but it was steady. So I accepted it. I fished off and on that summer.

That fall they laid me off, and I got unemployment. Me and Carole both did, so we come out good that winter. We was doing better now, paying our bills on time. We returned most of what we owed people and had a few dollars in the bank. But with both of us working, we was barely moving ahead. The museum job wasn't doing it. I worried that I'd never get out from behind the eight ball working there.

Late that winter—this would be in probably March 1986—Carole and me heard stories about fishing in Alaska. Bobby Cheeseman, a young fellow from St. Ignace, did it and made piles of money. He filleted fish on a factory ship what docked in them islands that stick out toward Russia. The company sold fish to Mrs. Paul's, I think. They'd fish in that Bering Strait and be at sea for weeks at a time.

I called Bobby Cheeseman's mother. She told me about it and give me the company's address. It was out of Seattle. I called them up and talked with Al in the personnel division. He said, "Come on out." This looked like a chance to score big. If me and Carole both went on the ship, we could bank a lot of money. I said, "I want to fish with you."

At that time it cost six hundred dollars to fly to that island from Seattle. We had enough money saved for me to go. I went to the Greyhound station and checked on getting to Seattle. I couldn't make it in time for that charter flight, so I'd miss this trip. Al told me to come next time.

I never did go to Alaska, but while I was thinking about it, I let some rumors slip around town about how I was going to quit my job at the museum. I made sure the story got out to the guys on DDA. Paul called me in one day—he was city manager by then—and he said, "What's this I hear about you leaving us and going to Alaska, eh?"

I told Paul the truth, but I laid it on too. "Paul," I said, "I just cannot make it on what you're paying me. I like the job, and you're good to work for. That ain't it. I just got to make more money."

Broken Dreams

"Well, Ron, what would it take to keep you?" he asked. "How much of a raise?"

"I don't know. I'll think on it and tell you tomorrow."

I went back and forth with myself about what to do. I talked with Carole for a long time, and we figured I should go for a $2 raise but be willing to settle for less, because I didn't actually have another job.

Next day, I drove down to the city hall and told Paul what I wanted. He said, "Ron, I checked around and we can't go that high, but I can pay you $6 an hour and give you medical insurance. I'll guarantee you ten months' work."

"OK," I said. "That seems fair to me. OK, and thanks." So I come out good there.

I heard that the DDA was going to try for some grant money to fix up the museum. In the spring I was on unemployment, and Carole wasn't getting many hours at the motel yet, so we were hurting money-wise. I wanted to get back on the job, but everything was a confusion because we didn't know about the grant money. I was waiting and waiting, but nothing was happening. Me and Carole was headed toward broke again.

I talked to Paul, and he saw that I was worried, I guess, because he give me the OK to go back to work on the living scene for the center of the museum. I wanted to put my canoe there, with an Indian family going about their everyday living. Paul said, "Sure," but when we went to the DDA meeting, they said, "Sorry, Ron. You better hold up till we find out about the grant."

A couple years before this, I went to federal court in Grand Rapids to be a witness in the fishing rights case maybe. I met this college professor there that was testifying about the historical aspects of Indian fishing. Dick was his name, a real friendly fellow. He taught archaeology at one of them big state universities. Well, him and his students got a dig going here in St. Ignace right next to the museum where I was working. Dick visited up to my house the next spring, and it wasn't long before we become friends.

The grant came through and we had a meeting about how to spend it. They figured we should have a committee that would hash out what was to be done at the museum. Dick came up for this DDA meeting, and began throwing his weight around as the so-called expert on Indians—the city had hired him as a consultant. I was put on the committee to divvy up the grant. Right away Dick began arguing with me. He said we should hire some design consultants, a big firm, professionals in the field. And he knew the people to do the job. Meantime, I'd be out of work, and nobody was saying, "Well, Ron, get back on the job." I could be gathering materials for the longhouse they wanted, instead of collecting measly unemployment. Dick said I got to wait for the university to draw up a plan.

They decided to hire a big consulting firm. At the time, I didn't care about that. I just wanted to get back to work. That's what I was thinking about. Later on I got to wondering why we didn't hire local people. But right then I was thinking about building a longhouse and getting a paycheck. After the meeting, I got arguing with Dick. He said I'd have to wait. He left town for the university.

I waited and waited for plans, but I got nothing from them university people. Meantime, Dick wrote up an interpretive theme, a plan for remodeling the museum. He never said nothing to the committee, that I know of. Now, the deal was that the committee was going to do a plan and send it out to different firms. Then they'd write back and tell us what they could do with it. But there wasn't no meetings. The committee didn't do nothing, and now we get an answer from two different firms. Dick's interpretive theme was *the* plan, and it was out for bids without us even knowing about it. I didn't like Dick's interpretive theme. He had things in there like the Chippewas thought Mackinac Island was the center of the earth. Crap.

I asked Paul what the story was about the committee and Dick's interpretive theme. He seemed evasive, and I think he must have called down to the university, because when Dick come back to St. Ignace a few weeks later, he invited me up to the Tepee Lounge, there on the hill right after you come off Interstate 75. Me and Dick had a couple beers and talked, just the two of us. We didn't drink much. I wasn't drunk, and neither was he. So I said, "Dick, what will this consist of where I'm going to work? What's to be done?"

He started talking puffed up. "Ron," he said, "there will be nothing like it in the whole United States. It will be Indian, just Indian. A longhouse sixty feet long—"

I broke in on him. "I don't want to interfere—"

Now he cut me off. "Don't," he said. "Just stay out of it, Ron. You'll be OK."

Dick was real serious now and being the big boss giving orders. I didn't feel like arguing, and I didn't understand what was going on. I knew Dick was worried about my doing something that would mess up his plans. Afterward I told Carole about what Dick had said, and she told me to watch out.

We had a committee meeting the next morning, and I asked Dick about the canoe. Was it going to be in the scene?

Broken Dreams

"Maybe," he said.

I looked right at him, and I told him, "It better be!" Now, this was not because I made it. It was because the canoe was one of the most unique things the Indians ever invented. They utilized it for everything: hunting, fishing, gathering rice, trapping, everything. So I forced the issue. "Put it in there," I told them.

That grant was for lots of money, and darn near all them dollars went out of town. There ain't many jobs in this place, and most of us is pretty poor, but there's talented people that live here. They could've done this work in the museum. I said to the committee, "This money ought to go to local people. They can do the job."

Well, Dick stomped on that idea. "Use the architect from Petoskey," he said. Hire out-of-town experts was his plan.

I went to a DDA meeting. I told them, "If you don't want to listen to my expertise, then I'll quit. No one listens to me."

It went on like this all summer, just a lot of hassle and bad feelings. It made me angry to see local people lose work to outsiders. I kept complaining to Paul and other DDA members, and it must have got back to Dick because when he come up from the university for his consulting he always ridiculed my work and I think he talked behind my back, too—dwindled me right down. I felt uncomfortable at the museum so I figured I should quit.

I did some little projects at the museum that fall. I fished the fall run too. I began to think I had better find another job. I wasn't sure yet just what I would do.

I'd see Rich Boss around town. He's a contractor and an architect. He'd kid with me and say, "When you going to come and work for me? Make some good money?" I've known Rich for years. I worked for him before. Carole's brothers worked for him, and Chris had a job with him the winter before. Rich works all over. He pays good, and he's a nice guy to work for.

I talked with Rich when he hired Chris. I told him about the stuff going on at the museum. He said, "Anytime you want it, Ron, you got a job with me." I thanked him because that give me security to make some moves at the museum.

When I decided to quit the museum, I talked with Rich. I knew definitely that I would be hired. I didn't know what I'd do. Most of it was carpentry, and I'm no carpenter. One Monday morning I brought Chris to the airport to fly to Mackinac Island, and Rich said to me, "What do you want to do?"

I told him, "I want to go to work for you as soon as I can."

I started that week. They were remodeling the Grand Hotel. I did mostly labor: moving building materials, hauling stuff they tore out. Mainly I was tending for the carpenters, making sure they had the materials they needed and cleaning up after them.

I made good money. It was a lot of hours, and he paid for room and board. It's hard to get a steady paycheck during winter, when there ain't much going on. I liked working for him too, and I was much happier being away from all that trouble at the museum.

I screwed my feet up working over there at the hotel. I couldn't afford no good shoes then, so I was working in them pac boots. We were putting in twelve and a half hours five days a week and six or eight hours on Saturdays. There wasn't enough support in them boots, with me being on my feet that much. I was walking here and walking there, carrying heavy stuff half the time. My feet and legs began to hurt, and soon I was in terrible pain. Hammer toes, the doctor calls them. Three toes turned numb on my left foot, and two on my right. That tendon is shortened up. The hurt is awful. I don't know what I'm going to do this winter. My feet still hurt, and there ain't no way to get relief. The doctor said to keep off my feet, but I can't do that.

Rich laid me off in late May. I been fishing since then. I fish in the mornings and do craftwork in the afternoon till Carole gets done at the motel. I fished perch most of the summer. I'm fishing salmon now and doing good. It's real hard work. We been lifting most every day a thousand pounds and more. I lost a lot of weight doing it, but I'm holding up OK. The arthritis in my back ain't bothered me. I'm glad about that. I'm worried about my feet this winter. I hope I can take the pain.

Taking Stock

When I was a boy, nobody ever took me by the hand and showed me the path toward becoming a man. I had to find it on my own. It wasn't no easy job. You seen how I lost my way sometimes. But I'm proud of what I done with my life, and I figure I'm pretty near free from the curse my mom and dad put on me when I was young. I don't worry about them things no more. Well, not very often.

Back then, the way my life was going, it seemed great being the toughest guy in town and having everybody know it. I didn't see that most people feared me and didn't want me around. But I learned in prison that my fists wasn't going to do it and that for as mean as I was, other guys was meaner and some was crazy, like the one in Cusino what bashed that poor fellow with a bar because he was mad about bologna.

So you remember how I made a plan for myself: to find a woman, get married, and raise a family. I decided if I found a good woman, I would be faithful to her and not sneak around. I've been married twenty years and never went out on Carole, not messed with no other woman.

It may sound like a fairy tale — to fall in love and live happy ever after. Well, that ain't the way it was. Me and Carole had our battles. Them is between me and her and not none of your business. If you been married, you know what I'm talking about. There's been conflicts, but I always had faith in her. Her love has helped me be a better person than what I was. Without her, I don't know what would've happened to me.

Carole and I is partners. We decide things together — talk it over and figure out what to do. We share the work in the house. I don't have no use for them that want their wives to wait on them. I cook and clean and do dishes when Carole's working, and she does the same for me when I'm on the job. Everybody helps.

I've tried to provide for Carole and Chris—keep a roof over them and food on the table. Like you seen, it ain't always been easy. I worked hard doing it. A man should work for his living. I don't care what he does—work is work—but you got to do it. There's too many people on welfare that just live off it. They're parasites to the public. Stand on your own feet, I figure.

I worry sometimes. I'm so backed up academically that if my physical status goes, I don't know how I'd support myself. I'm edging toward fifty years old. I got this trouble with my feet and arthritis in my spine. A few weeks back the X ray showed some spots on my lungs, so I quit them cigarettes again. But I just don't know what I'd do. I wouldn't want to be no welfare loafer.

Some folks figure it's what people do that counts. I can't see that. I figure it's how they do it, their style. I don't think one man's no better than another man because he does some fancy job or owns lots of stuff. Most of them people is nasty and real clever at using other folks. You know the ones I'm talking about. I'd sooner trust the man that works with his hands. In my early life, the authorities was the white-collar, suit-and-tie people. That was the ones abusing me. It just grew on me not to trust them. My life since then hasn't changed my mind none, like working with them university people.

People today think that you got to make piles of money. They measure your worth in dollars. Material things get stressed too much. Closeness in the family and having good friends is more important than the size of your paycheck. People is more important than owning things.

I've tried to teach Chris some good values, to help him like I never was. He knows that I love him. I'm happy with the way he has growed up. Most of all, I'm proud that he has warm feelings for other people. He's very sensitive to what's going on, and that's unusual for a teenager, I think. Let me tell you a story so you'll understand what I'm talking about.

This was several years ago. Carole's friend was lost in a bottle, and she forgot her son's birthday. Chris decided that he would give her son Billy a party. Chris had a savings account, and he asked Carole if he could get twenty-five dollars out. She said, "Sure. What do you want it for?"

He said, "To give Billy a birthday party. He's feeling bad about his ma not giving him one."

They got the money, and Chris planned the whole thing. He

bought some toys, a cake, hot dogs, potato chips—got everything in line for a party. I wished I'd had a camera. He hooked his wagon loaded with this stuff to his three-wheeler, rode down the hill, and give Billy a party. I was so proud. Somewhere Chris had learned to have compassion. If you remember how I growed up, you understand how good I felt about what Chris done.

To me, family should look out for each other—parents and kids, brothers and sisters, everybody helping. Mostly my family was not like that. Floyd helped me, and Donna did too, but they's about the only ones. I don't go to my family for help—not for material things or for someone to talk to, tell my troubles to. There's not that kind of relationship. I guess there never will be. It's too late for that now. My family don't do nothing together. The few times we've got to deal with each other, we end up fighting and mad, with hurt feelings.

I remember when my dad died. He was in the hospital up here at Mackinac Straits. I went to see him. He looked OK at first and was in good spirits. I visited him several times. He'd had a stroke, but he pulled out for a while. Chris was real young, so this would've been around 1968. My dad was in the hospital for quite a spell because he was real sick. I think he was there, got out, and then went back in. Finally his heart just give out. He was dead. I felt sad. I felt—well, I didn't know just what. I'm hunting for the words, but I can't find them.

For a while I had thought it would be good for the family to be together at the funeral. But I was wrong. It was awful, like it was always awful, not good for nobody. It fired up old hatreds.

A few days before the funeral my twin brother, Donny, come home from the West Coast. Right away my brother-in-law Sonny was after him. He told Donny, "You come here and just flop. I suppose you got no money at all."

Donny gave it back to him: "I come here to bury my father. I'll pitch in for the funeral. We'll all help."

Cheap Sonny was worried about a few bucks. And he thinks he knows everything. So a big argument broke out. People was screaming at each other, and the family ain't hardly been together yet. During all that time there was tension, not because my dad had died but because my family could just no way get along with each other.

Donny was late for the family portrait. Everybody was mad at him, yelling. Sonny was running things again and pissing people off. We had the dinner after the funeral at Carole and I's house. My brother Tommy got drunk and beat up my little brother Leonard, so

Some folks figure it's what people do that counts. I can't see that. I figure it's how they do it, their style. I don't think one man's no better than another man because he does some fancy job or owns lots of stuff. . . . I've tried to teach Chris some good values, to help him like I never was. He knows that I love him. I'm happy with the way he has grown up. Most of all, I'm happy that he has warm feelings for other people.

I had to be the peacemaker. I gave him a backhander and told him to leave Leonard alone. He come up here just to get drunk, I think. He never cared for our dad, just used him. Anyhow, all this awful stuff was going on while I was trying to get my feelings straight about my father's death.

We wanted to get a headstone for my dad's grave. Nobody's got much money, so I asked them to pitch in a few dollars for the stone. I was going to collect the money and buy it. Not long after, Tommy spread the story that Carole and I took the money and got drunk with it. Well, there wasn't no money. Nobody had give us nothing.

I don't know why Tommy would do that, but it's the way he is. I caught him over on Prospect Street a few days later. I grabbed him and asked him why he was telling all the lies. I could see fear in his eyes. He was sitting in his car, parked there, so I reached in the window and snatched his keys. I grabbed him by the throat and squeezed his Adam's apple till he couldn't breathe or talk—nothing. "You bastard!" I yelled. Then I let loose of him.

Bob Hendrick, an old buddy, was there too, with his wife. She'd been gossiping like Tommy. "You bitch!" I shouted. "You shut up too!"

Then Tommy began screaming at me. I told him, "Anytime you want to be brothers, you can enter my home, but till then you shut your mouth."

Finally the headstone thing got so bad that we just never bought one. I guess my dad is lying in an unmarked grave to this day, but I don't know for sure. I don't go near graves; they give me bad feelings. Since the funeral, I never been back to where he's buried.

My mother got real sick one time not long after my dad died. Her appendix burst. She was awful sick. Here came these feelings again. I told you about how I had hated her when I was young, but she was my mother and now she was in bad shape. I didn't know what to feel. I'm not even sure today what I feel about her. Possibly she was dying there in the hospital in Petoskey, so—whatever I felt—Carole and I went to visit her.

Here was Sonny Huyck again, running things, or at least trying to. He was arranging the visits, saying "You go first, you go second," like that. I was upset and crying, but I was getting real mad too. My sister seen how things was going, and she got Sonny quiet for a time. I didn't know what was going on inside me yet. I never got to know her. Now she was dying and a stranger to me. I wanted to be left alone to get control of myself.

I went to see her after a while. She looked bad, really tired, and her skin was an odd color. At that moment I didn't hate her no more, but I didn't love her neither.

She got better, and over the years things have mellowed some. She visits me and Carole. She baby-sat Chris years ago, but she wasn't really a grandma, if you know what I mean. And the stingy side come out when she charged us for baby-sitting her grandson. I was furious about that. Deep inside, I was hoping some good family feelings would grow, but I was being stupid, I guess, because it will never happen.

But, you know, it's strange. When we was broke and had no money at all, she gave us fifty dollars. From a person as cheap as she is, fifty dollars is a lot, and she had no way of knowing when we'd pay her back. It's hard to make sense out of family things. I guess nobody never gets what they want, do they?

Today it's still hard for me to talk to her or even be around her. I mean, we can't reminisce about the good old days when I was a little boy, can we? I don't like to touch her. I can't put my arms around her or kiss her. That part isn't there for me, and it never will be. But it's in my heart to forgive her if I can. I hope so. Old hatreds die hard.

When I was first married, she'd come to visit and say stuff that would rile me up. I'd want to hit her, sort of pay her back for the old days, wake her up. I didn't do nothing, though, or say anything either. I kept them feelings to myself, bottled up, not knowing what to do with them. One time I remember wanting to grab her by the hair and drag her out of my house, right into the street.

I see my mother every now and then. She comes by the house. We have a relationship, but I don't know quite how to describe it. I'm not sure what she feels toward me. I don't hate her no more, but my feelings ain't clear. I try to make things between her and me as good as I can.

I hope someday I'll find it in my heart to love her, but I don't know if I will.

Afterword *by Robert Doherty*

The Hard Times beckon in Empire, lurking in the curve where you swing right and head up the hill toward the sand dunes. Not that these were hard times for Ed and Chet. Chippewas in their early twenties, the two men had been fishing in Lake Michigan, just off the beach where Highway 209 dead-ends after it goes through Glen Haven. They gillnetted lake trout and whitefish by the old pilings to the left, and they had some big lifts out of deep water too. In all, they had more than a ton of fish iced down in the back of Ron's truck. And they were feeling good—good to be off the beach and good because Ron would pay them a fat bonus when he saw the lifts they had made.

Ed and Chet stopped in at the Hard Times to have a couple of beers and watch the fights on TV. Then they would head north. Jim, the crew boss, took off with Mindy, looking forward to having her in a bed for a change instead of on the beach or in her car. Funny about Jim—young guy, had a nice wife and kids up north, but he could never get enough of Mindy. He hardly went home at all anymore.

Ed and Chet drank schnapps and beer. It was a lousy fight on TV, so they shot some pool and kept drinking. The fight ended at three. Chet was getting loud, and Ed was working to talk at all, his words coming real slow and sort of mushy. Ed dribbled beer down the side of his face onto his yellow Lake Superior State College T-shirt, where it settled in a dark stain.

Drunk, Ed and Chet finally headed north around five o'clock. But they never made it to the fishery in Mackinaw City. Remarkably, they got as far as Elk Rapids before they wrecked.

Chet didn't remember anything but falling asleep in the truck and waking up in a field full of fish. Ed said the rear end of the truck started swaying and he lost control. More likely, he fell asleep. He never hit the brakes at all; there were no skid marks on the road. Apparently the truck took a slow left turn across the highway, then bounced over the ditch and through a fence before the left front slammed into the ground. The windshield popped, and the two men flew out. The truck cartwheeled, with fish going every which way. Then it lay over on its side, one front wheel spinning slowly, the smell of gas spreading. Ed and Chet lay in the grass, out cold.

Headed south toward Elk Rapids, a beige Buick slowed and then stopped near the spot where the truck had gone off the road. Nobody got out for a moment. Then the driver opened the door and stood on the gravel-strewn shoulder of the highway. Balding, about fifty years old, and wearing white shoes, seersucker pants, and a white knit shirt, he looked up and down the road. Nothing was coming. He opened the trunk of his car. The first time, he got two nice trout, about six pounds each. Then he walked into the field, grabbed a box full of whitefish, and headed back to his car. As he set the box in the trunk, his wife yelled, "Car coming!" They spun off south as a black car showed in the distance. Two other cars stopped.

"Wonder if he's dead?"

"Naw. He's breathing."

Ed heard them talking way off somewhere, so he opened his eyes. Vaguely, he saw a woman carrying two trout by the gills and heading for the highway. Groggy and a bit drunk, Ed lay there wondering what to do.

"Want to sell some fish?" the man asked.

Ed didn't answer. The man grabbed a box of whitefish and struggled toward his car, then drove off.

Driving south toward Elk Rapids, Chuck Williams saw the accident and thought he recognized the smashed truck. He stopped to help his fellow Indians if he could. Chet had stumbled to the edge of the road, where Chuck saw him.

"Chet, what happened? Where's Ron? Are you hurt?"

Chet stared at Chuck for a moment, trying to figure out if he was hurt. "I'm OK," Chet said. "See how Ed is. I'll call Ron and get help."

Chuck walked into the field to where Ed lay.

"Ed, you OK? Ed, come on. Wake up. Jesus, Ed, wake up."

"Who's that?" Ed said. "Yeah, I'm OK, I guess. That you, Chuck? Man, am I glad to see you! Where's Chet?"

"He's all right. Back's full of glass, head's cut, but he's not hurt bad. He went up the road to call Ron, to that house over there. What happened? You sure tore this field up. There's fish all over the place."

We better pick them up before it gets dark. It's not good to be here after dark."

"Right. We better get out of here. You got your truck?"

"No."

"Oh, God." Ed's face twisted in pain as he pushed himself up.

"Ron'll get a truck. Let me look at your back. There's blood on your shirt. Let me see." Chuck lifted the shirt. "It's a mess," he said. "Skin's dug up real bad on your shoulder there. You better see a doctor when you get north. Cop car coming."

With lights blinking up top but no siren, the sheriff's car was coming too fast. It ripped into the gravel shoulder, throwing stones, and slammed to a stop. The cop in the car reached up above the visor to get his sunglasses. A fat man, he had trouble getting around the steering wheel. "Antrim County Sheriff" was written on the door.

"Have some trouble, boys?" He paused. "I see you been fishing. Lots of trout there. Need help?"

"Yeah. Could you call a tow truck for us?"

The cop nodded. "You guys pay for it?"

"No. Insurance will pay," Ed answered.

The cop nodded again. "Anybody hurt?"

"No."

"You driving?" The cop looked at Chuck.

"No. He was," Chuck said, pointing at Ed. "I just got here."

The cop looked at Ed and said, "Let me see your driver's license." Ed handed his wallet to the cop.

"No," said the cop. "Take it out of there." He looked at the license. "OK. Is that your truck?"

"No. I work for the owner. I'll get the registration. It's in the truck." The cop followed Ed, eyeing the fish as he went. He looked at the registration, walked back to his car, and talked on the radio for several minutes.

The cop struggled out of his car again and puffed over to Ed and Chuck. "Tow truck's on its way," he said. "Should be here soon. Boys, if I could, I'd throw your asses in jail. I can't do that. Let me tell you, though, you'd better get out of here before people see those trout. You know how they feel about Indians gillnetting all the fish. Somebody'll get mad and shoot you maybe. Better get out of here before dark." The cop drove south, throwing gravel and dust until he was out of sight.

In the house up the road, Chet slouched in a kitchen chair. Faced toward the ladder-back, he draped his arms casually over the top rung, but his bony-white knuckles betrayed tension. The woman who lived there cut Chet's bloodstained shirt off and gently cleaned the cuts. Chet displayed no signs of pain, but his eyes bulged and showed too much white. "I got to use your phone again," he said. "OK?"

"Sure."

He dialed and waited. "Ron. We wrecked. . . . No, not drinking. . . . We're OK. . . . Naw, we was not drinking. Lifted the nets late. Pulled them out and left them at George's. . . . Yeah, about five miles north of Elk Rapids. The boat's at George's. We're OK. . . . Can you get a truck? . . . Chuck stopped, and he's with Ed and the fish. Just get a truck and some—. . . Bullshit. We wasn't drinking. The truck's totaled. . . . We'll get the fish up by the road."

The woman smiled at Chet when he put the phone down. "You should see a doctor," she said. "You've got some bad cuts. They need stitches, and they could get infected."

"Thanks. Here's money for the phone. Really, thanks a lot. I got to go." Uncomfortable with her tenderness, Chet rushed out the door and walked back to the wreck.

Ron couldn't sit still. He stalked the room, smoking one cigarette after another. He flopped in his TV-watching chair momentarily but soon bounced to his feet and renewed his pacing. I didn't know Ron very well then; I'd only met him briefly twice before. But I knew a lot about him because I had been listening to his tape-recorded autobiography. I had come to Ron's home in Michigan's upper peninsula so that he and I could start writing his life story, but nervous the way he was now, he was thinking only of Ed and Chet and his wrecked truck.

I'd been fascinated by Ron's tape recordings. Now I watched him move about the room, trying all the while to relate the man before me to the vicious fighter described on the tapes. Six foot two, thin now that he was lifting nets all the time, Ron moved with an easy grace. He was incredibly strong. The muscles in his back stretched his white T-shirt, and his long, scar-covered arms were well defined, like a weight lifter's. He was an imposing man, frightening in a way.

I remembered the day before, Saturday afternoon, shortly after I first arrived at his house. Ron's wife, Carole, had gone out with their son, Chris. Ron and I had sat talking in his living room while he half watched "Wide World of Sports" on TV. He had the sound off and only glanced at the screen from time to time to see what was on. Our conversation wandered, mostly with me asking questions and him giving answers. Suddenly something on TV grabbed his interest. He started toward the set but stopped right in front of me.

"You like boxing, Bob?" he asked.

Memories of Ron's self-described brutality flashed through my mind. I thought he wanted us to put on the gloves. Terror seized me. I couldn't speak. Ron looked at me, sensed my fear, and laughed.

"No, Bob, I don't want to fight with you," he said. "Boxing on TV, I mean. Do you want to watch the fights on TV?"

I swallowed hard, trying to regain control and avoid looking foolish. "Sure," I said.

Now I studied Ron's face. From the side his long French nose stood out, but from the front his flashing deep-blue eyes drew first attention. It was only after a second and careful look that I noticed the high cheekbones, black hair, and dark skin that betray Ron's Chippewa ancestry. People unfamiliar with Indians might think him a white man.

After being silent for several minutes, Ron burst into a tirade against Ed, Chet, and Jim. "Goddamn those guys," he said. "They been drinking. I know they been drinking. They pulled those nets this morning and went to the Hard Times. Jim ought to know them guys are trouble. Christ, once they get drinking, they never stop. Bet he had that woman down there, went off to Rogers City with her. Just can't keep it in his pants. And he left those two idiots with all those fish and my truck. I know they been drinking."

Ron usually did his own fishing. He kept his crew in line that way. But he had hurt his back the week before and couldn't lift nets, so he hired the three young guys to fish for wages and shares, using his gear.

Ron went back to the phone and made a call. "Bud there?" he asked. "He's at a wedding? Could you call him? . . . Yeah, this is Ron. I need his truck. . . . Ed and Chet wrecked my truck down below near Elk Rapids. . . . Naw, Jim's off poking Miss Rogers City." Ron told the whole story as he knew it, piling detail on detail. "Well," he said finally, "if you'd call Bud about the truck." He hung up.

Ron called someone else. "Hello, Al?" It was Saturday night, and Al wasn't home. Ron launched into the story again, though the person on the other end already knew about the accident. After Ron hung up, the phone rang.

"Yeah, they wrecked it all right. Near Elk Rapids," Ron said. "I sure could. . . . There's maybe a ton of fish. It'd go in your truck OK. We'll get ice at Bell's." Ron told the story once more very precisely, with the details but without embellishment. "About fifteen minutes. . . . OK."

Ron hung up and turned to me. "Will you drive my car down there?" he asked. "It'd be good to have the car if there's trouble. I'll go with Jay in his truck. Carole will show you the way."

Carole quickly put the living room in order before we left. Satisfied, she grabbed her purse off the table, surveyed the now tidy room, and hurried out the door. To this point, she had said only a few words to me and seemed overcome by shyness. In a way, I was too. I felt uncomfortable about the long ride ahead, because the two of us seemed momentarily tongue-tied. We were to remain clumsy with each other long after Ron and I had become friends, but eventually, when the mutual awkwardness disappeared, Carole and I found good feelings for one another. I came to admire her. She was good for Ron. She steadied him and quieted his volatility. He was lucky to have married such a warmhearted and loving woman.

Carole looked like an Indian. Round-faced, with black hair, high cheekbones, dark eyes, and coppery skin, she was slim now but inclined to put on weight because of an unpredictable thyroid. Her Ottawa ancestors had fought assimilation to the point that her family contained only Native Americans. As a full-blood, she was a rarity among eastern Indians, most of whom have intermixed with non-Indians.

Carole led me outside to her Ford Thunderbird. She handed me the keys and asked me to drive, so we got in and headed down South Airport hill toward town. Ahead, three miles offshore and looming on the eastern horizon in the weird light of the evening sun, was Mackinac Island, a popular and fancy summer resort. I swung right on State Street, St. Ignace's only major thoroughfare. Carole said nothing. We quickly settled into a silent two-hour drive. As we passed through St. Ignace and climbed the hill to get on Interstate 75 and cross the Mackinac Bridge, my mind wandered.

I thought about St. Ignace, the town where Ron and Carole had lived all their lives. A tiny community of twenty-six hundred people, St. Ignace has a thousand-year history. Indians gathered there in a fishing village long before Europeans arrived in the Americas. White men have lived along that Lake Huron harbor since 1671, when Father Marquette established a mission among the Hurons. Old though the town is, the region around it flourished only briefly during the lumbering era and is mostly uninhabited second-growth woods today, much of it in Hiawatha National Forest. Formerly a fishing community and a departure point for railroad and car ferries, St. Ignace now depends on tourist dollars lured north each summer by Mackinac Island.

Motels line State Street. Some are luxurious, such as K Royale, the Heritage Inn, and the Georgian House, and some are plain, like Miles Cabins. But in midsummer they're mostly full. No Vacancy signs begin flashing in early afternoon. Restaurants, bars, and curio shops dominate the half-mile-long downtown business district, where State Street hugs the waterfront. In July and August those businesses hum with activity and spawn lots of minimum-wage jobs. But in the fall, tourists stop coming, businesses close, and jobs, however menial, disappear. By midwinter, 40 percent of the local residents are typically out of work. The lucky ones collect unemployment; the rest turn to welfare and Aid For Dependent Children.

St. Ignace hasn't become gentrified-cute yet. The process is under way, but tourism already hides the gut-wrenching poverty that torments numerous town dwellers, many of them Chippewas. A drive up Maloney Hill to the land above the touristy waterfront quickly reveals the other St. Ignace, where simply surviving can be a struggle. St. Ignace is a place of stark and troubling contrasts between a mostly white middle class and a mostly Indian underclass. Ron and Carole didn't belong to either group. At the moment they were Indian middle class, but even a little bad luck could send them tumbling back into the bleak day-to-day struggle from which they had temporarily escaped. Through no fault of their own, Ron and Carole lived precarious lives in which commonplace guarantees succumbed to luck, and fate often rendered people powerless.

Carole and I drove across the bridge to Mackinaw City, bought some gas, and turned south on U.S. Highway 31. There was not much traffic as the sky darkened. It had become a black moonless night by the time we got to Petoskey. We sped through nearly deserted Charlevoix, and it wasn't long before our headlights picked up Ed and Chuck, standing at the side of the road.

"That you, Ronny?" Ed seemed surprisingly composed.

"No," Carole said. "He and Jay'll be here soon, with Jay's truck. They went to Bell's to get ice. You OK?"

"Yeah."

"Where's the truck?"

"Towed to Elk Rapids. There's a car coming. Better get down. We ain't had no trouble, but white people are crazy around here. I got a gun in my car."

"It's slowing down. Must be Ron and Jay. Yeah, it's them."

The men loaded the fish into Jay's truck. Ed and Chet said they had thirty-four boxes, but there were only twenty-eight now. Passersby must have gotten the rest; mostly they'd taken whitefish. It was around 11 P.M. now, and each time a car was spotted, everyone worried about it, especially if a couple of cars came together.

But no car stopped, and nobody shot at us. In about twenty minutes the truck was packed.

Jay drove north toward Mackinaw City. All the while, Ron cross-examined Ed and Chet, trying to get their stories straight. He picked at each detail, wanting to know what happened.

"Ambulance came, huh?"

"Yeah. We refused to go with them. Figured to guard the fish. Fire truck came too. Hosed down the truck. Put water in the gas tank."

"When did you pull the nets?"

"Around noon."

"Well, where in hell you guys been all this time? Drinking at the Hard Times. You been drinking. You never could hold your beer. You idiot, you fell asleep. It's a wonder you ain't dead. You wrecked my truck."

"We wasn't drinking. The back of the truck just started swinging. I lost control."

By the time they got to Mackinaw City, Ron seemed more relaxed, content with what he knew. And maybe he remembered some of the crazy stuff he'd done when he was young. Ron unlocked the door to the fishery and tossed some fiberglass boxes out behind the truck. "Throw them loose fish in the boxes," he said. "Let's get at it."

Ed, Chet, and Ron all worked at gutting fish in four deft motions: slit down the belly, cut up into the gills, press the knife against the guts, and pull. Then the fish was ready to be packed. Chet hacked at the fish. His knife wasn't sharp, and he was only half there anyway. Ron gutted twice as many fish as the other two together.

"Start packing, Ed," Ron said. "I'm far enough ahead. I can keep up with you."

A cop car stopped in the driveway outside the door. Two city cops were inside. "You all right in there, boys?" one of them asked. "Pretty late tonight, huh?"

"No problem."

The cops drove off. Ed got some waxed cartons with "Michigan Fish Producers' Association" printed on the side. Chet shoveled shaved ice into each box. Ed weighed the box and ice and then started packing the gutted fish in the box, just one kind of fish in a box. Chet put fifty pounds of fish into the box, added more ice, closed the box, and started again. Ron was really going with his knife now, rhythmically gutting the fish, moving so fast you'd think he'd cut himself. In an hour, they were done. There were thirty-seven boxes—1,850 pounds of dressed fish.

"You want to go home or what?" Ron asked. "It's almost two o'clock."

"Leave me at the Homestead," Chet said. "We'll make it by two. I want to drink me some Seven-Ups." He was ready to get drunk again. Ed wanted to go home. Ron was pretty calm now, his anger softened by time and hard work. Ron left Chet and Ed off and went home.

Chris and John, Carole's nephew, had fallen asleep on the floor with the TV on. Chris woke up. "A lot of people called about the truck, Dad," he said. "The phone's been ringing all night."

"OK. You better get to sleep. We all better get to sleep. Everything's OK, Chris. We'll get the truck tomorrow. I'm going to bed. Bob, you can sleep in Chris's room. He and John'll be OK out here."

I walked down the short hall to Chris's room at the far end of the house—a typical bedroom for a ten-year-old boy, with two twin beds, a bureau, sports trinkets, and a .410 shotgun resting in the corner. Carole must have straightened it up, though. Ten-year-olds don't keep orderly rooms like this one. Exhausted after a long tension-filled day, I took my clothes off and flopped on the bed, hoping for sleep. The room was blazing hot. Carole had lit the wood stove when we got home, and the heat swirled down the hall. I closed the door and slid the window open. A dog howled in the distance, and I heard the west wind in the balsams. The chilly air felt good and I relaxed some, but I knew sleep would be a long time coming.

I thought about the first time I met Ron, in early May 1979, just twelve months before this. I had been in Sault Ste. Marie, Michigan, researching a book on Native American treaty-right fishing. In the early 1970s, Chippewas and Ottawas in northern Michigan had begun to reclaim Native American rights that had gone unexercised for a hundred years or more. Based in Sault Ste. Marie but drawing members from all over Michigan's upper peninsula, the Sault Ste. Marie tribe of Chippewas was establishing at the same time its sovereignty as an Indian nation not subject to the jurisdiction of the State of Michigan. Fishing rights played an important part in that organizational process, provoking high emotions and bitter feelings between Indians and non-Indians while simultaneously fostering in-group solidarity and pride among Native Americans.

In 1971, Chippewas claimed their treaty fishing rights and began netting, contrary to state rules. They used gill nets; caught lake trout, a species reserved for sportfishers; refused to buy commercial fishing licenses; and otherwise disobeyed Michigan fishing laws. After a brief period of indecision, state officials became uncompromising enemies of Indian fishing. Governor William Milliken, Attorney General Frank Kelley, Congressman Robert Davis, and Howard Tanner, the head of the Department of Natural Resources, gave speech after speech that portrayed the Indians as greedy anti-environmentalists whose gillnetting threatened to destroy the state's multimillion-dollar Great Lakes fishery. State and local police arrested treaty fishers; confiscated their boats, motors, and nets; and otherwise harassed them. Court cases followed, with Indians usually on the losing end. One Native American served a jail sentence after being convicted for treaty fishing, and many Indians paid fines and lost valuable equipment.

Eventually, after two long battles in court, the Chippewas and Ottawas won victories in the state and federal supreme courts that recognized their treaty rights and severely limited state power over them. Nevertheless, state leaders refused to accept the validity of treaty rights or the court decisions and continued their verbal attacks on Indian gill-netters. Vigilante groups stepped up efforts to intimidate Native American fishers. Night riders threatened to burn out a Charlevoix wholesaler who bought Indian-caught fish, and they fired shots through his living-room window. Anonymous phone-callers menaced the children of Indian fishers.

In all, an ugly situation had prevailed in May 1979 when I spoke with Dan Green, the attorney for the Sault tribe. I had chosen to interview Green because he was a knowledgeable, though partisan, observer of the conflicts surrounding fishing rights, and he had intimate knowledge of the issues, legal and otherwise. Toward the end of the interview, I told Green that I wanted to talk with some tribal fishers. He suggested Ron because Ron had advanced Indian rights, primarily by being a point man who had opened new waters despite the potential danger, but also because he was an articulate spokesperson for members of the Sault tribe who did not live on tribal land.

Two days after I spoke with Green, I called Ron from a pay phone in St. Ignace. I explained that I was a university professor writing a book about treaty fishing and that Dan Green had suggested that I talk with him. "Sure," Ron said. "I'd be glad to talk to you," and he explained how to find his house. "I'll see you in a couple minutes."

I found Ron's place easily. It was a small prefab ranch house with a shed at the west end that housed the fishery. A yellow boat lay on a trailer in the middle of the lawn, piled with fishing gear, ropes, wooden boxes packed with nets, and a dozen gray fiberglass fish boxes. I smelled rotten fish. A fisherman lived here, no doubt about that. As I looked inside the house, I could see two deep-green, big-leafed, five-foot-tall potted plants framed by white curtains. Farther back in the room, I saw a man moving about, but no one had come to the door when I parked in the driveway. I knocked on the aluminum storm door.

"Come on in. It's unlocked," a man's voice told me, so I opened the door and stepped into a large airy living room. Ron sat at the table in the dining area at the back of the house. He was doing something with his hands, but I couldn't see what. He walked over to me, introduced himself, and shook hands. It was the beginning of a long and wonderful friendship, though neither of us knew at the time.

"Let's sit back here," he said. "We can talk while I finish carving some bone pipes I been working on. Want a cup of coffee while we talk?"

"Sure," I said. I looked around. The big lived-in room with upholstered couch and chairs, a mix of antiques, and modern mahogany tables hinted of a warmhearted family. I felt at ease. Ron returned with the coffee. Happy and talkative, he slid into a long conversation in which he did most of the talking.

I asked Ron if he had encountered trouble with vigilantes, the police, or state game officials while he fished under Chippewa treaty rights. "Damn right," he said. He described several confrontations with those enemies of Indian fishing. He told the stories skillfully and in detail, concentrating on the people—their emotions, what they said, their threats of conflict and violence. Later, when I looked at my notes, I realized that however spellbinding he was, Ron had related a series of disconnected episodes. He had seldom linked the people to the context of a situation, and the episodes bore no relationship to one another. Eventually I realized that Ron's manner of telling stories reflected his episodic sense of reality and that we thus had some difficult editorial problems to solve. During that first interview, though, I was captivated by his narrative skills.

Ron talked for more than an hour, and I quit trying to take detailed notes. Clearly, he was worth a return visit. I asked him if I could come back and tape-record his stories. "Sure, anytime," he said. But then I saw a look of puzzlement and concern flash across his face—a tightening around the eyes. Something was wrong.

"What's the problem?" I asked.

"I'm writing a book too, you know. There's a guy helping me, and I'm going to have to talk with him, I guess. I don't know. I ain't heard from Paul in more than a year."

Curious, I asked Ron to tell me about his book. "I taped it out—my life story from when I was a kid."

"What do you mean by 'taped it out'?"

"Oh," he said, "I tape-recorded my autobiography. I sat in that chair right there, late at night, all by myself. My wife and son was asleep. You know, you can't do it with people around, listening. I had the lights off, just the TV on with no sound. And I talked into the tape recorder—taped it right out."

"How many tapes?" I asked.

"I don't know. Maybe twenty."

"What's on those tapes, Ron? Tell me about them." For the next hour and a half Ron told me his life story up to about age twenty-five; he was now about forty. I listened without taking notes. He related dramatic episodes as before. Taken together, they described an awful life—child abuse, heartless parents and public institutions, attempted suicide, fighting and brutality, prison—but after enduring such horrors, Ron had reformed himself, helped by Carole's love. It was quite a story of degradation and redemption, a man's struggle to overcome his tragic childhood. I could see a first-rate book, one that would be both fun and challenging to work on.

I told Ron that I would like to listen to his tapes, if he could get them back, and that I might be willing to help him write his story, provided he could end any arrangements he had made with Paul. I drove home to Pennsylvania, and a couple of weeks later a package containing twenty-one hour-long tape recordings arrived at my University of Pittsburgh office. I called Ron and told him the tapes had shown up and that I would listen to them as soon as possible. He said that Paul had given up any interest in them.

I listened to all the tapes over the next several days. They contained remarkable stories, mostly about fights Ron had been in. Ron had not numbered the tapes, and he seldom indicated dates. He seemed to have little sense of time or of life as an interconnected developmental process. I found it hard to relate the stories to one another, even at the simplest level of putting them in chronological order. But the stories were powerful enough to warrant a try at the book. I called Ron and told him I would like to help him write his book and that I would come back to St. Ignace to talk with him in late summer. We met that August 1979 and agreed to go ahead and work together and that we would deal with royalties, authorship, and copyrights when we had a finished manuscript.

AFTERWORD

In the fall I received a research grant from the university's Central Research Development Fund to transcribe Ron's tapes. I hired Joe and Helen Rishel to do most of the transcriptions and did some myself. We meticulously wrote down Ron's words, though Joe and Helen, as faithful Catholics, refused to record Ron's blasphemy, and we soon agreed to eliminate most of the profanity because repetitive foul language served no purpose. With those two exceptions, we transcribed everything exactly as Ron had said it.

Now a year had gone by since I first interviewed Ron, and I was back in his house, lying sleepless in his son's bed, hoping in the next few days to begin shaping Ron's tape recordings into a publishable book. Somewhere in the midst of such memories, I fell asleep.

Carole rose early the next day. Chris and John were still asleep on the living-room floor, so Carole moved quietly in the kitchen, making coffee.

"Ron still in bed?" I asked when I got up.

Carole nodded yes. "There's coffee in the kitchen, Bob, if you want it. Ron'll be up soon. He's awake."

Ron stumbled into the room, heavy-eyed. "Morning," he said. He was a night person. "Want a cup of coffee? Oh, you got some." The phone rang. "They wrecked it all right," he said, "totaled her." Ron knew more now, so he related a different version of the accident than he had the day before. Ron retold the story of the accident a half dozen times that day, each time in detail. Other people also retold the story. Ed and Chet had things a bit different from Ron, but not much. By nightfall the story of the accident had spread. It was a good story, full of white racism, that would be retold many times. Ron hung up the phone. "You hungry?" he asked me.

"Yes."

"You hungry, Chris? John? Want some ham and eggs?" The boys nodded. "Got to go to the store. Want to come, Bob?"

We drove down the hill toward St. Ignace. Ron turned toward town, and the driver of an approaching car waved at him. Ron pulled over, and the other guy backed up.

"Heard about your truck, Ron. Need help?"

"Naw. Got to get fishing again, though, so I need a truck. We can use Jim's if he can get her going. The fuel pump busted last fall, and he let her sit all winter, but we'll get her going. I ought to kick Jim's ass. I ain't seen him yet. You know, he left them two guys with my truck and a ton of fish. He knew they'd get to drinking." Ron had forgotten about the store for the moment. He shut the T-Bird off and walked over to the other car. He told the story again, details and all.

People in the store knew too, the cashier and a stockboy. But

Ron wanted to eat—his stomach rumbled with hunger—so he told a shortened version.

After breakfast, Ron felt like talking, not about the accident but about himself, his life. Ron and I went back to Chris's room, where no one would overhear us. He was willing to talk with me in the room but otherwise wanted absolute privacy. Listening to his first batch of tapes, I had often felt uncomfortable, as if I were eavesdropping on an intimate conversation between psychiatrist and patient. I sometimes thought that Ron used the tape-recording process therapeutically to rid himself of unwanted and emotion-laden experiences. The tape recorder acted as a surrogate psychiatrist. I had never asked Ron if he used the tape recorder for therapy or if he saw any relationship between his emotional state and his desire to talk to the tape recorder. He did tell me that he had made the twenty-one tapes with a minimum of calculation, simply talking and letting his mind run free. On the other hand, each of his stories had an inner logic—a beginning, a middle, and an end. I hoped now to link the individual stories together in a coherent narrative.

I set up the tape recorder on the floor and began asking Ron questions from a list I had prepared: When did you live in the junked-out car? How old were you? Were you in school or working at that time? Where did you eat? Why do you think your mother ignored you and left you out there in the cold? I had a hundred or so such questions, most of which sought to establish context or to provide transitions between episodes. I asked him if he thought his parents treated him cruelly because he was not his father's son. He told me that the idea had occurred to him but that he did not think it to be the case.

Ron and I talked for about ninety minutes before he began to lose his concentration; then we quit. We had three similar sessions over the next several days. I went home with nearly six hours of recordings. During the first of those sessions, I would ask Ron a question and then let him talk freely without interruption until he decided he had exhausted the subject. When I allowed him to control the sessions this way, Ron often shifted away from my questions and began to relate stories about fighting or his abused childhood. He repeated some episodes, and when I compared them with the originals, I was pleased to discover that they bore a close resemblance. It didn't prove that Ron was telling the truth, only that he had well rehearsed "official" versions of his stories.

Over the next several years, I tried to verify Ron's stories and came to believe that he was truthful at least to the extent that each of us has an individual perception of an experience that does not quite accord with the perceptions of others who shared that experience. I did discover that in a few instances Ron had left out some of the really awful things he had done as a young man and that he would not reveal the details of his relationship with Carole.

During the second recording session, I tried to keep Ron focused on my questions, and I cut him off when he strayed from the subject I wanted him to talk about. At the time, I didn't think much about what I was doing. I had simply decided that Ron's stories wouldn't constitute his life story until they were connected to one another. In fact, I had begun to shape the manuscript according to my own conceptions of human life, not Ron's.

I recall one such conversation in which I put ideas in Ron's head, but I cannot remember if it took place during these sessions, and I'm not sure just how it affected him. I asked Ron if he could remember when he first realized he was a Chippewa and, more generally, when he became aware of being an Indian in some larger sense. My questions led us into a long, rambling conversation about race and class in St. Ignace. As a social scientist, I often looked for racial influences in situations where Ron did not. He seemed oblivious to behavior I thought clearly discriminatory or racially motivated. For example, I asked him about juvenile gang wars in St. Ignace. He saw no racial dimensions to them until I pointed out that all but one member of his Little Acre gang was an Indian, whereas the opposing Wilson gang had no Indians in it. Later Ron told me that maybe race had played a role, but he wasn't sure if it was important.

Ron became aware that he was an Indian when his mother sent him to a home school for Native Americans when he was eleven years old. But he had taken only a passing interest in his heritage until the fishing rights conflict heated up some twenty-five years later. The battles over treaty fishing raised Native American consciousness and fostered in-group feelings among the Indians, especially in the face of non-Indian hostility. Treaty fishing offered solid economic opportunities in a region where steady work was hard to find. But the opportunities were open only to people who could prove descent from members of a historical Chippewa or Ottawa band that had survived to the present and gained federal recognition as a legitimate Native American group. As a consequence, men and women who wanted to fish had to learn genealogy and family history, publicly avow their Native American descent, and join a recognized Indian group. Ron and many like him learned about their heritage as a result and became identified as Indians.

When the fishing controversy boiled over in the late 1970s,

whites bitterly complained about the inequalities inherent in treaty rights. It seemed un-American that Indians could freely violate laws that other U.S. citizens had to obey. How could the federal courts create "supercitizen" Indians? Didn't the constitution guarantee equality? So as not to appear a fool, Ron learned enough history and law to answer such questions and to defend his rights against their critics. The controversy forced assimilated Indians like him to learn about their long-neglected heritage. As a consequence, many Chippewas and Ottawas became knowledgeable historians and genealogists, and it's a rare Native American who doesn't know his or her family's past. And yet I see little evidence that this recently acquired knowledge has sensitized Native Americans to the full impact of race prejudice and discrimination upon their lives any more than it led Ron to see race as a factor in the gang wars he fought as a boy.

Later that afternoon, after we had quit our second session of tape recording, Ron's friend Tom towed the truck north from Elk Rapids and parked it in the yard. Ron called State Farm, his insurance agency, and the adjuster promised to look at the truck on Tuesday. But the adjuster called late Tuesday afternoon and said he couldn't make it before Thursday. After breakfast Wednesday, Ron and I sat and talked in the living room, drinking coffee. It was a sunny day and had gotten quite warm by midmorning. Someone knocked at the door.

It was Carole's nephew Ed, who had wrecked the truck. Stocky and broad-faced like Carole, he was pure-blood Ottawa and showed it. No one could possibly have mistaken him for a white man. Ed was a lot of fun, a charming young man despite his excessive drinking. He was remarkably intelligent, had a wonderful sense of humor, and was absolutely fearless. He and Ron had become close friends during the several years they'd fished together.

Ed and Ron talked for a while. Ed wanted his share of the money for the fish they'd packed Sunday night. Ron got Ed to tell about the accident again but didn't accuse Ed of drinking. Mostly Ron wanted assurance that his boat and nets were OK, and he wanted to establish the details of the story. Ron laughed when Ed told about the guy who wanted to buy the fish, and Ed remembered that the farmer wanted $250 for damages to his field. Ron ridiculed greedy white people.

When Ron paid him, Ed subtly separated himself from the other people in the room—Carole had visitors too. He moved back and toward the door a bit. He seemed to follow the conversation but didn't take part; he just stood back, away from the others, saying nothing. Ron asked Ed if he wanted something to eat or drink some coffee, but Ed shook his head no.

"Want a ride home, Ed?"

"Sure. Be fishing tomorrow?"

"Yeah. Got to get Jim's truck running."

Ron took Ed home and returned in about twenty minutes. He got some coffee and started talking again.

"I wish you could've met Carole's parents," he said. "They're dead now. Real nice people. It was strange that even though they got along good and was kind to each other and everything, they could no way live together. They split up when Carole was young, and she became like the mother to her younger brothers that was living at home, Calvin and Little Ron. When we got married, them boys come to live with us. Carole looked after her dad too, cooked and cleaned for him. She run the house from the time she was thirteen years old and got her first job a year later. Her dad told me she give him her paychecks to help the family and only kept ten dollars a week for herself. Except for a few years there when Chris was young and later when I was fishing, she's worked in motels and run a household ever since she was a little girl.

"Carole's mom and dad took good care of her. She never went hungry or nothing and was always dressed nice. Not like me. And she don't remember kids teasing her the way they razzed me. Carole never felt discriminated against, and she shows her Indian more than me, so I got to believe my troubles was on account of being raggedy." Ron abruptly stopped talking, stood up, stretched, and headed to the kitchen for more coffee.

I found what Ron had just told me hard to believe, and later, when I knew Carole well, I asked her several times about her experiences with prejudice and discrimination. She insisted that she had never encountered either one. Perhaps she was right, but she also had an inner strength that may have blinded her to racism. Regardless of Carole's perception and experience, as far as I could see, prejudice and discrimination pervaded northern Michigan, though they were usually well hidden.

I also pressed Carole to tell me about her mother and father. She hesitated to answer and usually spoke in generalities, but her descriptions, however vague, revealed warm feelings for both parents, despite their separation from each other.

Her affection for her father was particularly apparent. He had been a powerful figure in her life, a strong steady man who brought her a sense of stability, security, and self-worth. Talented, energetic, and hardworking, John Shomin had earned his living as a craftsman, making furniture and Indian artifacts. He designed small wooden totem poles and created jigs for them so that they could be mass-produced. For years St. Ignace Indians painted Shomin's totem poles, which the white owner of the factory sold as "genuine Indian-made" crafts. Shomin's meticulous work habits and the sense of beauty and proportion that made him a talented woodworker carried over into his private life, or perhaps it was the other way around. Regardless, he left Carole with an artistic bent, a feel for color and design. And he instilled in her a need to keep her life and home in good order, both literally and emotionally.

Carole and Ron always spoke warmly about Carole's mother, Evelyn, who was loving, funny, high-spirited, and happy. Yet Evelyn remained a shadowy figure. Carole never mentioned that she resented her parents' separation, and she maintained close ties with the half-brother and half-sister born to her mother after the breakup. It was hard to know how Carole's mother affected her or what impact her parent's separation had upon her.

Ron came back from the kitchen with his coffee. "Nice out today, ain't it?" he said. "The woods are nice today, with that breeze and the sun."

"Do you need stuff out of the woods for your longhouse?"

"Well, yeah, I'd like to peel some bark. Since it's warm like this, the sap'll be up and the bark'll be loose. It was pretty tight the last time I was out. Been waiting for a day like this. You want to peel some bark?"

"Sure."

Ron drove out of St. Ignace north on a two-lane road through deep woods. Cedar trees grew mostly in low-lying areas, but pine and birch prospered in the better-drained upland. Not one big tree had survived lumbering days. A few had grown to maybe two feet in diameter, but most stood at eighteen inches or less. Most of the area around St. Ignace was woodland like this.

Ron pulled into a driveway, talked with a young woman in the house for a few minutes, and drove around behind the house into an open area. He and I walked into the woods. "Hear that?" he asked.

"No."

"Partridge drumming. I seen them doing that. Making an idiot out of himself trying to get a female. Well, ain't much different than us, is it?" Ron laughed. "A good tree's about the size of that one, but smooth, with no eyes or branches. There's one."

Ron used an old hunting knife and a broken-handled ax to cut

AFTERWORD

through the bark of the cedar tree all the way around, about seven feet high and then down near the ground. He held his knife against the bark, whacked it, pulled the knife out, and started again. He finished the cuts, took the ax, and drove it into the tree at the upper cut. Then he pulled the ax straight down in one deft motion. Pale yellow inner bark showed. Ron pressed the axhead under the bark and around the tree. The six-by-four-foot sheet came off easily, and he set it in a sunny spot to dry.

He stripped nine trees, quickly and with the same grace with which he had gutted fish. Then the knife broke. "Too bad," he said. "Sap's up, and it's stripping easy. Got to quit. Come on. We'll take the bark over to the park, and I'll show you the longhouse." We got the cedar sheets Ron had cut and rolled them together. They oozed stickiness. Sap clung to the edges, and cedar smell filled the air.

From above St. Ignace on the ridge west of I-75 is a breathtaking view of the straits and the Mackinac Bridge. The Father Marquette State Park runs along the crest, with the auditorium and exhibit hall about one hundred yards down the hill toward the bridge. Ron was building a longhouse inside the exhibit hall.

"Bring the bark inside," he said. "We'll lay them on the floor next to the wall over here so they dry OK and don't curl. The longhouse is in the other room. The frame there is white ash. I cut it green and bent it to shape—lashed it like that to dry sort of hooplike. The bark goes over the frame, and then I'll fasten it down with red willow strips and white ash splints along there. A real longhouse like in the olden days would be much bigger than what I'm building here, but there ain't enough space. They're going to put a mirror in there to make everything look bigger."

I left St. Ignace the next day, drove home, and began transcribing the new tapes. When they were done, I combined the new transcriptions with the text from Ron's original tapes. I could see how some minor tinkering on my part would produce a connected narrative, but I also recognized that the text could not be left as Ron had dictated it, even with the profanity removed. Some further editorial changes seemed necessary.

As any speaker will, Ron frequently repeated himself and used the same word over and over again. He also tended to make false starts—to begin a sentence with one idea and then abruptly shift to a different one, having never completed the first. Without asking Ron, I decided to edit the transcriptions to make them more readable. I began to think about Ron's prose as a writer would. I found that I was so familiar with Ron's speech patterns that I could write the way he talked and that no one could tell the difference except Ron and me. I edited the text, changing words, deleting most of the false starts, and cutting out the repetitions.

I didn't change much by doing this, but I did eliminate at least one-half of Ron's text. I dropped many of Ron's stories, especially descriptions of his fights, which seemed infinite in number. I told Ron what I had done, and he quickly agreed to everything except for the removal of the fight stories. He said that for several years his life had been given to brawling and that people who read his book should understand that, even at the risk of numbing them or inspiring hatred for him. He was probably right, but I decided to eliminate at least 90 percent of the fight stories.

I read the new edited version and found its narrative flow pleasing, though I could see where some of the episodes would benefit from more detail. Overall, the manuscript still lacked a purpose. I couldn't see what its point was or why anyone ought to read it. I asked Ron why he had wanted to write a book about himself, and he told me that he hoped to encourage parents to love their children and treat them respectfully so they wouldn't end up suffering the way he did. I saw something different. I saw a man's struggle to overcome the curse of his origins—poverty and unfeeling parents. In its present form, the manuscript met neither of our objectives, and I didn't know what to do about it.

I found the connections between the two parts of Ron's life difficult to fathom but believed that they would clarify the manuscript's meaning, if only I could understand them. During a period of about two years—beginning in 1965 with a second prison stint and ending shortly after his marriage to Carole and the birth of his son—Ron had transformed himself from a vicious bully to a decent and warmhearted husband and father. The totality of the change seemed unbelievable, yet I knew it had taken place and felt I needed to know why.

I often asked Ron about his reformation, and he always told me that Carole's love had brought it about. Clearly, Carole cared for Ron in a manner outside his previous experience, and her unwavering support had brought him a chance to cast off feelings of personal vulnerability and worthlessness. Ron's marriage provided structure and orderliness to his life. He had a wife, a child, family responsibilities—a home, in other words. It was a haven unlike any he had known before. Carole was also a patient listener who allowed Ron to talk without passing judgment upon him. She just let him go on until he had vented his emotions. She was, in effect, a skilled counselor as well as a loving companion.

Nevertheless, however dominant Carole's role in Ron's redemption, other factors played important parts too. Ron decided to save himself before he met Carole. He was in jail and facing a second prison term for violating parole — he had savagely beaten a man and snapped the man's collarbone during a drunken brawl. Prison did not rehabilitate Ron in any ordinary sense, but the terrifying prospect of more lockup time with unpredictably violent men convinced him that he must change his life so that he would never have to go back. In prison, Ron shaped a new life plan. Carole helped him realize that plan, but he had created it on his own.

From time to time I asked Ron to explain this critical period of his life to me. In all, we had talked at length about it a dozen times or more, but I never got the information I wanted. Indeed, Ron seemed baffled by my questions. He lacked the words and concepts to describe what had happened. He could not explain his redemption. Like love itself, it seemed mysterious and magical to him and, finally, to me as well. How could it be otherwise?

In the fall, I began sending letters to Ron in which I asked him to talk about specific events or topics. I wasn't sure what to do, but I wanted him to describe his life after he had gotten out of prison the second time and reformed himself. So I asked him to tell me about the jobs he had had, the places he'd lived, how he got involved in Indian fishing, and so forth.

During that winter, Ron recorded another eighteen tapes. There were thirty-nine hours of recordings now, plus the six hours we did together, roughly twelve hundred pages of text if fully transcribed. Ron did the tapes two or three at a time. I listened to the recordings as soon as I got them, and then I sent Ron a new set of questions. That process went on through the winter and affected the content of all the tapes. Ron also told me that he had begun to plan more than he had before, often composing short outlines to guide him. I think he had to organize his thoughts because, for the most part, he was no longer telling stories that had a logic developed from frequent retelling over the years. Ron still retold stories, but after the first half dozen tapes, most of my questions sought to establish context and transitions between episodes, just as they had before. By the spring of 1981 the manuscript had doubled in size, the first half composed of Ron's stories expanded by my efforts to get him to establish contexts and make transitions, and the second half made up of his responses to my theme-centered questions.

In late April 1981 I drove north to visit Ron and Carole. I enjoyed being with them, and I wanted to help Ron get his recently purchased trap-net rig ready for fishing. I also hoped to do some question-and-answer tape recording the way we had the year before.

The alarm clock in the next room whirred me awake. I heard Ron get up. It was about five-thirty in the morning. I slid the window open and listened for wind in the trees. Outside, birds sang in the half-light that paled the east. There was no breeze, so Ron would lift the gill nets he had set in Lake Huron out front of the St. Ignace Harbor. I smelled the hounds, Lucy and Suzie, in their pen under the window.

There was no need for me to get up yet because, as a white man, I couldn't fish with Ron and his nephews Ed and Tuffy. But I was wide awake. I pulled on my jeans and walked into the living room.

Ron had brewed coffee and offered me some. Soon Tuffy drove up, his maroon Pinto frosty in the spring morning chill. He parked on the front lawn and came into the house. Ed was with him, smelling of beer and cigarette smoke from the night before. He was quiet and probably drunk yet.

Tuffy was talkative. "The lake's flat, Ron," he said. "It's smooth, but the wind's coming. There's glare ice in the harbor. The ducks is froze in. We're going to get a big lift today. I know it. My dad got ten hundred pounds yesterday."

Ron asked Tuffy if he wanted coffee. Tuffy nodded yes and walked into the kitchen to help himself. Silence prevailed except for the radio, tuned to station JML from Petoskey. Charlie Daniels howled that he was "still in Saigon." Ed drummed a careless rhythm, his fingers tapping the wooden chair arm.

With his long French-Indian nose, Tuffy looked like a Paquin. In his early twenties, thin, and about six feet tall, he had been an all-state basketball player at St. Ignace High. He detested school, though, and never went to college. Tuffy married his high school sweetheart right after graduation and lucked into a high-paying job as a deckhand on the *Chief Wawatam,* a grungy boat that ferried railroad cars across the Mackinac Straits. Working on the *Chief* the last four years, he had paid for his wife's education at Central Michigan University and saved some money too. His wife was to graduate in a month. But the *Chief* fell to hard times and had been dry-docked a week ago. Tuffy lost his job. He was lucky to have work fishing with Ron. With unemployment higher than 30 percent in Mackinac County, decent jobs were hard to find.

Ron stood up, and Ed and Tuffy followed his lead. Ron opened the front closet and pulled out three pairs of oilers, bib-fronted rubber overalls that keep fishers dry as they lift their nets. Ron teased Ed as they all pulled on their oilers. "Goddamn it, Ed," he said. "The

AFTERWORD

gloves with paint marks is mine. You left yours in the boat. Don't grab mine. Yours is froze in the boat, and they stink." This well-established routine went on every morning, and usually Ed came back rapid-fire, casting aspersions on Ron's ancestry and sexual habits. But hung over as Ed was that morning, he just grinned and shoved Tuffy's warm dry gloves deep into his coat pocket.

The three men went outside. Ron started his truck, got out, and scraped the frost off the windshield. Unaware that Ed has his gloves, Tuffy looked on the truck's dashboard and then poked through the junk on the floor: two Pepsi bottles, a Dr Pepper can, a broken flashlight, and a blanket. Puzzled, he walked to the trailered rowboat sitting in the yard and squinted inside. Ed's gloves lay on the bottom of the boat in the fish-scale clutter, but Tuffy didn't see his own there.

Ron turned his truck around and backed toward the trailer and boat. Ed lifted the trailer tongue off a stump and motioned Ron back. They'd done this hundreds of times. Ron maneuvered the truck to the right spot with casual ease. Ed slid the hitch onto the ball, locked it, and climbed into the truck. Tuffy moved in beside Ed and slammed the door, and Ron drove down the hill toward the lake. The sun hadn't risen yet, but the brightening eastern sky had chased the stars away. It was the start of a long day.

Standing in the doorway, I heard the truck clatter when it hit the rough pavement in front of the house next door, indicating a broken rear spring that Ron should fix. Ron, Ed, and Tuffy wouldn't be back for several hours. I relaxed now that they had left and the house was quiet. I slid into a big living-room chair, closed my eyes, and fell asleep.

"Chris! Chris! Get up. We overslept. Get up. Your dad didn't fix the alarm. It's seven o'clock. I'll take you to school. You won't make the bus," Carole wakened Chris.

Carole walked into the living room, unruffled by the early morning chaos. "Hi," she said. "Did Ron wake you?"

"Yes, but I wanted to get up and fix buoy lines while he's lifting."

Carole moved to the kitchen and fixed Chris's breakfast: toast and jelly, orange juice, Frosted Flakes, and milk. Heavy-eyed, Chris stumbled to the table. Even after his quick shower, he was only half awake and wanted to be left alone. He was mad about missing the bus. He liked to get to school before classes started, so he could play basketball with the other eighth-grade boys.

"Ready, Chris?" Carole asked. She wanted to go. Chris mumbled something and nodded yes.

"I'll be back in a couple hours," Carole told me. "I've got some things to do. You need anything at the store? I'm going to my sister's for a while and then to the Super Value."

I shook my head. "No, thanks."

Carole and Chris drove off. I went outdoors into the front yard. The sun had begun to melt its way across the front yard, leaving the shady areas frosty white. I heard the wind hiss in the balsams across the road. Beginning gently in the morning and rising to gale force by midafternoon, the wind had blown west for four days. Even now in the early morning, a few whitecaps ruffled the lake, and at the far reach of vision the water rolled across the edge of the sky. If the wind increased, Ron, Ed, and Tuffy would have a tough time lifting nets. There would be no danger, but it would be hard work to pull into the waves.

I looked around the yard. Behind the small ranch house a gill-net reel was perched, half hidden at the edge of the trees. Carole had wrapped three nets around the reel to dry the green moss debris caught in them. She would rub the moss out that afternoon probably, untangle the snarls, and box up the gang of nets so Ron could set them again. She had overhauled nets yesterday by dipping the snarls in hair conditioner. I laughed to myself when I remembered her joyful chatter as she deftly picked apart the hair-conditioned snarls.

To the west of the house, two dark brown sheds sat, one behind the other. Presently stuffed with four trap nets, the box-shaped building in the rear once served as a cooler on a refrigerated truck. Ron could store iced-down fish in the cooler, but so far he hadn't used it. The low-slung front building housed an ice-making machine, a storage bin for ice, and a place to gut fish. The cooler and the ice machine allowed Ron to process and wholesale his own fish.

Aluminum corks cluttered the ground in front of the sheds. Net boxes lay askew beside the driveway. Bottles that had been tossed into the woods glinted in the early morning sun. At the edge of the trees, a green boat full of water rusted as the wind pushed an empty Pennzoil bottle across the oily surface.

Ron had once fished out of that small boat. Then he welded steel along the gunwale, raising the sides so he could carry more fish. When he launched the high-sided boat and stepped in, it flipped, tossing him into the lake. He had raised the center of gravity so much that the once-trustworthy craft had turned vicious. He trailered the boat home and dumped it in the yard. It had sat there two years now, rusting and breeding mosquitoes.

At the east end of the house, Lucy barked. She'd seen the ducks swimming in the pothole next door. Two mallards had settled in the snowmelt pond a few days ago, and the bored rabbit hound yelped at them haphazardly all day long. Lucy and Suzie lived in a chicken-wire pen Ron had built along the edge of the house. Their pen couldn't be seen, hidden behind three black snowmobiles parked at the edge of the yard. But at night they were noisy. They would whiff a raccoon or another dog, yap a few times nervously, and then burst into full-throated baying.

I heard Ron's truck clacking, protesting the rough pavement and lack of care. Ron swung it into the yard.

"Do any good?" I asked.

"Oh, not too bad. About six hundred pounds of whitefish. Ed, take them up to the fishery, will you?"

Ed nodded agreement, backed the boat into the yard, unhitched it, and drove away. The rest of us went into the house. Ron stripped off his oilers and dumped them just inside the front door. Not wanting to anger Carole, Tuffy threw his into the closet. Ron got some coffee, lit a cigarette, and eased into his chair.

"It's just whipping out there," Ron said, complaining about the morning's work. "Damn the wind! And them guys from Bay Mills set all around us. Buoys up the ass. Nets right down the lake, where they won't catch a fish, not one. Somebody set over the top of our nets, so we didn't get no fish on the outside end. Blowing like this, their nets'll tangle, ball up, and roll right down the lake. Them guys just use cinder-block anchors. I wish they'd get out of here. We busted our ass pulling into the wind. Damn, it's ten o'clock in the morning, and I've already done a day's work. I bet we won't get sixty cents a pound for them fish either."

Carole gunned her car in the driveway and skidded to a stop. She loved to hot-rod. A quick frown pinched her face when she opened the door and saw Ron's oilers, but she stepped over them without saying anything, half-smiled a hello, and went into the kitchen to start breakfast. As a girl, she had fixed the family meals, becoming an expert cook in the process. Now she prepared hearty, good-tasting meals in no time at all. I smelled bacon cooking and heard Carole stirring something, wooden spoon whacking metal pan.

Carole called us to eat the meal of bacon, pancakes, butter and syrup, orange juice, and coffee. Hungry after working on the lake, Ron and Tuffy gulped down several pancakes. Ron ate too fast but stopped abruptly when he realized how quickly he'd eaten. With work to do, he didn't want stomach trouble. He left the table, lit a cigarette, and walked into the living room to relax in his chair. He fell asleep quickly, his cigarette still burning in the amber pebbled-glass ashtray on the table beside him. Tuffy said something to Carole, went out the door, and drove away.

Ron and I had settled into a daily routine, fixing his trap-net boat. He'd nap for a half hour or so after he lifted his nets in the morning, and then we'd work nonstop until six or seven in the evening, when we ate dinner. He'd rest after dinner, usually relaxing, smoking, watching TV. Then we'd go back at it for a couple of hours, often finishing after dark. For a week and a half now, Ron had labored at least twelve hours every day, what with lifting gill nets, fixing his boat, and getting trap nets ready.

Ron slept for about an hour. When he woke up, he said, "OK, Bob?" He was set to return to work. We had almost finished the boat, and he hoped to launch it tomorrow. We went to work.

Later, Carole called us to dinner, a feast of fried chicken, mashed potatoes, gravy, green beans, and coleslaw. We dug in.

"This is really good, Carole," I told her. "You're a hell of a cook."

Pleased, she smiled. We'd done this before. "What'd you expect?" she said with a chuckle.

Chris wasn't hungry and left the table a few moments after we sat down. Ron ate quickly and retired to his chair and cigarettes. Carole cleared the plates off the table but left the food while I continued eating. She wanted to clean up and watch "Jokers Wild" and "Jeopardy," but she didn't say anything. She'd leave the mess till later if she wasn't done when the game shows came on.

We watched TV for an hour. Ron and Carole took pleasure in competing with the contestants, quickly answering most of the questions. Ron dozed off for about twenty minutes during the second show, gently snoring as he rested. He woke as the show ended; it seemed as if he'd set some inner alarm. I'd seen him do that often. A brief nap lifted him.

"Come on, Bob," he said. "Let's get that net ready."

Chris had disappeared after supper, but he hung around now, the way he did when he wanted something. "Dad," he said, "Brad and them went smelting last night. Smelts run at Nun's Creek and Pine River around one o'clock. They got a lot." Chris wanted to dip smelt that night.

"I got to get this net done," Ron said. "I don't know, Chris. I'm tired."

"Aw, Dad, all them guys is going. I'll get up and go to school and everything."

"Look, Chris, I don't know."

Ron's anger didn't bother Chris. He had just about won and he knew it. He'd wait a few minutes and try again. He sauntered away and began toying with a corner of the net we were straightening.

Trap nets have three parts: the lead, the heart, and the pot. Ron and I had the heart and pot spread on his front lawn. We had put the pot in good order, with corners together, top and bottom lines running parallel. Ron was repairing mesh that mice had eaten. Most trap-netters douse their nets with pepper when they store them, but Ron hadn't known that when he put his nets away the previous October. Mice had chewed holes in the mesh to get fluff for their nests.

Ron worked quickly with his seaman's needle and nylon twine. His sewing hand swung in short arcs, ducked into the mesh to tie one half hitch and then another against the first, and then arced again to catch another mesh. He tied off the twine and cut it. He had repaired the hole.

"Grab those bridles, Bob." Ron motioned toward two loops spliced to the junction between the pot and the heart. "Pull them out. OK. Looks all right, eh? See any holes?"

"No. It's fine, as far as I can see. Let's check the points." Ron worked along one side of the net, running top and bottom lines through his hands, checking lines and mesh. I did the same thing on the other side. The heart flared as it approached the lead and then angled sharply in two mesh walls—the points, which kept the fish moving toward the tunnels in the center of the heart.

"Watch it, Dad! Jeez! I fixed them." Chris had straightened the points while we fumbled with the heart. "Come on, Dad. Let's dip smelt tonight, huh?"

Impressed with Chris's cleverness, Ron agreed. He probably would have anyhow. "OK. We'll go to Hoban's Creek. But I want to load the lead first. We got time. Get your ma, and turn on them lights."

The lead was a forty-foot-high nylon-mesh fence. When it was set, it stretched several hundred feet from the heart toward shallower water. Fish bumped into the lead and moved naturally toward deeper water into the trap net. Ron backed his truck toward the west corner of his house, where we had piled the lead several days before. It was about eight o'clock, not quite dark. Chris turned on the floodlights, and he and Carole came out of the house.

"You and Chris take the corkline, Bob," Ron said, "and me and Carole will get the leadline. Pull the net way to the front, and lay the corks side by side. We'll stack the mesh in between. This lead's twelve hundred foot long. Keep pulling toward the front so we get her all in."

Chris and I had the easy job. Chris stood on the ground, feeding line and mesh to me in the truck. The plastic floats on the upper line, or corkline, slipped easily along the mesh without hanging up, but the weights on the lower line, or leadline, kinked the rope and snarled in the mesh. Ron and Carole kept pace with us, though. Carole's hands moved quickly, throwing some mesh over, pulling some line through. She instinctively knew what to do to remove snarls. With a few deft movements, she straightened out tangles that looked unmanageable to me. She fed line to Ron, and he stacked the lead weights much as I had placed the floats along the opposite side of the truck. We loaded the lead quickly. Ron could set it tomorrow if we launched the boat.

Hoban's Creek doesn't amount to much. Most of the year, it meanders out of the woods, under the highway, and into Lake Huron. But now, swollen with snowmelt runoff, the creek ripped along, carrying messages to smelt waiting in the lake, luring the small fish into the stream to spawn. All over northern Michigan, smelt surged unpredictably into the streams, filling them with fish. For a few minutes, a half hour maybe, the smelt would jam the creek, but then, suddenly, they'd be gone. The silvery fish might reappear in a few hours, but sometimes they wouldn't show up for several days. No one could tell for sure when the smelt would rush into the streams. The uncertainty added to the fun of dipping.

The oily smelt make delicious smoked fish, and they're awfully good fried, but mostly people dip them for the fun of it, to celebrate north-country spring, whoop it up with friends, and drink a lot of beer. Smelt usually run in the wee hours, so dipping offers people an excuse to stay out and have a good time.

A small crowd had gathered along the creek when we drove into the motel parking lot. Ron swung toward the rear of the lot near the lake. We could see people along the stream, a couple wrapped in a blanket drinking a jumbo beer, kids running around, a family sitting on a picnic table in front of a fire they'd built. Somebody yelled, "Knock off the lights!" Ron doused his headlights and mumbled something about stupid city folk. "Crap!" he said. "Them fish'll come when they want. Ain't no lights going to change their minds."

"Here they come! The run is on!" a teenage boy yelled down by the lake. "Here they come!" Everybody grabbed their nets and rushed to the creek. Two men ran out of the motel, carrying Coleman lanterns. Dressed in waders, they plunged into the creek. Heads down, they eyed the bottom as they walked upstream. Water rushed around their ankles, and the lanterns hissed as the men looked for smelt in the eerie light. "There's no run," one of them growled. "Goddamn it. Stop doing that! What the hell's the matter with you?"

"Let's try that pool on the other side by the bridge," Chris said. "Remember that time, Dad, when we dipped all them smelt, and nobody else got nothing?" Chris and Ron headed across the bridge and into the hemlock grove that edged the stream. Along the road a guy and girl were making out in a pickup truck. She broke out of a long kiss, rolled down the window, and yelled, "Hey, Ronny, anything doing down there?"

"Naw," Ron said with a chuckle. "There's better action where you're at."

Chris hurried along the creek, stopping every few steps to shine his flashlight into the water. "They ain't going to run tonight, Chris. Let's go home." Ron had had enough. "Will you drive, Bob? I'm awful tired."

Ron and Chris had both dozed off by the time I turned into the yard and stopped. Ron stumbled out of the truck and into the house. "We're not lifting nets tomorrow," he said. "Art's going to move the boat in the morning. He'll be here about nine, so sleep in. See you in the morning." I went to bed. Chris, fully clothed, had already fallen asleep in the other bed. I heard Ron snoring next door. I pushed the window open to get some air, lay down, and dropped into a sound sleep.

I didn't hear Chris get up the next morning. The hounds woke me, yapping at the pothole ducks. It was eight o'clock, time to get up. Ron was up, sitting in his chair, smoking and drinking coffee. Although he was energetic on the mornings he lifted, he often loafed for a couple hours after waking on other mornings. I knew he'd be nervous today till Art moved his boat. Ron had driven the boat onto the trailer, given it a shot of gas, shot across the top, smashed into his truck, and left the boat crosswise on the trailer. After Art left, Ron and I would fix the keel and launch the boat. Carole was talkative, but Ron didn't say much, a sure sign he was worried.

Art arrived at 9:05. He parked his blue pickup behind Ron's truck, went over to the boat, and walked around it, looking carefully at its cockeyed lean. Ron immediately came to life and went outside to talk with Art. I went out too but didn't enter the conversation between the longtime friends.

"God, how'd you do that, Ron?" Art asked.

Ron explained, as the two men inspected the boat, figuring how to lift it. I couldn't hear what they said to one another, but down the hill I heard *beep, beep, beep*. It was Art's son, Wade, coming with a big front loader—the family owned a construction company. Art spoke with his son a few minutes, and then Wade climbed into the machine. Everything went to hand signals then, what with the beeping and the roar of the engine. Using hand signals, Art instructed Wade. Within a few minutes they had Ron's boat sitting straight on the trailer. Wade drove away.

"I'll get that clock one of these days," Art said. He had swapped some stuff for an antique clock of Ron's. "You'd better beef up that trailer tongue. It looks shaky. You'll be OK now. Go ahead and launch her, but fix that trailer before you take her out in the fall."

Ron was happy to see his boat sitting straight. "Thanks, Art."

Art smiled, his wrinkly good-natured face full of warmth. "Sure," he said. "Hey, bring me some fish when you lift, eh? I got to go."

After Art left, Ron and I straightened the keel quickly. I braced an angle iron along one side, and he blasted the other with the end of a six-foot pipe. A few crinkles remained, but the boat would handle all right. That afternoon, we launched it without trouble and loaded a trap net to be set the next day. Ron worried about leaving the net lying on the deck all night. The year before, some pranksters had moved lines around, and he had set with the points crossed. He lost two days' labor pulling the net out, straightening it, and putting it back in the lake.

Ron, Ed, and Tuffy lifted gill nets the next morning, ate breakfast, and headed onto the lake to set the trap net. No one had tampered with the net, so the set went easily. Ron yelled a lot and got excited, and Tuffy screwed up a few times, dropping anchors before he should. Considering the three men's inexperience, they did remarkably well, getting the net properly set. They had six more nets to go.

That night Ron, Carole, and I drank some beers and got drunk, celebrating the start of a new season.

I left St. Ignace the next day without doing any tape recording. I figured to come back and record in late May. I drove home to Pittsburgh to work on my fishing rights book. I talked with Ron on the phone a few times over the next several weeks and lent him some money when he told me he couldn't make the payments on his house and truck. I knew he hadn't caught many fish the previous winter and had gotten behind, so I didn't think much about his needing money during the spring run, typically a flush time for fishers.

Busy with my own affairs, I lost touch with Ron during late May. I'd picked my son up at college and he and I had driven north

AFTERWORD

to Platte Lake near Traverse City, where we rented a cabin for the summer. He had a job hauling canoes for an outfitter who ran trips on the Platte River, and I hoped to finish writing my book. The next two days, I rushed around, visiting friends I hadn't seen since the preceding summer. I called Ron to see if I could visit with him and Carole on the Tuesday after Memorial Day weekend.

"Sure," he said. "It'll be good to see you." I explained that I had some things to do in Traverse City and wouldn't get to St. Ignace until late afternoon. "Well, I want to lift nets in the morning," Ron said, "so that'd work out good."

I turned left at the Tiki Campground sign and climbed the hill toward Ron's house. I liked Michigan's upper peninsula and looked forward to seeing Ron and Carole. I laughed to myself when I saw their yard. Fishing gear was everywhere, just as it had been when I left a month before.

I parked behind Ron's truck and walked toward the house, my feet squishing in the clay driveway. No one came to the door to greet me. They never did. I don't know why. They never said good-bye either. Ron and Carole usually avoided emotion-laden situations, typically keeping their feelings to themselves. I saw Ron inside, so I jerked open the storm door and walked in, wiping my clay-covered boots on the mat near the door. "How are you doing, Ron?" I asked.

"So-so. How about you?"

"Fine, really. Happy to be away from the city and back up here. Oops! Hold on. I'll get the door." The west wind had pried the storm door open and slammed it against the outside wall, ripping the safety chain loose. The latch had broken last fall, and the door burst open whenever it wished unless you closed it carefully by simultaneously lifting and pulling. One of these times a strong west wind was going to rocket the door off its hinges and into the woods.

I closed the door and turned back to the room. Ron sat in his chair, his right hand spread on the arm, squeezing the cloth, his fingers digging in. A cigarette burned in his left hand, bluish smoke drifting over his head. My eyes and throat burned. He had smoked a lot. The ashtray to his left brimmed with crumpled butts. I wondered about his greeting. I'd never heard him say "So-so" before. He had two typical greetings: "Oh, not too bad" and "Good! I'm doing real good."

Carole and Chris sat on the couch. Neither said anything at first. Chris's eyes caught mine, and he smiled. "Hi, Bob," he said. He said something to Carole that I didn't hear and left the room. Carole got up, went into the kitchen, and came back. I walked into the kitchen to get a cup of coffee. As well as I knew Ron and Carole, I felt awkward now, out of place, but the feelings would pass when the three of us had been together long enough to reaffirm our ties. Soon Carole would be teasing the way she always did.

There was no coffee in the pot. I looked in the plastic crock above the sink for some to brew. I jiggled the lid and looked inside. "There's no coffee, Bob," Carole said. "I've got to get to the store. There's tea in the cupboard on the other side. You know where. Put three bags in the coffee maker."

Carole knew I loved coffee, and her voice conveyed an unstated apology. I found the tea bags, put three in the coffee-stained basket, filled the Mr. Coffee with water, and turned it on. When the tea had brewed, I poured myself a mugful. "You want any tea, Ron? Carole?"

"No. Help yourself, Bob," Carole answered.

I opened the refrigerator to get some milk to lighten my tea, but there wasn't any. There wasn't much of anything else either, just mustard, ketchup, some relish, and a can of peaches. Carole heard me in the refrigerator. "If you want milk, Bob, get the condensed in the cupboard."

We talked for a while. I carried the conversation, an unusual occurrence, and there were frequent and prolonged silences. It was almost six-thirty, and I felt very hungry. The house was foodless, so I suggested that we go out to eat, my treat. I'd often done this in the past. "Do you want to eat at Miller's Camp?" I asked.

"I don't care," Ron responded. He often said yes in this way. Ron liked Miller's Camp, even though twenty years before he had nearly killed a man there, stabbing him in the eye with a pool cue. The food was good, and I figured a few beers would loosen Ron and Carole up.

Carole led the way into Miller's Camp, with Chris and Ron behind her, and me in the rear. She hesitated a moment in the empty dining room, as if to ask if any of us wanted to eat there and then headed for a booth in the bar, where a dozen or so people sat drinking and talking. We ordered something to eat. I got fish, Ron and Chris had burgers and fries, and Carole wanted shrimp in a basket. It seemed odd for a fisherman's wife to eat shrimp, but she frequently ordered them when we went out. Ron asked for gravy on his fries, which struck me as unappealing, but given his mood, I kept my mouth shut. He hardly seemed ripe for teasing.

"Want to shoot some pool, Mom?" Chris asked. He stood up and searched his pockets for a quarter. Carole looked at Chris and said something to him with her eyes.

"Here, Chris," I said. "I've got some quarters if you want to play." I gave him a couple of quarters, and he headed for the pool table in the back of the dining room. I heard the balls drop, and in a moment Chris came back to the booth. "Come on," he pleaded. He and Carole left to shoot a game.

Ron and I drank two beers each, not saying much. When the waitress brought our food, I went to tell Carole and Chris that they could eat. Chris quickly knocked in three striped balls, sunk the eight ball, and returned triumphantly to the booth. He rarely out-shot his mother, so he was elated. He wolfed down his two cheese-burgers, swallowed his fries and his mother's fries, ate most of her shrimp, and went back to the pool table.

We finished eating, left Miller's Camp, and dropped Chris at John's house, halfway down Maloney Hill. "How about drinking a few beers and listening to some music?" I asked. "Mackinaw's playing at the Nicolet tonight."

"I don't feel like music tonight. We could go to the Homestead for a while if you want." Ron's spirits lagged at the bar. He remained morose. We had drunk several beers, and usually he'd be wound up by now, laughing and talking with people he knew. And ordinarily Carole would get pretty goofy after a few drinks. I enjoyed going out with the two of them. We always had a good time. But not tonight.

At the Homestead I ordered a second round of beers. When the waitress brought them, Ron made no effort to pay. His eyes caught mine for a moment, and he looked down. I paid for the three cans of Miller's. I had bought the first round too, and I knew something was wrong, because, no matter what, Ron paid his own way and a little more. Ron and Carole seemed uncomfortable. I asked them if they wanted to leave, and both of them nodded yes. We drove home.

Ron turned on the TV when we got inside. A little drunk, I fell asleep in the chair, woke up, excused myself, and went to bed. In the morning I'd find out what troubled Ron and Carole so much.

I woke early. I heard the radio—music from JML—and knew that Carole was already up. I got up and went out into the living room. Carole was reading the *National Enquirer*. "Get a cup of tea if you want, Bob," she said. "Ron'll be up soon."

Ron stumbled in a few minutes later, looking half out of it, the way he did on mornings when he wasn't lifting nets. He got some tea, lit a cigarette, and settled into his chair to wake up. I waited for more than an hour before I asked him what was bothering him. It wasn't a good idea to press him about anything when he first got up.

"What's wrong, Ron? Something's bothering you. What is it?"

"I'm broke, flat broke. No money at all. Not a penny. I owe people all over. I can't make my payments. I'm behind on my truck and on the house." Ron stopped. I understood yesterday's events and felt stupid and ashamed for having missed all the clues. Proud as they were, Ron and Carole wouldn't ask for help.

"I don't understand, Ron. The trap nets aren't working? Or what?"

"You know Brooks. He fishes out of Mackinaw City. He's got trap nets up the ass. He planted all around me, surrounded me. The fish couldn't get to my nets if they wanted to. Shit! I could give them a map and an invitation, and they'd still end up with Brooks. I'm not catching many fish since he showed up, a few hundred pounds a week, maybe. But that ain't the worst of it. The wholesale price for whitefish is twenty-five cents—two hundred fifty dollars for ten hundred pounds of fish. I can't live on that. By the time I pay Ed and Tuffy, I got a hundred and fifty dollars left, which won't even take care of my boat."

I felt the tears rise in my eyes and roll down my cheeks. And for a moment I felt his pain. I knew how much importance he attached to his family's well-being. "I'm sorry, Ron. I didn't know."

"I didn't want to lay my troubles on you," Ron said. "You helped us before, and I couldn't ask again. Damn. I don't know what to do. But I got to do something or I'm going to lose everything—my house, the truck, Carole's car, my boat, the nets, everything. Everything I worked for all these years, gone."

Usually Ron got mad in situations like this, working his anger into a full-blown rage. He'd rant against the people who denied him opportunity, who frustrated his ambitions. And then he'd lash out against people who had abused him as a youngster, usually ending in a tirade against his mother. I knew the uselessness of arguing with him when he got like that and was prepared to let him rage for a while till he calmed down, an hour or so usually.

But Ron had slipped beyond anger into despair. His resources used up, he couldn't see any way to get out of his dilemma. His temper never flared. He just sat there, looking at me with his eyes unfocused, smoking one cigarette after another. He seemed to have lost hope.

I waited several minutes. "How many pounds of fish are you catching each week?" I asked.

"Maybe ten hundred, about that much most of the time."

"Not bad if you could get a decent price for them. Somebody's making money. Down below in Traverse City and around there, whitefish fillets sell for around four dollars a pound. You get twenty-five cents. In between, there's money to be made."

"Yeah. I sold smoked fish before. Smoked it and sold it to Tom

AFTERWORD

mostly, in Brevort. He smokes his own now. Does good too."

"At twenty-five cents a pound, you're never going to make money."

"No, I ain't. I can't figure the price going so low and just staying there. Canadian fish, I guess, and them fish buyers in Chicago. That's what's being said at the fishery. But I don't know. I wish the price would go up. I can't ever remember it being down so long. Hell, ten years ago I got more money for my fish than they're paying me now."

"Could you sell smoked fish now instead of wholesaling your catch at the fishery? Sell it yourself. You've got that ice machine and the cooler. Get the ice machine fixed, and you could sell your own fish, couldn't you?"

"Yeah. I'd have to build a smokehouse. But it's tough to sell fish near here, with so many fishermen around. That deal with Tom worked out good, but it'd be hard to find another one like that."

"How about down below? There's nobody fishing out of Traverse City, as far as I know. The only fisherman in that area is Carlson in Leland. You could undersell him, I'm sure. I'd help you sell fish down there and look around for places."

Ron pushed himself erect, his interest rising.

Ron and I forgot about the manuscript that summer. He and I got his fish business going again. He made good money during the tourist season, but by late fall he was broke again and struggled to avoid deep depression, which threatened to submerge him in hopelessness. He could easily lose everything he had worked for and fall prey to chronic poverty. From time to time I encouraged him to record some more tapes, but he had no stomach for it. We didn't work on the manuscript again for several years.

I probably could have renewed Ron's interest in the manuscript if I had tried hard, but I still wasn't sure what should be done. Meanwhile, Ron's economic situation worsened. His life was on the skids, and it hit a tragic bottom when Ed drowned while fishing through the ice with him. As a friend, I felt Ron's pain when he phoned me and told me about Ed's death. But as a scholar who was trying to record Ron's life story, I wondered what the disintegration of Ron's life meant. Had the awful curse of his childhood seized him once more? Taken him by the throat? The manuscript sat untouched.

I finished writing my fishing rights book in January 1987 and submitted it for publication. That spring I told Ron that I wanted to begin working on his story again and that I would keep at it until we had a publishable book. He and Carole had reasserted control over their lives in 1985. Each had gotten a wage-paying job, so Ron's normally good spirits had returned. Ron and I spent three question-and-answer recording sessions over the next few months. I began at page one of the manuscript and kept integrating new material and asking questions until I had shaped a coherent whole that I thought honestly portrayed Ron's life. The stories are Ron's, and virtually all the words are his too. The structure reflects a struggle between his and my conceptions of life.

I've learned a lot from Ron over the years. Born to middle-class privilege that takes the basic necessities for granted, and possessed of an Ivy League graduate education, I had never had a close friend who differed so much from me. In time I came to appreciate his point of view and to see that it usually made greater sense of his world than mine did. I felt humbled sometimes by Ron's common-sense wisdom, his breadth of skill, and his remarkable memory, cultivated to compensate for his inability to write. And I have felt the warmth of Ron's commitment to his wife and son. His awful childhood taught him the strength of love and the importance of being a loyal husband and nurturing father. Ron Paquin's life story describes how this ordinary man came to be extraordinary.

Several people read the manuscript. Depending on their values and interests, they commented on various subjects: the horror-filled reform schools and prisons, the greed and insensitivity of middle-class professionals, how a decultured Indian rediscovered his heritage, the healing power of a woman's love, and the curse of a mother's indifference. They're all described here, and each merits attention, but taken as a whole, the book is justified by Ron's portrayal of common people.

However extraordinary his life, Ron's experiences are typical of many eastern Native Americans who rediscovered their native heritage in the 1970s, often through reading books written by white anthropologists. As a boy, Ron did not think of himself as an Indian, but he does now. Because he was cut off from his cultural heritage during his formative years, his life story departs from the mainstream of American Indian autobiographies. There's no nostalgia for the old ways, no waiting for an Edenic past that never was and never will be again. Nobody's caught between cultures or trying to preserve tradition. Ron has written a different sort of autobiography, Indian to be sure, but primarily the story of a poor man who happens to be Chippewa. He lets the reader see life through the eyes of America's working poor who survive precariously between poverty and middle-classness.

Nearly eighteen million American families struggle in the same

AFTERWORD

economic niche occupied by Ron, Carole, and Chris. Though from diverse backgrounds, the members of these families have much in common with the Paquins. They are disproportionately nonwhite and undereducated. They rely upon more than one household income. They have a sequence of jobs rather than careers. They have little economic security, so they live in terms of a monthly cycle devoted to buying food, paying utility bills and the rent, and making car payments. Each month the routine begins again—stretching scarce resources in an attempt to get by. After the electric bill is paid, will there be enough left to replace the car's unsafe brakes?

Such invisible and largely inarticulate men and women see the world as an uncaring place in which people like them don't count for much. And yet they don't want to live as parasites. They believe in work and discipline. They disapprove of able-bodied loafers who exploit government programs like welfare and Aid For Dependent Children. They want to be autonomous and self-supporting and to have decent jobs so that they can take care of themselves and their children. They suffer with the ever-present fear that even a little bad luck—an accident or ill health—could shatter their lives.

Ron describes himself as a poor man. He often prefaces statements with the phrase "Well, a poor man like me." He identifies with working people who labor with their hands but disassociates himself from the lazy nonworkers below and the white-collared workers above. He believes the last two groups to be parasitic exploiters and his enemies. Ron articulates a class interpretation of America. In a way, he speaks for millions of Americans, the working poor who seldom get a chance to speak for themselves.

Carole Paquin died on a bleak Tuesday afternoon in mid-November 1989, killed by a massive heart attack while she slept. Her sister Milly found her lying in bed. Unable to wake her, Milly ran to the door, screaming for help. Hunting in the woods nearby, Ron had heard nothing when the foreboding seized him. He found the path and ran toward home but froze in disbelief as he cleared the trees and heard Milly sob, "Carole's dead."

That weekend nearly three hundred mourners crowded into Dotson's Funeral Home. A few stoic ones hid their feelings. Others wept uncontrollably. In the spring, when the ice gave up the earth, Carole was buried next to her father and near her brother, facing east to seek the first light.

IN MEMORIAM

I have suffered many torments in my life but none so bad as losing Carole. I went into shock after she died, and when I came out of it I could not face the reality that she was gone and would not be there no more forever. I started to black out all the time—pass right out—and people would find me crumpled on the floor. I could not sleep or eat. I lost forty pounds in one month. I often felt that life was not worth living without her, and for a long time I did not feel I could go on. I thought about suicide.

I'm doing better now. Chris has helped me a lot and Carole's family, too. I keep busy and I'm trying to get some structure back in my life. But I miss Carole very much. She will always be first in my heart.

Ron Paquin lives in St. Ignace, Michigan, where he works in the Museum of Ojibway Culture. Formerly an activist on behalf of Native American fishing rights, he no longer earns his living on the lakes. But he continues to fish commercially during the spring and fall runs, and in the winter he does some craft work to make a few dollars during the slack season and to keep in touch with his Chippewa heritage. Paquin has struggled emotionally since his wife's death and hard times are seldom far from his door.

Robert Doherty, a professor of history at the University of Pittsburgh, has written several books, the most recent of which is *Disputed Waters*. In it he examines American Indian treaty fishing rights in the Great Lakes. Doherty's connection with the north woods began with his grandfather, a lumberjack in Michigan during the early twentieth century. An avid naturalist, Doherty has spent most of his summers in the north country, the last ten researching Chippewa and Ottawa history.

Doherty and Paquin met coincidentally in 1979. They became friends and soon entered into the decade-long collaboration that became *Not First in Nobody's Heart*.